**JOURNAL FOR THE STUDY OF THE NEW TESTAMENT
SUPPLEMENT SERIES**

73

Executive Editor
Stanley E. Porter

JSOT Press
Sheffield

SACRED SPACE

An Approach to the Theology
of the Epistle to the Hebrews

Marie E. Isaacs

Journal for the Study of the New Testament
Supplement Series 73

For Pat

The scriptural quotations in this book are from the ecumenical edition of
the Revised Standard Version of the Bible copyrighted 1971, 1952 and
1946 by the Division on Christian Education of the National Council of
the Churches of Christ in the USA, and are reproduced by permission.

Published by JSOT Press
JSOT Press is an imprint of
Sheffield Academic Press Ltd
The University of Sheffield
343 Fulwood Road
Sheffield S10 3BP
England

Typeset by Sheffield Academic Press
and
Printed on acid-free paper in Great Britain
by Billing & Sons Ltd
Worcester

British Library Cataloguing in Publication Data

Isaacs, Marie E.
    Sacred Space: An Approach to the Theology of
    the Epistle to the Hebrews.—(JSNT
    Supplement Series, ISSN 0143-5108; No. 73)
    I. Title II. Series
    227

    ISBN 1-85075-356-3

CONTENTS

ACKNOWLEDGMENTS

My interest in the Epistle to the Hebrews came about initially more by necessity than choice, when, nearly 20 years ago, as the most recently appointed Lecturer in the Biblical Studies Department of Heythrop College, it fell to me to teach those areas of the New Testament not already spoken for by my more established colleagues. At the time I did not appreciate what a piece of serendipity that would prove to be, but now I should like to thank my then Head of Department, John Ashton, for obliging me to grapple with one of the most stimulating (if neglected) books of the New Testament.

Thus the genesis of this particular study was *not* a doctoral thesis but the exigencies of university undergraduate teaching. I gratefully acknowledge the contribution made to my understanding of Hebrews by the students I have taught over those years. In fact it was they who originally suggested that I should write on the topic. One in particular, Elizabeth Mott, deserves special mention for phoning me with persistent regularity, long after her graduation, to ask whether the writing was coming along well, and if not, why not. Her encouragement has meant much to me. I hope that my current students, however, will not be too disappointed to discover that this is *not* 'the book of the lectures' which they therefore need no longer attend! In spite of which I trust that it will prove of use to them.

I should also like to thank my colleagues at Heythrop College. The constructive comments and criticisms made of my paper on 'work in progress' by members of the Senior Seminar proved invaluable at a crucial stage in my thinking. Particularly I am indebted to my colleague, Tom Deidun, editor of the *Heythrop Journal*, who read and commented on each chapter as it was written. I absolve him from any responsibility for either the errors or opinions of the finished product. Nonetheless I know that I owe much to his scholarly judgment and insight.

Given the constraints of university teaching and administration in

Britain today it becomes increasingly difficult to find time for a sustained piece of writing and research. *Sacred Space* was written in fits and starts over a period of some five years. I am especially grateful, therefore, for the sabbatical leave granted me in the Michaelmas term of 1989. This gave me the opportunity to give Hebrews my undivided attention for a few months. During that time John and Irena Kirkpatrick generously gave me the use of their home in the Laurentians, which proved a perfect environment in which to write. I am grateful for their kindness. I would also like to thank Dean Donna Runnalls and the Faculty of Religious Studies at McGill University for welcoming me as Visiting Scholar during that sabbatical term in Montreal, and especially Tapas Majumdar for his ever-willing and efficient assistance in helping me to use the library there.

Without the expertise of Heidi Furcha and Sami Kahn in Montreal and Annabel Clarkson in London I would have found it difficult to move from the quill to the word processor. They valiantly deciphered my handwriting and transcribed it onto computer disks.

I am grateful to Sheffield Academic Press and the Series Editor David Hill for agreeing to publish a manuscript broader in scope than most in their JSNT Supplement Series.

Much as I owe to the academic community, my greatest debts are personal. It was the encouragement of my friends which spurred me not only to begin but to complete this work. Above all I must thank Patricia Kirkpatrick for never letting me lose sight of what I set out to do, and believing that I could achieve it.

Marie E. Isaacs
Heythrop College
London University
January 1992

ABBREVIATIONS

AB	Anchor Bible
BASOR	*Bulletin of the American Schools of Oriental Research*
BJRL	*Bulletin of the John Rylands University Library of Manchester*
BNTC	Black's New Testament Commentary
CBQMS	*Catholic Biblical Quarterly* Monograph Series
CJT	*Canadian Journal of Theology*
CRINT	Compendia rerum iudaicarum ad Novum Testamentum
EncJud	*Encyclopaedia Judaica*
ExpTim	*Expository Times*
FRLANT	Forschungen zur Religion und Literatur des Alten und Neuen Testaments
HeyJ	*Heythrop Journal*
HNT	Handbuch zum Neuen Testament
HTR	*Harvard Theological Review*
ICC	International Critical Commentary
IEJ	*Israel Exploration Journal*
Int	*Interpretation*
JBL	*Journal of Biblical Literature*
JSNT	*Journal for the Study of the New Testament*
JTS	*Journal of Theological Studies*
LCL	Loeb Classical Library
MNTC	Moffatt NT Commentary
NCB	New Century Bible
NICNT	New International Commentary on the New Testament
NovT	*Novum Testamentum*
NovTSup	*Novum Testamentum* Supplements
NRT	*La nouvelle revue théologique*
NTS	*New Testament Studies*
RB	*Revue biblique*
RevQ	*Revue de Qumran*
SBT	Studies in Biblical Theology
SNTSMS	Society of New Testament Studies Monograph Series
SR	*Studies in Religion*
StudNeot	Studia neotestamentica
TRu	*Theologische Rundschau*
TS	*Theological Studies*

WUNT	Wissenschaftliche Untersuchungen zum Neuen Testament
ZNW	*Zeitschrift für die neutestamentliche Wissenschaft*
ZTK	*Zeitschrift für Theologie und Kirche*

INTRODUCTION

'That strange old Epistle to the Hebrews; scarcely anyone reads it these days, save for the eleventh chapter'. With this confident opening to his essay an undergraduate managed in one breath to introduce and to dismiss our Epistle! What followed was in much the same vein and did nothing to redeem the situation. It was clearly the opinion of this particular student of theology that Hebrews resided on the higher and decidedly inaccessible shelves of the arcane—totally out of reach of the average twentieth-century reader.

To expose the brashness of this young critic is easy; to deny the validity of his complaint is not. It is undoubtedly true that for the majority of churchgoers, preachers and even biblical scholars, the Epistle to the Hebrews is hardly one of the New Testament's more central works. Christian tradition early claimed it for the apostle Paul, which assured its place in the canon of Christian Scripture. Yet such an ascription also had its disadvantages, not least that its unique voice went largely unrecognized. Even in this century, with the emergence of a scholarly consensus which accepts Hebrews' independence, still in many books on New Testament theology it is either omitted altogether or included as an addendum to Paul. Much the same can be said of the New Testament syllabuses of many theological colleges and universities in the UK.

Hebrews is indeed strange to the modern reader. It represents a conceptual world which is quite foreign to us, and our undergraduate rightly drew attention to the fact. One major difference, obscured by the apparent accessibility of modern English translations, is that it was originally written in koine Greek. To move from the one language to the other, moreover, involves more than a simple exchange of alphabets and vocabulary. We need to appreciate that the world-view of the original text is just as foreign to us as the language in which it is expressed. As the means whereby a people organize, conceptualize and articulate their experiences within a specific point in human history, language—any language—is inevitably particular to its own time and place. In the case of an ancient writing this is more evident. We recognize that translation is needed, that there is a gap between the text and ourselves which needs to be spanned. For all its failings, the historical-critical method, which until recently has dominated twentieth-century biblical studies, has at least taken seriously the distance between the world of the text and that of the modern reader. For proponents of the New Hermeneutical school,[1] of course, therein lies its main weakness—that it emphasizes the gap without providing the necessary means to bridge it. On the other hand, to attempt to overcome the hermeneutical problem by collapsing the distinction between the world of the text and that of the reader is surely to ignore the particularity of language itself.

This study is not intended as a closed book to all but those who read Greek. Hence the Revised Standard Version of the biblical text is cited throughout. Since *Sacred Space* is largely an exegetical work, however, I make no apology for constant recourse to the Greek text.[2] If nothing else it reminds us that we are dealing with a text which is indeed foreign to all of us!

Which is not to give way to the despair of the theology student with whose words this introduction began. What follows is an attempt to make the Epistle to the Hebrews more rather than less accessible to the modern reader. Paradoxically, I believe that this can best be achieved by accepting the text on its own terms rather than ours. I have tried therefore to expound Hebrews as I believe it would have been heard by a first-century, rather than a twentieth-century, audience.

As an ordained Christian minister serving a local church, I am all too aware of the preacher's need to make Scripture relevant to today's world. Yet at the same time, as a university teacher, I also take to heart the stricture with which Ernst Käsemann prefaced his *Commentary on Romans:*

---

1. For an introduction to and critical evaluation of this approach, see A.C. Thiselton, 'The New Hermeneutic', in *New Testament Interpretation: Essays in Principles and Methods* (ed. I.H. Marshall; Exeter: Paternoster Press, 1977), pp. 308-33.

2. *Novum Testamentum Graece* (ed. E. Nestle and K. Aland; Stuttgart: Deutsche Bibelgesellschaft, 26th edn, 1979).

> The impatient, who are concerned only about the results or practical appli-
> cation, should leave their hands off exegesis.[1]

I think that Hebrews has much to contribute to contemporary theology, which has neglected it to its own impoverishment. Nonetheless,
the specific aim of this particular study is more limited. It seeks to
understand the Epistle in its original context, rather than to contemporize or reinterpret it. It is, therefore, primarily a historical enterprise. Which is not to claim some spurious 'objectivity' in my
approach to the text. For if it is true that the text is the child of its
age, so too is the exegete. We bring to our reading of an ancient text
the presuppositions of the time and culture of which we are a part.
Who I am, therefore, conditions what questions I ask of the text,
which in turn colours what I see there. So, for example, for all its
exegetical rigour, Käsemann's study of the Epistle to the Hebrews,
begun as it was in 1938 while its author was imprisoned by the Nazis,
could not but be influenced by the events taking place in Germany at
that time. Käsemann has since acknowledged as much:

> By describing the church as the new people of God on its wandering
> through the wilderness, following the Pioneer and Perfecter of faith, I of
> course had in mind that radical Confessing Church which resisted the
> tyranny in Germany, and which had to be summoned to patience so that it
> could continue its way through endless wastes.[2]

Such an admission by no means invalidates any attempt to understand the theology of Hebrews in its original setting, however. Rather
it reminds us that we are dealing with a writing which is itself overtly
theological, the product of an author who was himself, like Käsemann,
grappling on the one hand with his inherited religious traditions and
on the other with his contemporary experience, in order to make
sense of them both. What was contemporary for him is, of course,
now ancient history for us, and the sermon which he originally
preached to the specific situation of his congregation has become part
of the on-going canon of Christian Scripture. We cannot pretend that
these things do not affect the way we understand Hebrews. Yet it is

---

1. E. Käsemann, *Commentary on Romans* (London: SCM Press, 1980), p. viii.
2. E. Käsemann, *Kirkliche Konflikte*, I (Göttingen: Vandenhoeck & Ruprecht,
1982), p. 17, cited in the Translator's Preface to E. Käsemann, *The Wandering
People of God: An Investigation of the Letter to the Hebrews* (Minneapolis:
Augsburg, 1984), p. 13.

my hope that this attempt to read the Epistle within a viable first-century context, far from consigning it to the limbo of antiquarian study, may do something towards recapturing something of the immediacy of its message.

In choosing 'sacred space' as a way into the thought of the Epistle to the Hebrews, I am not venturing into the realms of comparative anthropology, although I have been sensitized to the importance of notions of sacred space and sacred time in a number of different religious traditions by such works as Mircea Eliade's *The Sacred and the Profane*.[1] Jonathan Z. Smith, a historian of religions who has applied anthropological insights to some of ancient Israel's biblical traditions,[2] has reminded us that for the exegete,

> it is not sufficient merely to name the text; rather it is necessary both to locate a text within a history of tradition and to provide some sort of explanation of the process of continuity and change.[3]

In the case of the Epistle to the Hebrews that means that, in order to appreciate its author's theology, we must understand both the religious traditions which he inherited, and the processes which led him to mould them into this particular articulation of the gospel. Since we can be sure of neither, it is not surprising that commentators have arrived at very different interpretations of our Epistle. What follows is but *one* approach, offered as a contribution to the debate, not *the* definitive reading of the text.

1. M. Eliade, *The Sacred and the Profane: The Nature of Religion* (New York: Harcourt, Brace, 1959). For a critical evaluation of Eliade's work, see Jonathan Z. Smith, *Map is not Territory: Studies in the History of Religions* (Leiden: Brill, 1978), pp. 88-103; *idem, To Take Place: Toward Theory in Ritual* (Chicago: University of Chicago Press, 1987), pp. 1-23.
2. Smith, *Map is not Territory*, pp. 104-28; *idem, To Take Place*, pp. 47-73.
3. Smith, *Map is not Territory*, p. xi.

Chapter 1

A TEXT IN SEARCH OF A CONTEXT

1. *Identifying Hebrews' Central Theme*

It is now almost 80 years since Alexander Nairne published his insightful study of the Epistle to the Hebrews, *The Epistle of Priesthood*.[1] This was an appropriate title, since for Nairne 'the priesthood of Christ is the main theme of the Epistle'.[2] Its author's principal message is, 'Think of our Lord as a priest, and I will make you understand'.[3]

The centrality of the theme of Christ's priesthood for Hebrews is indubitable, and Nairne did well to draw our attention to it, but whether all else in the Epistle is to be subsumed under it is another matter. Nairne's work was not alone in its preoccupation with this theme. It represents a longstanding tradition of interpretation which has focused almost exclusively upon priesthood in Hebrews. It is this motif which has fuelled subsequent theories of the atonement and, perhaps more contentiously, has provided a model of Christian ministry within the church—a priesthood 'after the order of Melchizedek'.

This study, however, is not principally concerned with the subsequent use to which the church in its 'many and various ways' has subjected the Epistle to the Hebrews. Of course, no exegete is *sui generis*, standing uniquely alone and apart from previous traditions of interpretation. Every biblical scholar must recognize this fact, not only to pay due deference in acknowledgment and footnotes to one's elders and betters, but in order to understand one's own preoccupations and

1. A. Nairne, *The Epistle of Priesthood* (Edinburgh: T. & T. Clark, 2nd edn, 1915 [1913]).
2. Nairne, *Priesthood*, p. 136.
3. Nairne, *Priesthood*, p. 30.

presuppositions. That said, however indebted to the secondary sources or the traditions of the past and bound by the presuppositions of the present, an exegete's principal loyalty is to the primary text. Measured against this, a preoccupation with the theme of priesthood does not do justice to the Epistle to the Hebrews, however understandable it may be within the context of the history of Christian doctrine.

Since Nairne, many studies and articles have been published[1] which concentrate on other aspects of the Epistle. Few of these, however, have followed him in attempting to integrate the whole of Hebrews under one 'head'. Ernst Käsemann's *Das wandernde Gottesvolk*[2] and Graham Hughes's *Hebrews and Hermeneutics*[3] are notable exceptions. Each has attempted to identify the Epistle's integrating factor, although for neither of them is it priesthood.

Käsemann sees the myth of the redeemed redeemer as the pattern which unites themes of pilgrimage, cult and priesthood. So the journey on which Christians follow their Lord is that of a pilgrimage whose goal is the attainment of 'rest', that is, mystical union with God. The redeemer, like the high priest before him, needs himself to be perfected/redeemed in order to lead others to this beatific state.

Graham Hughes's work, on the other hand, reflects our present decade's preoccupation with hermeneutical problems. It is not perhaps surprising, therefore, that he identifies the major concern of the author of Hebrews as the problematic of the relationship between the given of the past (i.e. the old dispensation of Judaism) and the revelation of the present (i.e. the new dispensation in Christ). For Hughes it is the attempt to forge a hermeneutical theory which would hold together past and present, which runs throughout the entire Epistle, uniting its disparate themes. In every section the author of Hebrews is seen as propounding a history of the Word, whereby the Old Testament is depicted as a history of promise which finds its fulfilment in Christ.

1. For an annotated bibliography of works published up to 1963, see E. Grässer, 'Der Hebräerbrief 1938–1963', *TRu* 30 (1964), pp. 138-256.
2. E. Käsemann, *Das wandernde Gottesvolk: Eine Untersuchung zum Hebräerbrief* (FRLANT, 37; Göttingen: Vandenhoeck & Ruprecht, 1939). All subsequent citations are from the English translation of the 2nd German edition (1957), *The Wandering People of God*.
3. G. Hughes, *Hebrews and Hermeneutics* (Cambridge: Cambridge University Press, 1979).

So these various emphases, whether upon priesthood, a redeemer myth, or a hermeneutic, can all be seen to reflect the concerns of the time of the exegete as much as if not more than that of the author of the Epistle to the Hebrews and his first audience. Morna D. Hooker[1] has reminded us that the very tools of the exegete's trade have been fashioned 'In His Own Image', and are far from being as objective or precise as we have led ourselves and others to believe.

Yet just as such strictures do not entirely invalidate modern exegetical method, so neither does criticism of previous attempts to grapple with the theology of the Epistle to the Hebrews imply that they have nothing to offer. It merely puts into perspective the partial and contingent nature of all exegesis.

2. *Hebrews' Structural Coherence*

However dated in some ways Nairne's book on the Epistle may seem today, he was nonetheless right to look for coherence in what is arguably the most well-structured of all New Testament works. Ceslau Spicq maintains that its basic form is that of the classical lecture.[2] Thus it opens with a πρόθεσις in which the author's chief propositions are stated (Heb. 1.1-4; these are recapped at 4.14-16; 8.1-2 and 10.19-22). This is followed (1.5–6.20) by a doctrinal introduction (the διήγησις) which leads into the major demonstrative argument (the ἀπόδειξις), that is, the exposition of Christ as priest and victim (7.1–10.18), together with the implications of that for the Christian life (10.19–12.13). Heb. 12.14-29 is the epilogue (ἐπίλογος) of the lecture. A. Vanhoye's work on the literary structure of Hebrews[3] has demonstrated its coherence even more clearly. Even if we do not necessarily accept all of Vanhoye's elaborate chiasms, we are forced to admit that, in form as well as content, this Epistle is no hotch-potch of unrelated themes, but a carefully argued and skilfully crafted piece of

---

1. M.D. Hooker, 'In His Own Image', in *What About the New Testament? Essays in Honour of Christopher Evans* (ed. M.D. Hooker and C. Hickling; London: SCM Press, 1975), pp. 28-44.

2. C. Spicq, *L'épître aux Hébreux*, I (RB; Paris: Gabalda, 3rd edn, 1952), pp. 33-38: 'Une lecture plus attentive permet d'y reconnaître une structure parfaitement classique' (p. 38).

3. A. Vanhoye, *La structure littéraire de l'épître aux Hébreux* (StudNeot, 1; Paris: Desclée de Brouwer, 1963).

sustained theological writing. To say this is not to claim thereby that it is a systematic treatise. The author's statements have undoubtedly contributed to subsequent attempts to generalize the Christian faith, but clearly his original purpose was to address 'a word of encouragement' (λόγος τῆς παρακλήσεως)[1] to a specific audience.

Most modern commentators would recognize the homiletic character of the Epistle to the Hebrews. So it has been classified by Spicq as a type of missionary sermon.[2] More specifically, H. Thyen[3] has seen it as typical of a homiletic tradition which had its origins in the Hellenistic-Jewish synagogue, and which can also be detected in other extant Jewish and Christian works of the period.[4] George Buchanan is even more specific when he claims that Hebrews is a homiletic midrash on Psalm 110.[5]

This does not, of course, indicate whether this sermon was originally oral or written. The form in which it has come down to us is as a written communication, but that does not mean that that was how it was first delivered. Not least we cannot ignore questions as to the original place of all or part of ch. 13, whether it was integral to Hebrews or a later addition, and therefore whether this book began life as an 'epistle'. These issues will have to be discussed in due course. The outcome of that discussion will not, however, affect the basic conclusion that Hebrews 1–12 is a sermon. Part of the problem in determining whether originally written or oral is that the Graeco-Roman culture of which it was a part was essentially oral in style and ideal, even in its written medium. It therefore abounded in rhetorical

1. Heb. 13.22. See F.F. Bruce, *The Epistle to the Hebrews* (New London Commentaries; London: Marshall, Morgan & Scott, 1965), p. 413: 'The phrase clearly denotes a homily'.

2. Spicq, *Hébreux*, I, pp. 18, 220.

3. H. Thyen, *Der Stil der Jüdisch-Hellenischen Homilie* (Göttingen: Vandenhoeck & Ruprecht, 1955). Since this work lacks a detailed index, J. Swetman has done a valuable service in bringing together its conclusions concerning the Epistle to the Hebrews in his article, 'On the Literary Genre of the "Epistle" to the Hebrews', *NovT* 11 (1969), pp. 261-69.

4. Thyen claims to find a similar homiletic pattern in all or part of Philo's *Leg. All.*, *4 Macc.*, *3 Macc.*, Tobit, Wis. Sol., *Test. XII Patr.*, James, Acts 7, *Barn.*, *Hermas* and the *Didache*.

5. G.W. Buchanan, *To the Hebrews* (AB; New York: Doubleday, 1972), pp. xii-xxii.

devices. Many of these are employed by the author of Hebrews. 'About this we have much to say',[1] 'Now the point of what we are saying is this',[2] 'What more shall I say? Time would fail me'[3]—these are commonplaces of the rhetorician's art.[4]

It is in the paraenetic[5] sections—those passages in which the author turns from the scriptural passages he is expounding or the theological point he is making to admonish his audience directly—that we most clearly hear the cadences of the preacher. Furthermore, these passages are not confined to the end of the work but abound throughout. And neither (with the exception of ch. 13, which consists of a series of pastoral instructions and personal notes more reminiscent of the ending of Paul's Epistles[6]) is the paraenesis of Hebrews a mere listing of diverse admonitions and exhortations. The paraenetic sections are closely integrated into the theological exposition, as, not least, the author's use of connecting particles shows.

The διὰ τοῦτο (2.1) with which he turns from his affirmation of Christ's supremacy over even the angels (which is the theme of 1.4–2.18) to address his audience directly is an emphatic introduction to an *a fortiori* argument. If the message declared by angels[7] is valid and to

1. Heb. 5.11.
2. Heb. 8.1.
3. Heb. 11.32.
4. For other stylistic and rhetorical features, see Spicq, *Hébreux*, I, pp. 351-78; M.R. Cosby, 'The Rhetorical Composition of Hebrews 11', *JBL* 107 (1988), pp. 257-73. Thyen (*Stil*, pp. 43, 45, 50, 53, 58-59) attributes some of these to the influence of the Cynic-Stoic diatribe.
5. For a definition of paraenesis, see M. Dibelius, *Geschichte der urchristlichen Literatur*, II (Berlin: de Gruyter, 1926), p. 65: 'Paraenesis is what one calls a listing together of diverse, often unrelated, admonitions in a homogeneous style of address' (my translation). More generally, the term can be used of exhortation directly addressed to the reader.
6. See F.F. Filson, *'Yesterday': A Study of Hebrews in the Light of Chapter 13* (SBT, 4; London: SCM Press, 1967), pp. 22-25, who thinks that the fourfold structure of Heb. 13—(a) varied teaching and injunctions, (b) formal benediction, (c) personal greetings and messages and (d) a closing brief benediction—can be paralleled by the endings of 1 Thessalonians, 2 Thessalonians, Galatians, 2 Timothy, Philippians, Romans (and 1 Peter).
7. Cf. Gal. 3.19; Acts 7.35. For evidence within Judaism of a belief in angelic mediation of the Torah, see M.E. Isaacs, *The Concept of Spirit: A Study of Pneuma in Hellenistic Judaism and its Bearing on the New Testament* (Heythrop

be obeyed, how much more must that declared by the Lord be heeded (2.1-4). In 3.1–4.13 the emphasis is predominantly paraenetic, interspersed with theological 'asides'. Here the author's scriptural exegesis is entirely at the service of his exhortation. In fact the section ends with a reminder that Scripture itself has an admonitory effect:

> For the word of God is living and active, sharper than a two-edged sword, piercing to the division of soul and spirit, of joints and marrow, and discerning the thoughts and intentions of the heart (4.12).

So the readers are exhorted to 'consider Jesus, the apostle and high priest of our confession' (3.1), who, like Moses, was faithful, and yet, unlike Moses, was a son rather than a servant in the household of God's people (3.1-6). 'Therefore' (διό 3.7) Ps. 95.7-11 is cited as a warning to his audience against falling into the unbelief of Israel in the wilderness. They are exhorted to seize the 'today' of the psalm and to beware 'therefore' (οὖν 4.1) lest they fail to enter into God's promised rest:

> Let us therefore (οὖν) strive to enter that rest, that no one fall by the same sort of disobedience (4.11).

Even that most explicitly paraenetic of sections, 5.11–6.20, is closely connected with the theological argument which precedes it. Thus it is the Melchizedekian high priesthood of Christ mentioned in v. 10 to which the περὶ οὖ in v. 11 refers, and which he finds difficult to explain to recipients whom he regards as immature. Hence it is his desire to expound Christ in terms of a priesthood 'after the order of Melchizedek' which leads him both to rebuke his readers for their lack of spiritual growth and to urge them to better things by reminding them that they are the heirs of God's promise to Abraham—a promise doubly sure since it was confirmed by an oath (6.13-20). This reminder of the fidelity of God leads back, via a reference to Jesus who has entered the holy of holies as a forerunner (vv. 19-20), to the theme which initiated this paraenetic section, that is, Christ's Melchizedekian high priesthood.

This is taken up immediately in ch. 7 and is further expounded in terms of Jesus as high priest and victim until 10.18. At this point we encounter another οὖν (v. 19), which links the theme of Christ's sacrifice with the following exhortation to perseverance (10.19-39).

Monographs, 1; London: Heythrop College, 1976), pp. 129-30.

Here the Epistle's solemn warning of the impossibility of a second repentance and re-admission into the ranks of the people of God (10.26-31)[1] is wholly dependent upon the preceding argument—that Jesus' sacrifice was superior to that of the Aaronic system precisely because it did not have to be repeated.[2] Only that which is not efficacious needs repetition. Since Christ's sacrifice did achieve what it intended, that is, to overcome the barrier between God and humankind, it did not have to be repeated. It was 'once' (ἄπαξ),[3] 'once for all time' (ἐφάπαξ).[4] Indeed, for the author of Hebrews to admit the possibility of a repetition of Christ's sacrifice would be to undermine the cultic model with which he is working. The corollary of Jesus' unrepeatable death is that he cannot deal with sin a second time. Therefore, having once abdicated from the community of faith, there can be no way back.

'But we are not those who shrink back and are destroyed, but those who have faith and keep their souls' (10.39). With these words of encouragement our author urges his readers to persevere in the faith, listing in ch. 11 those heroes of old who displayed such faith. With the emphatic τοιγαροῦν (for that very reason) he begins his final exhortation to perseverance (12.1-29):

> Since we are surrounded by so great a cloud of witnesses, let us also lay aside every weight, and sin which clings so closely and let us run with perseverance the race that is set before us, looking to Jesus the pioneer and perfecter of our faith (12.1-2).

It is this integration of doctrinal and paraenetic material which tells against any attempt to regard the two as separate entities. F.C. Synge[5] has contended that they originally constituted two separate written units: (1) a theological work whose theme was that of the 'Heavenly Companion'—here the author drew upon an existing collection of scriptural *Testimonia* in order to demonstrate to Jewish opponents that Jesus was the 'Heavenly Companion' mentioned in various Old Testament passages; and (2) an exhortatory piece composed to convert

1. See also Heb. 6.4-6.
2. Heb. 9.12-14, 25-28; 10.11-14.
3. ἄπαξ; cf. Heb. 9.26, 27, 28. With regard to the high priest on the Day of Atonement see Heb. 9.7.
4. ἐφάπαξ; cf. Heb. 7.27; 9.12; 10.10.
5. F.C. Synge, *Hebrews and the Scriptures* (London: SPCK, 1959).

those Jews who were as yet only loosely attached to a Christian syna-gogue.[1] There are major problems with Synge's thesis, however, not least with his assumption that Hebrews employed an existing *Testimonia* collection.[2] Above all there is the unlikelihood that the theological and paraenetic sections were originally intended for two different audiences. Any attempt to divide the two types of material is not only unnecessary for an intelligible reading of the book, but does violence to its very structure. That structure demands a unified reading, not least because it is a powerful medium for the author's message—that an understanding of the person and work of Christ is essentially related to an understanding of the present life of the people of God.

It would therefore seem evident from any study of the structure of the Epistle to the Hebrews that its paraenesis and its theology cannot be considered apart from each other. Yet this realization by no means solves all the exegete's problems since in many ways it would be easier if the integral nature of the various sections of the Epistle could be ignored. We might then at least be able to separate issues of its original audience from those of its doctrinal content. As it is, trying to relate the two poses its own special difficulties.

3. *Problems in Determining the Epistle's Audience*

This brings us face to face with one of the most critical decisions to be made in reading the Epistle to the Hebrews, that is, determining the

1. Synge (*Hebrews*, pp. 43-53) assigns Heb. 1.1-14; 2.5-18; 3.1-6; 4.14–5.10; 6.13–10.25 to this 'Heavenly Companion' unit, and 2.1-4; 3.7–4.13; 5.11–6.12; 10.25-31; 12.18ff. to the 'Exhortation' unit.

2. Synge, *Hebrews*, pp. 53-55. R. Longenecker (*Biblical Exegesis in the Apostolic Period* [Grand Rapids: Eerdmans; Exeter: Paternoster Press, 1975], p. 180) believes that the catena of Old Testament passages cited in Heb. 1.3–2.4 was probably understood as messianic and brought together by the church prior to Hebrews. He does not, however, commit himself to a written *Testimonia* theory. Commentators vary in the number of Old Testament passages they believe to be cited in Hebrews—not least because it is not always clear exactly to which passage the author is alluding. Longenecker (*Exegesis*, pp. 164-67) lists 38 direct quotations together with a further 55 allusions. What would tell against a *Testimonia* theory is that, of these, some 20 passages are not cited in any other New Testament work, and even where Hebrews does have a common Old Testament passage it sometimes has a variant wording (e.g. Hab. 2.4 in Heb. 10.38; cf. Rom. 1.17; Gal. 3.11), or applies it in very different ways (e.g. Ps. 8.6 in Heb. 2.8; cf. 1 Cor. 15.27).

relationship between the situation of those addressed and the theological exposition of the author. Since the two are so interrelated, our view of its audience will largely condition our understanding of Hebrews' message. Yet the plethora of diverse and sometimes contradictory reconstructions of the Epistle's *Sitz im Leben* bears witness to the ambiguity of the evidence and the complexity of the problem. So, for example, Hebrews has been read as a missionary tract intended to convert Jews,[1] or alternatively as addressed to Gentiles already converted to Christianity, either to encourage them not to give up their faith,[2] or to reinterpret the Old Testament theme of the journey of God's people in terms of Gnostic mythology and thereby to present the Christian life as the soul's pilgrimage of faith, following the redeemed redeemer to an immaterial, heavenly world.[3] More traditionally, the recipients have been thought to have been Jewish Christians.[4] This is to interpret the superscription Πρὸς Ἑβραίους in terms of the ethnic origin rather than the present religious affiliation of the community to whom it was written.[5] In which case these 'Hebrews' are unlike those we find in Acts 6.1 who seem to be Semitic-speaking Jewish Christians. They would be closer to Luke's 'Hellenists',[6] since there is every indication that our Epistle came from

1. H. Kosmala, *Hebräer, Essener, Christen* (Leiden: Brill, 1969).

2. So W.G. Kümmel, *Introduction to the New Testament* (London: SCM Press, 2nd edn, 1975), pp. 399-401, who cites Kuss, Michel, Albertz, Feine-Behm, Henslow, Jülicher-Fascher, Marxsen, Michaelis, Schelkle, Wrede, Käsemann, Oepke and Schierse as those who postulate a Gentile audience. To this list should now be added H. Braun. E.F. Scott (*The Epistle to the Hebrews: Its Doctrine and Significance* [Edinburgh: T. & T. Clark, 1922]) and J. Moffatt (*The Epistle to the Hebrews* [ICC; Edinburgh: T. & T. Clark, 1924]) are rare examples of English scholars who have adopted this position.

3. Käsemann, *Wandering People*.

4. The view that Hebrews was addressed to a Jewish-Christian audience has been the accepted consensus among commentators from the very earliest times. According to Kümmel (*Introduction*, p. 399), the suggestion that it was addressed to Gentiles was not advanced before 1936 (by E.M. Roeth).

5. See Paul's claim to be a Hebrew in Phil. 3.5.

6. See M. Hengel, 'Zwischen Jesus und Paulus', *ZTK* 72 (1975), pp. 151-206; H. Windisch, '"Ελλην', *TDNT*, II, pp. 502-16; *contra* O. Cullmann, 'The Significance of the Qumran Texts for Research into the Beginnings of Christianity', in *The Scrolls and the New Testament* (ed. K. Stendahl; London: SCM Press,

and was written to a Greek-speaking milieu. We cannot be sure that 'To the Hebrews' is an accurate description of its original recipients, however. Although the superscription is to be found in all extant manuscripts, it must be borne in mind that it probably reflects a later interpretative tradition rather than forming part of the original work. It cannot, therefore, determine our conclusions as to its original recipients. Those who believe that the Epistle was originally written to Gentiles are obliged to ignore it altogether.

Yet even those who think that Hebrews was written to a group of Jewish Christians are by no means agreed as to what kind of Judaism they came from. Is it Palestinian or Diaspora, mainstream or heterodox? Increasingly scholars are becoming aware of the dangers of classifying the Judaism of the first century of the Common Era according to such simplistic distinctions. Hence we are now appreciating that the differences between Judaean and Diaspora Jewry in this period were of degree rather than kind.[1] Furthermore, at home and abroad there were movements within Judaism which had more in common with each other than with a shared topography or even a common language.

Neither is there agreement as to the author's purpose in writing to these Jewish Christians. Is he attempting, as R.E. Glaze[2] maintains, to get them to leave the synagogue and thereby make a complete break

---

1958), pp. 18-32, who equates 'Hellenist' with 'sectarian'. More recently, R. Murray ('Jews, Hebrews and Christians: Some Needed Distinctions', *NovT* 24 [1982], pp. 194-208) has suggested that 'Jews' should be kept to designate those who identified with Jerusalem and its Temple, over against 'Hebrews' which should be applied to those who were hostile to the same. He claims (p. 202) that our Epistle came from such dissenting circles and is therefore aptly addressed 'To the Hebrews'. Cf. F.F. Bruce, ' "To the Hebrews" or "To the Essenes"?', *NTS* 9 (1962–63), pp. 217-32. Murray's conclusions as to the provenance of Hebrews, however, are by no means integral to his discussion of nomenclature. His suggested usage of 'Jew' and 'Hebrew' has found little scholarly support and is not helpful in discussing our Epistle. Here Ἑβραῖοι seems more naturally to designate Christians of Jewish origin rather than to single them out as dissenters. Cf. M. Black, *The Scrolls and Christian Origins* (London: Nelson, 1961), p. 78.

1. See M. Hengel, *Judaism and Hellenism: Studies in their Encounter in Palestine during the Early Hellenistic Period* (2 vols.; London: SCM Press, 1974), *passim*, and works cited in Isaacs, *Concept of Spirit*, pp. 1-9.

2. R.E. Glaze, *No Easy Salvation* (Zachary, LA: Insight, 1966), pp. 13-29.

with Judaism, or is William Manson[1] correct in seeing the author's intention as the encouragement of a group of Jewish Christians to leave the safety of a *religio licita* and to embark upon a mission to Gentiles? Alternatively, others have seen the problem of the recipients not as an unwillingness to abandon an exclusively Jewish Christianity but as a desire to return to a Judaism which they had already left. On this interpretation the author is attempting to prevent apostasy to Judaism.[2] A re-emergence of nationalism at the outbreak of the Jewish War in 66 CE has been the favourite suggestion to account for such an impulse. George Buchanan[3] has depicted the recipients as a group of Diaspora Jewish Christians who had returned to Jerusalem to await the parousia. Its delay threatened the continuation of the group, some of whom were tempted to leave Jerusalem and abandon their Zionist hopes, while others were contemplating a return to the sacrificial system still operating in the Jerusalem Temple. Raymond Brown also[4] sees the threat of a reversion to the sacrificial system of Judaism as lying behind the Epistle, but he locates the recipients in Rome where he suggests that after 70 CE there arose among Jewish Christians a conservative movement to revive the cult—this time based on the wilderness tabernacle rather than the now destroyed Jerusalem Temple. C.F.D. Moule,[5] dating the Epistle before the fall of Jerusalem, has suggested that it was intended to explain why alone of all religions in the ancient world—pagan or Jewish—Christianity had no sacrificial system.

---

1. W. Manson, *The Epistle to the Hebrews: An Historical and Theological Reconsideration* (London: Hodder & Stoughton, 1951).

2. Among modern commentators see, e.g., Manson, *Hebrews*; Bruce, *Hebrews*; Buchanan, *Hebrews*; P.E. Hughes, *A Commentary on the Epistle to the Hebrews* (Grand Rapids: Eerdmans, 1977); and D. Guthrie, *Hebrews* (TNTC; Grand Rapids: Eerdmans; Leicester: Inter-Varsity Press, 1983). Cf. also B. Lindars, 'The Rhetorical Structure of Hebrews', *NTS* 35 (1989), pp. 382-406, who identifies the audience as a group of Diaspora Jewish Christians in danger of reverting to membership in the synagogue. The delay of the parousia has brought about a loss of confidence in the permanent purificatory effects of the death of Christ. Lindars dates Hebrews before 70 CE.

3. Buchanan, *Hebrews*, p. 266.

4. R.E. Brown and J.P. Meier, *Antioch and Rome* (London: Geoffrey Chapman, 1983), pp. 139-88.

5. C.F.D. Moule, 'Sanctuary and Sacrifice in the Church of the New Testament', *JTS* 1 (1950), pp. 29-41.

Scholars who have concentrated on the Epistle's teaching about Christ's supremacy over the angels have been inclined to see the author's purpose as corrective. So for F.D.V. Narborough,[1] Hebrews was written to offset an incipient Jewish Gnosticism similar to that attacked by the Epistle to the Colossians. This suggestion was taken up by T.W. Manson[2] who maintained that the first ten chapters of Hebrews was intended as a complete refutation of those tendencies which were later to develop into what J.B. Lightfoot classified as the Colossian 'heresy',[3] that is, the relegation of Christ to the rank of an angel, together with the maintenance of Jewish calendrical, ritual and dietary customs. Hence Hebrews 1–4 asserts the unique supremacy of Christ over all angelic intermediaries, and Hebrews 5–10 claims that he has superseded all Jewish ritual.

These are but some of the different approaches which have been taken vis-à-vis the possible recipients of the Epistle. 'Time would fail me' as our author would say, 'to tell of all the others!' I have outlined some of the major hypotheses, not in order to cover the history of previous research, but to give some indication of the widely diverse ways scholars have viewed the situation which Hebrews addressed. These in their turn have given rise to different understandings of what

---

1. F.D.V. Narborough, *The Epistle to the Hebrews* (Oxford: Clarendon Press, 1930).

2. T.W. Manson, 'The Problem of the Epistle to the Hebrews', *BJRL* 32 (1949–50), pp. 1-17. Manson believed that Hebrews was written by Apollos to Colossae before Paul wrote Colossians. More recently, R. Jewett (*Letter to Pilgrims: A Commentary on the Epistle to the Hebrews* [New York: Pilgrim Press, 1981]) has taken up this suggestion of a Lycus Valley setting for Hebrews. Following C.P. Anderson ('The Epistle to the Hebrews and the Pauline Letter Collection', *HTR* 59 [1966], pp. 429-48 and *idem*, 'Hebrews among the Letters of Paul', *SR* 5 [1975–76], pp. 258-66), he identifies it with the 'lost' letter to the Laodicaeans, written not by the same author as Colossians, but about the same time (55/56 CE), by Epaphras. According to Jewett both letters were intended to refute any Gnostic notion that the Christian was beleaguered by hostile forces, impeding the journey to the heavenly homeland.

3. J.B. Lightfoot, *Colossians and Philemon* (London: Macmillan, 2nd edn, 1876). The existence of any such 'heresy' at Colossae, however, has been called into question by M.D. Hooker, 'Were There False Teachers at Colossae?', in *Christ and Spirit in the New Testament: Studies in Honour of C.F.D. Moule* (ed. B. Lindars and S. Smalley; Cambridge: Cambridge University Press, 1973), pp. 315-32.

the author was saying to his audience. So, according to its supposed *Sitz im Leben*, Hebrews has been interpreted as principally either apologetic, corrective, polemical or exhortatory in tone and intention.

This has been made possible by the paucity of information to be gained from the paraenetic sections themselves. Unlike a letter, we gain no insight into its intended readers from Hebrews' opening, since it begins with a prologue rather than an epistolary address. The first indication we have of the situation of its recipients is at the beginning of ch. 2 where the danger of drifting is mentioned:

> Therefore we must pay the closer attention to what we have heard lest we drift away from it (2.1).

The readers are therefore exhorted not to desert the faith:

> Take care, brethren, lest there be in any of you an evil, unbelieving heart, leading you to fall away from the living God (3.12).

Rather, they should beware of failing, like faithless Israel in the wilderness, to enter God's promised rest:

> Let us fear, lest any of you be judged to have failed to reach it (4.1)... Let us therefore strive to enter that rest, that no one fall by the same sort of disobedience (4.11).

This vocabulary of drifting (παραρρέω), desertion (ἀφίσταμαι), falling short (ὑστερέω) or falling (πίπτω) is vague and unspecific. It gives us no indication as to what constituted a threat to their faith. Hence, as we have seen, it has been interpreted by commentators to substantiate theories of a Gentile audience in danger of reverting to paganism, or a Jewish one tempted to return to Judaism. Yet the most obvious concern of our author, and one that is too often overlooked in the debate, is that the group should not give up their Christian faith. He is more concerned to emphasize what they would be leaving rather than to discuss what they might be reverting to. Hence his warnings that no second repentance is possible (6.4-6; 10.26-31) and his exhortation to fidelity:

> Let us hold fast the confession of our hope without wavering, for he who promised is faithful (10.23).

An appeal to the faithfulness of God to his promise is therefore used as the basis for his call to a similar fidelity on the part of the group.

It is important to notice, however, that all this is only by way of warning. Unless one assumes that every sin and shortcoming mentioned by a preacher in his or her sermon, including atheism, necessarily has its proponents in the listening congregation, there is nothing to suggest that as yet this group had given up their Christian faith. What they are specifically rebuked for is lack of progress in understanding. They are berated as those who, although they by now should be teachers, are still in need of elementary instruction (5.13-14). This basic teaching, 'the first principles of God's word' (5.12 τὰ στοιχεῖα τῆς ἀρχῆς τῶν λογίων τοῦ θεοῦ), is enumerated at the beginning of ch. 6 as: repentance from deeds which lead to death;[1] faith in God; teaching about ritual ablutions;[2] the laying on of hands;[3] a belief in the resurrection of the dead[4] and eternal judgment. As this list stands there is nothing specifically Christian about any of its items. All form part of Jewish faith and practice of the period. How far, then, or in what sense, can they be described as 'the elementary doctrine of Christ' (6.1 τὸν τῆς ἀρχῆς τοῦ Χριστοῦ λόγον)?

J. Clifford Adams[5] has suggested that τοῦ Χριστοῦ should be understood as a subjective genitive, that is, that the recipients are being asked to leave behind the original words of Jesus and move on to a deeper understanding of his person and work in terms of a priesthood Christology. That the author is finding their spiritual immaturity a hindrance to his attempt to explain the significance of Christ's work

---

1. *Contra* Jewett, *Pilgrims*, pp. 95-96, there is no reason to suppose that behind νεκρὰ ἔργα lies the Pauline contrast between works of the Law and justification by faith, since nowhere else in Hebrews is such a contrast drawn. Although Hab. 2.2-4 is cited by both authors (Heb. 10.37-38; Rom. 1.17; Gal. 3.11), Hebrews does not do so within the context of a discussion of Mosaic Torah.

2. βαπτισμῶν (6.2) is unlikely to refer to Christian baptism since it is the genitive plural of the masculine noun βαπτισμός, whereas the usual New Testament word for baptism (βάπτισμα) is neuter. *Contra*, J.D.G. Dunn (*Baptism in the Holy Spirit* [SBT, 15; London: SCM Press, 1970], pp. 206-207) cites the variant reading βαπτισμῷ (masculine) at Col. 2.12 in support of understanding Heb. 6.2 as a reference to baptism. Nowhere in the New Testament is baptism spoken of in the plural, however. It is therefore preferable to reject this reading of Hebrews.

3. For laying on of hands as the transference of power and the bestowal of blessing in both Old and New Testament tradition, see E. Lohse, 'χείρ', *TDNT*, IX, pp. 424-34.

4. This seems to refer to a belief in the resurrection of the dead in general rather than to the resurrection of Jesus in particular.

5. J.C. Adams, 'Exegesis of Heb. 6.1ff.', *NTS* 13 (1967), pp. 378-85.

in terms of a Melchizedekian high priesthood is clearly stated at 5.11:

> About this we have much to say which is hard to explain, since you have
> become dull of hearing.

It is also true that it is the theme of Christ's high priesthood after the order of Melchizedek that he is anxious to move on to. Yet against Adams it must be said that it would be most unlikely that any New Testament author would make such a distinction between the words of Jesus and his own interpretation of them, let alone that he would classify the sayings of Jesus as elementary in comparison with his own more advanced understanding. Scholars can and do disagree as to the extent to which the earliest Christians felt free to put their subsequent interpretations of Christianity upon the lips of Jesus.[1] Yet even those who would see behind many of the sayings attributed to Jesus of Nazareth, the words of early Christian prophets articulating what they believed to be teaching inspired by the risen Christ, envisage thereby an appeal to the ἀρχή of Christ's earthly ministry,[2] not a claim that later insight either goes beyond or is in some way superior to the beginning. Therefore, even allowing for doctrinal and other developments which took place in the early church, these were not seen as introducing a distinction between the original meaning or teaching of Jesus and its contemporary application. Biblical authors, whether interpreting the Scriptures or the words of Jesus, made no claim to be introducing something new into their text; rather they claimed that they were unfolding what was always there, intended for those with God-given eyes to see from the beginning. Therefore Adams's interpretation would seem untenable.

The more obvious understanding of this verse would be to take τοῦ Χριστοῦ as an objective genitive, that is, that the teaching is about Christ rather than having him as its author. Difficulties with this only arise if one assumes that a content which is Jewish cannot also be 'about Christ'. Yet the Christianity which produced the Epistle to the Hebrews, far from seeing itself as a different religion from Judaism, viewed all God's revelation—in the past in which he spoke 'in many and various ways. . . by the prophets' (1.1), as well as the present,

---

1. See J.D.G. Dunn, 'Prophetic "I" Sayings and the Jesus Tradition: The Importance of Testing Prophetic Utterances within Early Christianity', *NTS* 24 (1977–78), pp. 175-98.
2. See 1 Jn 1.1; 2.7, 13, 14, 24; 3.11.

'these last days' (1.1)—as equally 'about Christ'. To fail to see this is to misunderstand the whole purpose of the author's scriptural exegesis, which is to demonstrate that the Old Testament is amenable to a christological interpretation. Indeed for him that is what it was always about.

His impatience with his readers, therefore, is not that they have stayed within Judaism rather than moved on to Christianity, nor that their understanding has remained at the rudimentary level of the words of Jesus, as Adams's interpretation would suggest. His complaint is that they have failed to see that the (Jewish) Scriptures themselves testify to the work and person of Jesus as Melchizedekian high priest. Hence they have not found in those Scriptures the encouragement they need at this time when their faith is flagging and their confidence in God's purposes is on the wane.

It could well be that they are castigated for their lack of exegetical insight because the group, rather than being general, was specialized in its composition. A. Nairne said of the Epistle, 'It smells of the study, not the open air of life where history is being made'.[1] Certainly there is much to suggest, in its concept and execution, that this treatise-like sermon had a study group as its intended audience. Some members had not been attending as assiduously as in the past (10.25), and our author exhorts them all to meet together and thereby to encourage one another 'to love and good works' (10.24). If it were addressed to a group in training for some form of Christian 'rabbinate', then it would explain not only our author's recourse to exegetical methods which he does not bother to explain or justify, but would give more point to his jibes: 'Solid food is for the mature, and those who have their faculties trained by practice to distinguish good from evil' (5.14), and: 'Those who by now should be teachers still need milk, not solid food' (5.12). There is no need to see here, with Helmut Koester,[2] an appeal to esoteric scriptural Gnosis; merely a somewhat irate Yeshiva rabbi, frustrated by a group of sluggish pupils

---

1. Nairne, *Priesthood*, p. 7.

2. H. Koester, *Introduction to the New Testament*, II (Berlin: de Gruyter; Philadelphia: Fortress Press, 1982), pp. 273-74. Although Koester believes that Hebrews was intended for the church at large rather than an elect group, he does state that it 'belongs to the same category as those writings of Philo of Alexandria that are esoteric and that seem to mediate deeper insight into Scripture for the initiate' (p. 273).

who have lost their initial enthusiasm and diligence. More importantly the author of Hebrews is afraid that they are in danger of losing their Christian vocation.

There is nothing in the Epistle which would suggest that the particular impulse for such negligence was the present experience of persecution. Mention of the group's sufferings (παθήματα) is clearly with reference to the past—the 'former days' (10.32)—a time soon after their initial conversion ('after you were enlightened'),[1] rather than a description of their contemporary experience. They are reminded of their previous endurance in the face of public humiliation and ill-treatment:

> sometimes being publicly exposed to abuse and affliction (θλῖψις), and sometimes being partners (κοινωνοί) with those so treated (10.33).[2]

Whatever the specific nature of such 'persecution'—and from the use of the word θλῖψις in 10.33 which in many other New Testament contexts is associated with persecution[3] it would seem reasonable to suggest that, even if not instigated by the state, the suffering endured by members of this group was in some way seen to be the result of their Christian commitment—it had not, either in the past or the present, resulted in death. 'In your struggle against sin you have not yet resisted to the point of shedding your blood' (12.4).

Commentators such as F.F. Bruce, who are anxious to locate the recipients of Hebrews in Rome,[4] see behind this passage (10.32-34) a

1. Although later works speak of baptism as 'enlightenment' (see Justin, *Apol.* 1.61, 65; *Dial.* 122), and the Syriac Peshitta translates both Heb. 6.4 and 10.32 as 'baptism', it seems unlikely that in either verse the author had baptism in mind. The language of φωτίζειν and cognates was commonly used as a metaphor for spiritual illumination (see Spicq, *Hébreux*, II, pp. 150-52). Even Dunn, who wishes to see in Heb. 6.2 a reference to Christian baptism (see p. 28 n. 2), denies that in this verse φωτισθέντας is synonymous with βαπτισθέντας. It means rather 'the saving illumination brought by the Spirit through the Gospel' (Dunn, *Baptism*, p. 210). R. Williamson ('The Eucharist and the Epistle to the Hebrews', *NTS* 21 [1975], pp. 302-303), on the basis of the structure of vv. 4 and 5, reaches much the same conclusion.
2. The language of partnership (κοινωνοί) and sympathy (συνεπαθήσατε) in Heb. 10.33-34 strongly implies that those to whom compassion had been shown were fellow Christians, suffering as a result of their faith.
3. E.g. Mk 4.17; Mt. 13.21; Mk 13.19; Mt. 24.9; Jn 16.33.
4. Bruce, *Hebrews*, pp. 267-69.

reference to the expulsion by Claudius of the Jewish colony from the Imperial city in 49 CE.[1] Since there is no evidence to suggest that Jewish Christians were distinguished from any other kind of Jews by the Roman authorities at this time, no doubt they too would have been affected by the ban. In attempting to identify the specific suffering referred to in Hebrews it is important, however, to bear in mind, as P.E. Hughes has said, that 'Our author. . . is not concerned here with afflictions that overtook Jews as such, which would be beside the point, but with the sufferings which his readers had endured in consequence of their having embraced the Christian faith'.[2] It is therefore highly unlikely that we have here a reference to Claudius's expulsion of the Jews from Rome.

Bruce is, of course, not the only proponent of the theory that Rome was the original destination of the Epistle to the Hebrews. In this century such a position has had some notable exponents including A. von Harnack, A.S. Peake, T. Zahn and W. Neil.[3] William Manson's Baird Lectures of 1949 were largely devoted to elaborating his thesis that the addressees of the Epistle were members of the church in Rome, which was itself predominantly Jewish in composition.[4] More recently, Raymond Brown has expanded Manson's thesis, drawing upon Hebrews and including it in his reconstruction of the Christian community in Rome in the first century. In *Antioch and Rome*[5] he rehearses the usual arguments for a Roman destination and concentrates on two major factors in the debate: (1) the external attestation to knowledge and use of Hebrews in Rome from an early date, and (2)

---

1. The date of the Claudian edict is disputed. R. Jewett (*Dating Paul's Life* [London: SCM Press 1975], pp. 36-38) argues for 49 CE, *contra* G. Lüdemann (*Paul Apostle to the Gentiles: Studies in Chronology* [London: SCM Press, 1984], pp. 6-7) who favours 41 CE.

2. See P.E. Hughes, *Hebrews*, p. 428.

3. P.E. Hughes, *Hebrews*, p. 17 n. 19. See also R.McL. Wilson, *Hebrews* (NCC; Basingstoke: Marshall, Morgan & Scott; Grand Rapids: Eerdmans, 1987), p. 14; H.W. Attridge, *The Epistle to the Hebrews* (Hermeneia; Philadelphia: Fortress Press, 1989), pp. 9-10. M. Rissi (*Die Theologie des Hebräerbriefs: Ihre Verankerung in der Situation des Verfassers und seiner Leser* [WUNT, 41; Tübingen: Mohr [Paul Siebeck], 1987]) identifies the recipients as Jewish Christians located in Rome, but separated from the main church there.

4. Manson, *Hebrews*.

5. Brown and Meier, *Antioch and Rome*, pp. 142-51.

Rome's reluctance to accept the Epistle as by the apostle Paul and to include it in its canon of Scripture.

In the first case Brown stresses not only that the earliest use of Hebrews (although not explicitly cited either by title or name) is made by Clement of Rome in his letter to the Corinthians (usually dated at the turn of the first century),[1] but that throughout the second century CE it is to Rome we must look for evidence of an awareness of the Epistle. Thus he cites the *Shepherd of Hermas*, the Old Testament commentaries of Hippolytus and the presbyter Gaius as utilizing it.

What is equally clear, however, is that the theological *Tendenz* of Hebrews is quite at odds with that of *1 Clement* and the *Shepherd of Hermas*. Brown is himself at pains to point out that 'Both *1 Clement* and *Hermas*, although using the wording of Hebrews, move in almost opposite thought-directions'.[2] This is particularly evident in the case of Clement who, in spite of his knowledge of Hebrews, was happy to use the model of the Levitical cult as the God-given exemplar of Christian ministry. Such an approach would, however, be anathema to the author of the Epistle to the Hebrews. For him, the Levitical pattern had found its end and replacement in Jesus—the Melchizedekian high priest. The situation is similar in the case of Hebrews' teaching on the impossibility of a second repentance and restoration to the community of a Christian who has once 'fallen away'.[3] When we come later to consider our author's attitude to this, we shall see that his so-called 'rigorism' is integral to his whole argument vis-à-vis the significance and efficacy of Jesus' soteriological role. Although it would seem that Hermas knew Hebrews,[4] in allowing restoration after one post-baptismal lapse,[5] his thought moves in a wholly different direction.

It is the combination of these two factors, that is, (1) knowledge of Hebrews from an early date in Rome and yet (2) its utilization by

---

1. See *1 Clem.* 36.2-5, Heb. 1.3-13; *1 Clem.* 17.1, Heb. 11.37; *1 Clem.* 17.5, Heb. 3.5. For a discussion of the problems of dating *1 Clement*, see H.B. Green, 'Matthew, 1 Clement and Luke: Their Sequence and Relationship', *JTS* 40 (1989), pp. 1-25. See also Attridge, *Hebrews*, pp. 7-9.

2. Brown and Meier, *Antioch and Rome*, pp. 147-48.

3. Heb. 6.4-6; 10.26-31. *Herm. Man.* 4.3 appears to be a reference to this particular teaching.

4. See *Herm. Vis.* 2.2.1-4.

5. *Herm. Vis.* 2.2.1-4.

Clement and Hermas in ways which go against the grain of the Epistle's theology, which provides Raymond Brown with the answer to that question most difficult for those who would accept Hebrews' Roman destination. 'If Hebrews was originally written to Rome why did it take the western church in general and the Roman church in particular so long to accept its Pauline authorship and thereby to admit it into the canon of Scripture?'[1] After all, as late as the fourth century CE Eusebius records that some had rejected the canonical status of Hebrews on the grounds that it was disputed by the church of Rome which did not accept that it was written by Paul.[2]

This self-same church father gives us, however, a very different picture of the Epistle's status in the eastern church. In Alexandria, from the third century CE onwards, at one and the same time it was both accepted as canonical and yet problems as to its authorship were acknowledged. The fathers of the east were clearly not prepared to accept its relegation, even it if did not originate from the apostle Paul. Yet equally clearly they associated it with the Pauline tradition. They adopted various means whereby the problems of Pauline authorship could be acknowledged and yet the canonicity of Hebrews be affirmed. Thus according to Pantaenus it was written by the apostle, but out of motives of reverence for the Lord who had been sent to the Hebrews, Paul, the apostle to the Gentiles, modestly omitted his own name.[3] Clement of Alexandria found another solution; the Epistle had originally been written by Paul in the Hebrew language, whereas what we have now is its subsequent Greek translation.[4] Even the church father who expressed most doubts about the authorship of Hebrews, Origen, concluded, according to Eusebius, that it nonetheless contained the

1. For the final acceptance of Hebrews by the western church, see Kümmel, *Introduction*, pp. 392-94.

2. Eusebius, *H.E.* 3.3; 6.20.

3. Eusebius, *H.E.* 6.14.

4. Eusebius himself also resorted to the theory that Hebrews was a translation of a letter originally written by Paul, although he believed the translator to be Clement of Rome, not Luke (see *H.E.* 3.38). In the Latin church Jerome (*De Viris Illustribus* 5) also upheld the view that Paul had originally written the Epistle in Hebrew. Anderson ('Epistle', p. 435) thinks it possible that Clement of Rome thought that Hebrews was by Paul. If this is true, however, it would run counter to Anderson's suggestion in 'Letters of Paul', p. 265, as to why, from the second century CE, Rome did not accept Hebrews, i.e. that Rome knew it to be a work independent of Paul.

thoughts of the apostle.[1] The Alexandrian church seems to have adopted what in many ways strikes us as a modern distinction, that is, that it was prepared to accept Hebrews as Pauline, although not, in the form in which we have it, by Paul. It was therefore regarded as carrying apostolic authority even if it did not emanate from the apostle.

No such distinction appears to have been allowed for by Rome, however. There the authorship and authority of the Epistle were treated as indistinguishable. So if it was not by Paul it was not canonical. When the west did eventually accept Hebrews as authoritative Scripture it was largely on the grounds of its association in the east with the Pauline tradition. Thus only gradually was Hebrews accepted as part of the Pauline corpus in the west.

For Raymond Brown this is explicable if the Epistle had originally been written to Rome but by someone other than Paul. Furthermore, its radical message about the end of the Levitical model of priesthood, sacrifice and cult place was 'never enthusiastically appropriated'[2] by the Roman church. This, allied to a recollection that Paul had not been its author, accounts for its failure in the early period to be incorporated into its canon of Scripture.

Attractive as this reconstruction is in many ways, there are a number of difficulties about its acceptance. We have seen that the Alexandrian church, for example, managed to reconcile problems of Pauline authorship with their acceptance of its authority—as indeed did the Roman church from the fifth century CE when it finally accepted it as by Paul. Why could Rome not have done so earlier? Undoubtedly the theology of the Epistle vis-à-vis priesthood would not have been particularly sympathetic to Roman Christianity, but neither would that aspect of its teaching have been any more palatable to the east. The point is that had Hebrews' teaching not been amenable to reinterpretation, it would not have become part of the canon of any part of the church, east or west, which went on to use the priestly, Levitical model as its paradigm of Christian ministry. Even if it had, therefore, been originally written to Rome, I fail to see how its anticultic stance would have precluded it from early acceptance into the canon there,[3] since on Brown's own admission this did not prevent

---

1. Eusebius, *H.E.* 6.25.
2. Brown and Meier, *Antioch and Rome*, p. 148.
3. Unless one accepts the thesis of G. Theissen, *Untersuchungen zum Hebräerbrief* (Gütersloh: Gerd Mohn, 1969), that Hebrews was written as a polemic

Roman adherents of the priestly model (from *1 Clement* onwards) from utilizing the Epistle. Neither would Rome necessarily be deterred by doubts about the Epistle's authorship. After all the church there was prepared to accept into its canon works 'by Paul' and 'by Peter' which modern scholarship would now judge to be by other hands. We have seen that Alexandrian scholars were not bereft of the skills of literary criticism; nor in the case of Hebrews were they unprepared for some of the problems which their application would pose. It would therefore be a gross over-simplification to claim that from the third century, Pauline *authorship* of the Epistle was universally accepted in the east. As Origen put it, 'As to who actually wrote the epistle God knows the truth of the matter'.[1] What was accepted was the letter's apostolic *authority*. Why such authority was not invested in Hebrews by the church in Rome is not known. Personally, however, I am unconvinced by the argument which says 'Because the church there knew from earliest times that Paul had not in fact written it'.

What early manuscript evidence we do have, moreover, would suggest Rome as the Epistle's place of origin rather than its destination.[2] The Chester Beatty Papyrus (P46), usually dated about 200 CE, places Hebrews after the Epistle to the Romans and before 1 Corinthians, perhaps because the scribe thought that it had been written by Paul after or during his Roman imprisonment. It is more likely, however, that Hebrews was placed second in the Pauline corpus on the grounds of its length—the principle on which P46 seems to have arranged the Epistles. On those grounds it should have come third, after 1 Corinthians, but the scribe probably did not want to separate the two Corinthian letters. Certainly the scribe of Codex Alexandrinus (A) in the fifth century appended 'written from Rome' to Heb. 13.25. On the other hand, all this evidence tells us about is how subsequent scribes

---

against developments which had already taken place in the church, whereby Christian ministry was being understood in terms of Levitical priesthood.

1. Eusebius, *H.E.* 6.12-14.

2. See W.F. Howard, 'The Epistle to the Hebrews', *Int* 5 (1951), pp. 84-86, who believes that Hebrews was written from Rome to Ephesus, and A. Ehrhardt, *The Framework of the New Testament Stories* (Manchester: Manchester University Press, 1964), p. 109, who suggests that it was written from Rome to Christians in Jerusalem to console them after the fall of the city in 70 CE.

speculated. That they were intrigued by the letter's original destination and origin is evident from the number of scribal variants which are to be found at the end of ch. 13. These include 'written from Italy via Timothy'[1] and 'written from Rome by Paul to those in Jerusalem'.[2] These seem to be glosses introduced to amplify the reference to 'those from Italy' (οἱ ἀπὸ τῆς Ἰταλίας) in the preceding verse (v. 24) who send greetings. This itself is an ambiguous phrase, indicating either Italian Christians who are presumably away from Italy and who send their greetings, or greetings sent from those in Italy. In the former case it could imply that Italy was the Epistle's destination and those who were from that land sent their regards home, whereas in the latter case it would be natural to infer that Italy was the place from which the letter was being written and greetings were being sent from there to another part of the Empire. The NEB's translation 'greetings to you from our Italian friends' well captures the ambiguity of the phrase.

Italy, or more specifically Rome, has even less to commend it as Hebrews' place of origin than it has as its destination. If it was written from Rome it becomes even more difficult to account for its slow acceptance there. Its theology does not accord with what we know of the views of the Christian community in Rome in the first century.[3] As far as the letter itself is concerned, as we have already seen, apart from a vague and general reference to persecution in the past in 10.32-34 which cannot be linked to the Claudian edict, nor (since this persecution did not ensue in bloodshed) refer to the Neronian persecution of Roman Christians in 64 CE, ch. 13 is the only internal evidence which would link Hebrews with Italy. Even there, as we have seen, the Italian connection is far from unambiguous since it could be either the Epistle's destination or place of origin, or neither. Even more crucial to our discussion of what we know of Hebrews' original audience is the issue of the integrity or otherwise of this last chapter.

Before we turn to that topic, however, we must first consider George Buchanan's understanding of Heb. 10.34b:

1. So the majority of Byzantine manuscripts.
2. So 81.
3. See Brown and Meier, *Antioch and Rome*, p. 147: 'If Hebrews came from Rome it would represent Roman views, and just the opposite is true'.

> You joyfully accepted the plundering of your property (τὴν ἁρπαγὴν τῶν ὑπαρχόντων ὑμῶν μετὰ χαρᾶς προσεδέξασθε) since you knew that you yourselves had a better possession and an abiding one.

Although he admits that this would more naturally be taken either as a reference to the confiscation of their goods by governmental order or as looting by the mob, Buchanan nonetheless suggests that it could refer, not to action by outsiders, but to the group's own practice of asking its members voluntarily to give up their possessions upon joining the community. Buchanan cites as a contemporary Jewish parallel the practice of the Qumran Covenanters whose members handed over all their belongings to the group as the last step in their final initiation.[1] His view of the recipients of Hebrews is that they were in many ways similar to the Qumran community. Thus he characterizes them as belonging to 'a very strict, communal monastic sect'.[2] Unlike those scholars who appeal to supposed Qumran affinities in order to uphold a Judaean destination for Hebrews,[3] Buchanan properly refuses to confine those beliefs which the recipients of the Epistle had in common with the Qumran community to a Palestinian milieu.[4] Rather he sees Hebrews as having been written to a group of Jewish Christians whose home had originally been the Diaspora rather than Judaea, but who in the vanguard of a Zionist theology had now returned to Jerusalem, there to await the establishment of the reign of God. Now, in view of the delay, they were losing hope and perhaps

1. See 1QS 6.22-23.
2. Buchanan, *Hebrews*, p. 256.
3. So Kosmala, *Hebräer*, pp. 1-43, who thought that the recipients were Essene-type Jews who had not yet joined the Christian community, although they had had some initial Christian teaching. Y. Yadin ('The Dead Sea Scrolls and the Epistle to the Hebrews', *Scripta Hierosolymitana* 4 [1958], pp. 36-55) agreed that they had come from an Essene background, but thought that they had already become converts to Christianity. See also C. Spicq, 'L'épître aux Hébreux, Apollos, Jean-Baptiste, Les Hellénistes et Qumrân', *RevQ* 1 (1959), pp. 365-90, who, in the light of Qumran material, revised his previous opinion (cf. his commentary) that Hebrews had an Alexandrian provenance. This later article suggests that Hebrews may have been written by Apollos to Essene-type Christians, some of whom may have formerly been Jewish priests and members of the Qumran community. Cf. K. Bornhäuser, *Empfänger und Verfasser des Briefes an die Hebräer* (Gütersloh: Bertelsmann, 1932), who, long before the Qumran findings, suggested that the addressees were converts from the Jewish priesthood.
4. Buchanan, *Hebrews*, pp. 260-61.

toying with the idea of taking part in the Day of Atonement ceremonies as a means thereby of effecting the coming of the kingdom.[1]
In the meantime they are beginning to resent the relinquishing of their
private property which they undertook when they joined the
community.

There are a number of problems about accepting Buchanan's thesis,
however, not least his particular reading of this verse. The use of the
noun ἁρπαγή (10.34) conveys overtones of violent seizure or forcible
confiscation. Even if, as Buchanan suggests, there were those among
the group who resented the practice,[2] this would hardly account for
the choice of the term by an author who was attempting to reconcile
them to a voluntary sequestration of goods, presumably for the
common weal! It seems far more likely, therefore, that 10.32-34
refers to a situation in the community's past in which their goods had
been looted and some of their membership had been imprisoned.

Those who, like Buchanan, want to locate this group in Jerusalem[3]
face further difficulties. It is true that the location of the addressees as
'in Jerusalem and Palestine' is the earliest identification we have,
occurring as it does in Chrysostom's introduction to his homilies on
Hebrews. Furthermore, with the discoveries at Qumran, a Judaean
setting has once more been revived by those who are struck by certain
similarities between the preoccupations of the Epistle and those of the
writings of the Covenanters. 'What Jewish group', asks Richard
Longenecker, 'would have held to a theology that combined the ven-
eration of angels, a Moses prophetology, the supremacy of the
Aaronic priesthood, the exaltation of Melchizedek, the portrayal of
the cult in terms of the wilderness tabernacle, and the vital importance
of the sacrificial system—and in this approximate order of ascending
significance?'[4] He finds his answer at Qumran.

---

1. Buchanan, *Hebrews*, p. 266.
2. Buchanan, *Hebrews*, p. 256.
3. To those listed by Spicq, *Hébreux*, I, p. 239 n. 1, should be added
G. Buchanan and P.E. Hughes.
4. Longenecker, *Exegesis*, p. 160. For others who also regard the Dead Sea
Scrolls as of major significance in our understanding of the background of Hebrews'
addressees see p. 38 n. 3, together with F.M. Braun, 'L'arrière-fond judaïque de
quatrieme evangile et la communauté de l'alliance', *RB* 62 (1955), p. 55;
J. Danielou, *The Dead Sea Scrolls and Primitive Christianity* (Baltimore: Helicon,
1958), pp. 111-13; D. Flusser, 'The Dead Sea Sect and Pre-Pauline Christianity',
Scripta Hierosolymitana 4 (1958), pp. 215-17; Y. Yadin, 'A Note on Melchizedek

Yet as we examine the Epistle to the Hebrews more carefully, we shall find that such a listing of similarities masks their fundamental differences. Not least, the particular combination of Davidic messiah and non-Aaronic priesthood which we find in Hebrews is not one present in the Qumran writings, but was evidently derived by our author from Psalm 110—the only other place where it occurs. This Psalm is missing in the catena of passages in 11QMelchizedek. Unlike Hebrews the Qumran community took issue not with the continuation of a Levitical priesthood but with the incumbents of the office of high priest under the Hasmonaeans, whom they did not accept as of true Zadokite descent. This was a dispute which went back to the second century BCE, when the high priest Onias III was deposed by his Tobiad rivals. Since they believed that the wicked priest had defiled the sanctuary,[1] the Covenanters eschewed the Jerusalem Temple, awaiting the time when once more it would be purified. Unlike Hebrews, which sees Jesus as having brought about the end of priesthood and cult *per se*, however, the Covenanters look to their restoration. Furthermore, the role played by Melchizedek is very different. In Hebrews it is his non-Levitical priestly features which are brought to the fore; in the Dead Sea Scrolls it is his eschatological function

and Qumran', *IEJ* 15 (1965), pp. 152-54. H. Braun (*Qumran und das Neue Testament*, I [Tübingen: Mohr [Paul Siebeck], 1966), pp. 242-78) lists most of the suggested parallels between Qumran and Hebrews. In Vol. II, pp. 181-83, however, he concludes that only in some common methods of textual citation and exegesis is there any true comparison. Although this work was written before the discovery of 11QMelch, in his more recent commentary, *An Die Hebräer* (Hanbuch zum Neuen Testament, 14; Tübingen: Mohr [Paul Siebeck], 1984), Braun is still of the opinion that Qumran is not Hebrews' principal conceptual background. He thinks that the Epistle has neither a Palestinian origin nor a Jewish Christian audience.

1. See 1QpHab 12.7-8; 10.10; CD 12.2. In their interpretation of the *Temple Scroll*'s plans for a renewed Temple in Jerusalem, scholars differ as to whether those plans are presented (1) as a second Mosaic Torah which will replace the first in the eschatological age (so B.Z. Wacholder, *The Dawn of Qumran: The Sectarian Torah and the Teacher of Righteousness* [Cincinnati: Hebrew Union College Press, 1983], pp. 1-32); or (2) as the ones originally given to Moses at Sinai which will be finally put into operation (so Y. Yadin, *The Temple Scroll: The Hidden Law of the Dead Sea Sect* [London: Weidenfeld & Nicolson, 1985], pp. 121-169). For a discussion of both views see J. Maier, *The Temple Scroll: An Introduction, Translation and Commentary* (Sheffield: JSOT Press, 1985), pp. 5-59. Either way, 11QTorah furnishes evidence of the Covenanters' disaffection with the Jerusalem Temple and their hopes for its reformation or replacement.

which is stressed. F. Horton has refuted the suggestion that Melchizedek is actually called messiah at Qumran,[1] nor does he believe that he was identified with the archangel Michael.[2] It therefore seems unlikely that the author of Hebrews raised the question of the relative positions of Jesus and the angels in order to refute some Qumranic notion that a Melchizedekian figure would inevitably be counted among the angels. Indeed it is most unlikely that our author is engaged in polemics at all vis-à-vis angels. He does not discuss them in the paraenetic sections of the Epistle, and where he does mention them it is not in a polemical tone. When each of the supposed affinities between Hebrews and Qumran is examined more closely, what emerges, therefore, is not evidence of a direct link, but of a common Jewish heritage.[3] Even George Buchanan, who places the recipients of Hebrews in Jerusalem, concludes that whereas the Qumran material may help clarify the background of the New Testament in general, it has not identified either the author or the readers of Hebrews.[4] So Qumranic affinities do not determine a Judaean setting for our Epistle.

Neither can we infer from our author's treatment of his selected biblical passages concerning the cult place, his proximity or otherwise to the Jerusalem Temple, since he confines his exegesis of the role of the high priest in the Day of Atonement ceremonies to the setting of the wilderness tabernacle. Although it has been argued from his use of past tenses in 9.1-2 that Hebrews was written after the destruction of the Temple in 70 CE, it has equally been claimed that the author's pre-

1. F. Horton, *The Melchizedek Tradition* (SNTSMS, 30; Cambridge: Cambridge University Press, 1976), pp. 78-79.

2. Horton, *Melchizedek*, pp. 80-82, *contra* M. de Jonge and A.S. Van der Woude, '11Q Melchizedek and the New Testament', *NTS* 12 (1955–56), pp. 301-26; G. Vermes, *The Dead Sea Scrolls in English* (Harmondsworth: Penguin Books, 2nd edn, 1975), p. 266.

3. So J. Coppens, 'Les affinités qumraniennes de l'épître aux Hébreux', *NRT* 84 (1962), pp. 270-71; J.A. Fitzmyer, 'Further Light on Melchizedek from Qumran Cave 11', *JBL* 86 (1967), pp. 25-41. W. Horbury ('The Aaronic Priesthood in the Epistle to the Hebrews', *JSNT* 19 [1983], pp. 43-71) attributes the affinities between Qumran and Hebrews to their common sacerdotalism, derived from the Pentateuch rather than from any direct connection.

4. G.W. Buchanan, 'The Present State of Scholarship on Hebrews', in *Christianity, Judaism and Other Greco-Roman Cults. Studies for Morton Smith at 60*, I (ed. J. Neusner; Leiden: Brill, 1975), pp. 299-330.

dominant employment of the present tense[1] clearly indicates that the Levitical cult was fully operative.[2] Careful attention to the text indicates the impossibility of basing one's conclusion as to either the Epistle's destination or date on the author's use of tenses. From his stance as an exegete his text is present.[3] Perhaps this can be best seen in a verse which might at first glance seem to indicate that the Jerusalem Temple was no longer in existence:

> By this the Holy Spirit indicates that the way into the sanctuary is not yet opened as long as the outer tent is still standing (ἔτι τῆς πρώτης σκηνῆς ἐχούσης στάσιν), which is symbolic (παραβολή) for the present age (9.8-9a).

From its context it is not clear whether πρώτη σκηνή is to be understood as a reference to the holy place in the tabernacle, that is, the outer division of the tent which is the first, and indeed except for the high priest on the Day of Atonement the only, part of the sanctuary encountered by the worshipper as in 9.2, 6,[4] or whether it is the Mosaic tabernacle as a whole as in 8.5; 9.11, 21; 13.10. In the former case the author would be (presumably) contrasting the wilderness tabernacle, which excluded all but Israelites even from its outer sanctum, with heaven itself, which Jesus has opened to all believers—Jew and Gentile. In which case Hebrews would be desacralizing all space, at least in the sense of making access to God fully open to all. This is an attractive suggestion but one which does not entirely fit in with our author's theology. Unlike the apostle Paul, Hebrews does not seem to be interested in the issue of the admission of Gentiles into the church. It is therefore unlikely that this passage should be read in this way. The alternative interpretation, whereby Hebrews is here contrasting the entire σκηνή of the Mosaic dispensation with its displacement by Christ seems preferable. As C. Spicq has described it, 'the Mosaic ritual was a parable in action'[5] of the fact that there was then no direct access to God, whereas in the now we have such a way opened by

---

1. Heb. 5.1-4; 7.27-28; 8.3, 4-5; 9.6-7, 9, 13, 25; 10.1, 8, 11; 13.10-11. Cf. also the periphrastic use of εἶναι with the perfect participle in 7.10, 23.

2. So P.E. Hughes, *Hebrews*, pp. 30-31.

3. Similarly, two authors whom we know were writing after 70 CE, Josephus (*Ant.* 3.151-224) and *1 Clement* both use present tenses of the Temple cult.

4. So Moffatt, *Hebrews*, II, p. 118.

5. Spicq, *Hébreux*, II, p. 254: 'Le rituel mosaïque était une parabole en acté'.

Jesus. Neither reading of the text, however, sees in it a statement about the present existence (or otherwise) of the Jerusalem Temple. ἐχούσης στάσιν does not here refer to mere existence, but to that which is legally binding.[1] As far as our author is concerned, Israel's cult place is no longer to be regarded as having any present status, since Christ, by entering the true tabernacle of heaven itself, has gained for himself and his followers true access to God. Hence it is the tabernacle's 'standing' in the sense of 'enduring status' which is the issue for our author—not the existence of the Temple. Having demonstrated that the tent of meeting has been superseded, then *mutatis mutandis*, it would follow that the same is true for its successors in Jerusalem, but our author does not overtly discuss the latter. Some scholars[2] have claimed that had he been writing after 70 CE it would be inconceivable that our author would not have made capital out of the Temple's destruction. Yet that itself is to presume that Hebrews was written as a polemic against Judaism. Even if that were the case (which I do not believe), we should remember that it is only with hindsight that the events of 70 CE proved to be so final for the Jerusalem cult. It was only with the defeat of the Bar Kochba revolt in 135 CE that all hope of its restoration (other than in a future messianic age) came to an end.[3] Between those two dates it would have been precarious indeed to bolster up a Christian soteriology by an appeal to an event which, like the destruction of the Temple in the past, might prove to be no more than temporary.

Far from indicating that Hebrews was written before 70 CE, therefore, Hebrews' preoccupation with the wilderness tabernacle may well be an indication of its post 70 CE date. It has long been noted that nowhere in the New Testament do we have an overt reference to the fall of Jerusalem. Very few scholars would follow J.A.T. Robinson[4] in inferring from this that all New Testament authors were therefore writing before that date. Rather, they see in the Synoptic Gospels

1. See Bruce, *Hebrews*, pp. 192, 195.
2. E.g. J.A.T. Robinson, *Redating the New Testament* (London: SCM Press, 1976), p. 204.
3. See K.W. Clark, 'Worship in the Jerusalem Temple after A.D. 70', *NTS* 6 (1969–70), pp. 269-80, whose reminder of this fact still holds good, even if his evidence for the continuity of the cult on the Temple site between 70 and 135 CE remains conjectural.
4. Robinson, *Redating, passim*.

covert references and indications of a knowledge of those events.[1]
Couched in the form of future prophecy and placed on the lips of
Jesus, the fall of Jerusalem is depicted, like the destruction of the First
Temple and the desecration of the Second, as divine judgment upon
Israel.[2] It could be maintained that Hebrews, partly due to the impact
of the destruction of Jerusalem, especially on Jewish Christians whose
natural focus would be the holy land and above all the sacred cult
place, set out to divert the focus of their attention away from the
Temple to the wilderness tabernacle upon which it was thought the
former was patterned. Our author wishes to go further and to show
the redundancy of even the Mosaic shrine. His message could then be
summed up as 'Shrinés come and go, but the only one you can trust is
heaven itself—that shrine in which our Melchizedekian high priest has
now entered and thereby gains access for all those who will follow
him'. That message would be powerful before or after 70 CE—but if
it is an aspect of human nature that we become more attached to that
which we have just lost, then at least part of Hebrews' preoccupation
with offering an alternative to Judaism's sacred territory might be
accounted for by its comparatively recent loss.

This suggestion that Jewish Christians would need an alternative
interpretation of the Scriptures which dealt with sacred space does not
necessarily imply that they are to be located in Jerusalem—although
there is no *a priori* reason why Christian converts from Diaspora
Judaism could not be in Jerusalem. Indeed we know from Acts 6.19
that the capital had several Greek-speaking synagogues, presumably
for the benefit of non-Judaean visitors.[3] It is true that Diaspora
Judaism, by its 'spiritualization' of the cult, paved the way for a non-
Temple-based religion both in Judaism and Christianity,[4] but I think

---

1. E.g. Lk. 21.20-24; Mt. 24.2; Mk 13.2, 7(?).

2. This is most clear in Matthew's Gospel, where the parable of the marriage feast
(Mt. 22.1-14, especially v. 7) which precedes the 'woes' against Israel's religious
leaders (23.1-36), culminates in the lament over Jerusalem (23.37-39) and the
prophecy of her destruction (24). Israel's prophetic tradition also linked the fate of
Jerusalem with God's judgment on Israel. See Mic. 3.10-12; Jer. 7.30; Ezek. 5.1-
17; Isa. 63.15–64.12.

3. See J. Jeremias, *Jerusalem in the Time of Jesus* (London: SCM Press, 1969),
pp. 66, 69.

4. See H.A. Wolfson, *Philo*, II (Cambridge, MA: Harvard University Press,
1947), pp. 241-48.

Jacob Neusner overstates the case when he writes of Philo of Alexandria, 'I doubt whether his religious life would have been greatly affected had the Temple been destroyed in his life-time'.[1] In spite of the fact that for Jews such as Philo it was the synagogue rather than the Temple which was the stuff of their daily worship, nonetheless of their own volition they sent money for the continuation of the cult, made regular pilgrimages to Jerusalem and cited the splendours of its shrine and the impressiveness of its liturgy as part of Judaism's supremacy over the Gentiles.[2] But this further indicates the problem of trying to locate the addressees of the Epistle to the Hebrews; its preoccupation with the sacred space could equally well be addressed to those living inside or outside Judaea. Perhaps this is what lies behind the suggestion of a Palestinian rather than a Judaean provenance for our Epistle.[3] It at least takes seriously the fact that the recipients and the Epistle's author are Greek- rather than Semitic-speaking. It also does justice to the author's priestly preoccupations. Apart from those undoubted facts, it is exceedingly difficult to be more precise about Hebrews' destination and date. Perhaps it would therefore be more profitable to look to the Epistle not so much for what it tells us of its audience as for what it tells us about its author.

4. *'Placing' Hebrews*

In attempting to 'place' Hebrews we should bear in mind that, like most writing, it tells us more of its author than of its audience. With little unambiguous evidence provided externally or internally as to its original recipients, it would therefore seem prudent to ask what we can infer from the Epistle about the author of this sermon. From the plethora of names which have been suggested (Luke[4] or Clement of Rome[5] translating Paul, Barnabas,[6] Apollos[7] and even Priscilla[8]) at

1. J. Neusner, *Early Rabbinic Judaism* (Leiden: Brill, 1975), p. 35.
2. Philo, *Prov.* 2.64 (= Eusebius, *Praep. Ev.* 8.14.389b); Josephus, *Apion* 2.193-98. We must not forget also that some Jews adhered to a non-Jerusalem Temple, e.g., that at Leontopolis in Egypt, which was not destroyed until 73 CE.
3. E.g. Caesarea or Syrian Antioch (Spicq, *Hébreux*, I, pp. 249-52).
4. Clement of Alexandria (in Eusebius, *H.E.* 6.14).
5. Eusebius, *H.E.* 3.38.
6. Tertullian, *De Pudiata* 20 refers to the Epistle to the Hebrews as by Barnabas. That this was a view held by some is mentioned by Jerome, *De Viris Illustribus* 5, although he himself attributed the work to Paul. (See the superscription in the

first sight this might seem an equally fruitless task. Would we not once more be chasing the same old hares around the same old track—with the inevitable outcome of never catching our quarry? Perhaps not, if we do not start by trying to select the most likely candidate from a list of those mentioned in the New Testament. After all, although our author seems to have been known to his audience, he does not signify his name nor use any of the devices associated with pseudonymity. As we have it, Hebrews is an anonymous work, soon associated with the Pauline tradition, although not in the opinion of the vast majority of contemporary New Testament scholars by Paul or even predominantly 'Pauline' in theological *Tendenz*.

Far more important than the name of the author is what we can say about his background, education, preconceptions, religious traditions and preoccupations. It is about these that we need to know if we are to be able to place this enigmatic text in its original context and thus arrive at an understanding of its distinctive theology.

The most obvious conclusion that we can arrive at about our author is that he was Greek-speaking. Of all New Testament works this one displays the most sophisticated literary style.[1] We have already noted some of the rhetorical devices he employs (pp. 18-19). His use of alliteration—πίστει πεποίηκεν τὸ πάσχα καὶ τὴν πρόσχυσιν τοῦ αἵματος—is unfortunately not conveyed by the English 'By faith he kept the passover and the sprinkling of blood' (11.28). Furthermore,

Vulgate, *Epistola Pauli ad Hebraeos*.) This century, upholders of Barnabas's authorship include F. Blass, *Die Brief an die Hebräer* (Halle: Niemeyer, 1903); M. Dibelius, *Der Verfasser des Hebräerbriefes* (Strasbourg: Heitz, 1910); and Bornhäuser, *Empfänger*. Manson (*Hebrews*, p. 170) more circumspectly states that there is nothing intrinsically against Barnabas as its author.

7. This was the opinion of Martin Luther. Among its modern exponents are Spicq, *Hébreux*, I, pp. 209-11, Manson, 'Problem', pp. 1-17, and H.W. Montefiore, *The Epistle to the Hebrews* (BNTC; London: A. & C. Black, 1964), pp. 23-28.

8. A. von Harnack, 'Probabilia über die Adresse und den Verfasser des Hebräerbriefes', *ZNW* 1 (1900), pp. 16-18; R. Hoppins, *Priscilla, Author of the Epistle to the Hebrews and Other Essays* (New York: Exposition, 1969), pp. 11-116.

1. See P. Wendland, *Die urchristlichen Literaturformen* (Tübingen: Mohr [Paul Siebeck], 1912), p. 307; M.E. Thrall, *Greek Particles in the New Testament* (Leiden: Brill, 1962), p. 9.

our author seems at home in the general cultural milieu of the
Graeco-Roman world, as can be seen in his view of the role of education in the Christian life. In depicting this he uses metaphors drawn
from agriculture[1] and athletics.[2] Although none of these images is
unique to Hebrews, J.W. Thompson maintains that nowhere else in the
New Testament do we find them used to illustrate intellectual
progress.[3] For Thompson this furnishes evidence of our author's debt
to Greek *paideia*. Be that as it may, as A. Nairne said more generally
of Hebrews, 'It belongs quite naturally to a circle of men who have
had a hellenistic education'.[4] Among such men would be included
those who translated the Hebrew Scriptures into Greek and wrote such
works as the Wisdom of Solomon and the *Letter of Aristeas*. Philo of
Alexandria would also fall into this category. It is to these circles of
educated thought that Hebrews would seem to belong.

With the recognition that 'Hellenism', whether defined linguistically
or culturally, is not a phenomenon to be confined to the Diaspora have
unfortunately come simplistic statements as to its extent in first-
century Judaea. So, for example, J.A.T. Robinson appealed to recent
evidence of the presence of Greek in first-century Palestine to uphold
an early, apostolic, Palestinian provenance for 1 Peter and James.[5] It
was certainly timely for some of our cherished scholarly shibboleths
to be challenged—not least the equation of 'Greek' with 'late', that is,
post 70 CE. Greek fragments (including fragments of the Scriptures),
some of which may date from the first century CE, have been found in
the caves at Qumran.[6] There were Greek-speaking synagogues in
Jerusalem itself.[7] J.N. Sevenster, from his investigation of knowledge
of Greek among Jews living in Palestine at that time, concludes that

1. Heb. 6.7.
2. Heb. 5.14; 10.32; 12.1, 11.
3. J.W. Thompson, *The Beginnings of Christian Philosophy: The Epistle to the
Hebrews* (CBQMS, 13; Washington, DC: Catholic Biblical Association, 1982),
p. 38.
4. Nairne, *Priesthood*, p. 31.
5. Robinson, *Redating*, especially pp. 132-35.
6. See J.T. Milik, *Ten Years of Discovery in the Wilderness of Judea* (London:
SCM Press, 1959), pp. 31-35; *idem*, 'Le travail d'édition des fragments manuscrits
de Qumrân', *RB* 63 (1956), pp. 52-54; R.P.D. Barthélemy, 'Redécouverte d'un
chainon manquant de l'histoire de la Septante', *RB* 60 (1953), pp. 18-29.
7. See p. 44 n. 3.

even among the general populace there would have been a smattering of the language.[1] This is a long way, however, from claiming the kind of fluency necessary to produce such works at 1 Peter, James and Hebrews. The Greek of the general Jewish populace, revealed in Greek inscriptions and tombstones, was often semi-literate. Josephus is far more to be believed when (no doubt partly excusing his own necessity for assistance with the Greek language) he tells us that the Jewish masses were less inclined than other nations to learn foreign languages.[2] So the significant question to ask is not whether a Judaean could have known enough Greek to 'get by' in a territory governed by a Roman administration, and living cheek by jowl with Greek city states whose status had continued beyond the political decline of their Hellenistic founders. The important thing to know is whether our author betrays any signs of struggling with a foreign tongue. And all scholars are agreed that no such indicators are present in Hebrews.

Our author is heavily indebted to the Jewish Scriptures—yet he seems to have no immediate knowledge of them in Hebrew.[3] Of the 38 quotations and 55 allusions listed by Richard Longenecker, only six do not agree with either LXX[A] or LXX[B]. On the other hand, 14 agree with the LXX against the Masoretic text.[4] Furthermore, some of our author's exegetical points are clearly dependent upon a Greek version rather than the original Hebrew text. So, for example, the point that is made about a covenant only being effective upon the death of the testator (9.16) has meaning only because the Hebrew—*berîth*—has been translated in the LXX by the ambiguous διαθήκη, meaning testament/will as well as covenant. Heb. 1.6, 'Let all the angels worship him' (καὶ προσκυνησάτωσαν αὐτῷ πάντες ἄγγελοι θεοῦ), is not to be found in the MT but is taken from the LXX Deut. 32.43. In the Deuteronomy passage the LXX speaks of sons (υἱοί) rather than angels

---

1. J.N. Sevenster, *Do You Know Greek? How Much Greek Could the First Jewish Christians Have Known?* (Leiden: Brill, 1968), pp. 176-91. Cf. S. Liebermann, *Greek in Jewish Palestine* (New York: Jewish Theological Seminary of America, 1942), most of whose evidence (since he was writing before the Qumran findings) is taken from the second century CE or later.

2. *Ant.* 20.264.

3. See Longenecker, *Exegesis*, p. 169; A.T. Hanson, *The Living Utterances of God: The New Testament Exegesis of the Old* (London: Darton, Longman & Todd, 1983), p. 105.

4. Longenecker, *Exegesis*, pp. 164-69.

(ἄγγελοι) of God.[1] It is possible that our author has arrived at his reading by conflating the Deuteronomy text with Ps. 96.7 (προσκυνήσατε αὐτῷ πάντες οἱ ἄγγελοι αὐτοῦ). Obviously a tradition which described angels as 'sons of God'[2] would not have suited our author's argument that the Son is superior to angels because *he* is Son and as such is the recipient of their worship.

It is also evident that were the author of Hebrews relying on the Hebrew text of Ps. 104.4, he would have been unable to use it as the basis of his argument for the supremacy of the Son over unstable, changeable angels. In the MT the psalmist is extolling the power of God to use any and every element in the created order as vehicles of this power: 'Who makes the winds thy messengers and flames of fire thy servant'. The Greek translation, however, is far more amenable to our author's purpose of stressing the transient nature of angels: 'Who makes his angels winds and his servants flames of fire' (ὁ ποιῶν τοὺς ἀγγέλους αὐτοῦ πνεύματα καὶ τοὺς λειτουργοὺς αὐτοῦ πυρὸς φλόγα,[3] LXX PS. 103.4).

So far we have established that the author of Hebrews is to be placed among those who would have read the Hebrew Scriptures in Greek, which was probably their mother tongue. Furthermore, we have shown that this Greek-speaker came from the ranks of the educated. Even Ronald Williamson, in his refutation of C. Spicq's thesis that the author of Hebrews was directly dependent on Philo, has to acknowledge that the evidence compels us to accept that 'the writer of Hebrews drew upon the same wealth of literary vocabulary and moved in the same circles of educated thought as a man like Philo'.[4]

This, of course, does not, as Williamson has pointed out, demonstrate that our author was a 'Philonist'.[5] James Thompson has also

1. The LXX reads 'angels' (ἄγγελοι) rather than the MT 'sons' at Job 1.6; 2.1; 38.7.

2. For angelic beings described as 'sons of God' see Gen. 6.2, 4; Job 1.6; 2.1; 38.7; Ps. 29.1; 82.6; 89.7.

3. The LXX reads 'flaming fire' (πῦρ φλέγον) rather than 'flames of fire' (πυρὸς φλόγα). Our author has probably altered his text in order to perfect its parallelism with πνεύματα.

4. R. Williamson, *Philo and the Epistle to the Hebrews* (Leiden: Brill, 1970), p. 296.

5. *Contra* Spicq, *Hébreux*, I, ch. 3, 'Le Philonisme de l'épître aux Hébreux', pp. 39-91.

joined with those who believe that Spicq claimed too much for the parallels between Hebrews and Philo. Yet he believes that 'Williamson has not demonstrated that the two writers do not belong to a common conceptual world'.[1] For Thompson it is the metaphysics of Middle Platonism which provides the key to understanding the Epistle. Therefore it is to our author's predecessor Philo on the one hand, and subsequent Christian Platonists such as Clement of Alexandria and Origen on the other, that we must look if we are to appreciate the conceptual world of Hebrews. According to Thompson it is here that we find features which distinguish Hebrews both from the literature of first-century Judaism and other New Testament writings. L.K.K. Dey's *The Intermediary World and Patterns of Perfection in Philo and Hebrews*[2] also presents Philo as the principal intellectual point of comparison with our author. Dey argues that Hebrews' presentation of Christ as the one who attains access to God is best seen in terms of the Philonic conception of perfection as immediate, unmediated access to God, granted to such exemplars as Isaac, Aaron, Moses and Melchizedek.[3] Since, in Middle Platonic cosmology, access to God involved going beyond the second order intermediary world, the author of Hebrews needed to show that Jesus was not himself merely an intermediary. Hence he discusses the respective status of Jesus over against other intermediaries and exemplars of perfection, such as angels, Moses and the Aaronic high priest.[4]

Yet to view Hebrews exclusively through the spectacles of Hellenistic metaphysics does not seem to be the answer to the enigma of this Epistle. To say this is not to subscribe to the equation of either 'Hellenistic' or 'metaphysics' with all that is 'mad, bad and dangerous to know'! Unfortunately, such pejorative sentiments, albeit not expressed overtly, sometimes seem to lie just below the surface of otherwise apparently reasonable debate. I think Thompson quite properly detects such in Williamson's inference that were Hebrews to contain metaphysical reflections it would thereby fall outside the general

1. Thompson, *Beginnings*, p. 10.
2. L.K.K. Dey, *The Intermediary World and Patterns of Perfection in Philo and Hebrews* (Missoula, MT: Scholars Press, 1975).
3. Dey, *Intermediary World*, pp. 68-72.
4. Dey, *Intermediary World, passim*.

stream of early Christian thinking.[1] Similarly Longenecker concludes his discussion of the provenance of Hebrews by claiming that parallels with the thought of the Qumran Covenanters demonstrate that our Epistle is 'Jewish' rather than 'Hellenistic'.[2] If he means by that 'Jewish' rather than 'Gentile', then that would be a wholly acceptable conclusion—though not one necessarily arrived at via Qumran. If he means Palestinian rather than Diaspora, then this piece of linguistic imprecision has more disturbing implications, because it would imply that even a Hellenistic (Diaspora) Jew was not quite 'kosher'!

My discontent with those who wish to look wholly to a Hellenistic Jew such as Philo for the conceptual background of the Epistle to the Hebrews is not that I am averse to metaphysics. Nor that I regard Hellenistic Judaism as 'unorthodox'. Indeed if by 'Hellenistic' one means Greek-speaking, then on any reckoning our Epistle must be viewed against such a background. Yet the major problem with those who have searched the literature of Hellenistic Judaism for parallels is that inevitably they find what they are looking for. There is much wisdom in Williamson's remarks:

> It is my considered judgement that Spicq, among other things, isolates the linguistic aspect of the problem to the point where he loses sight of the basic differences of outlook and attitude between the two authors.[3]

Henry Chadwick, in his 'St Paul and Philo of Alexandria',[4] also reminded us of the danger, when comparing authors, of concentrating on the similarities and ignoring the dissimilarities. Asserting that the author of Hebrews and Philo came from the same kind of Jewish, Greek-speaking, educated milieu,[5] therefore, must not blind us to the fundamental differences that exist between them. Apart from the most

---

1. Thompson, *Beginnings*, pp. 160-61.
2. Longenecker, *Exegesis*, p. 164.
3. Williamson, *Philo and Hebrews*, p. 9.
4. H. Chadwick, 'St Paul and Philo of Alexandria', *BJRL* 48 (1966), pp. 286-307.
5. H.W. Montefiore (*Hebrews*, pp. 9-11) believes that the author of Hebrews may have known Philo. Cf. Moffatt, *Hebrews*, p. lxi; Hanson, *Living Utterances*, p. 111. S.G. Sowers (*The Hermeneutics of Philo and Hebrews* [Zürich: EVZ-Verlag, 1965], p. 69) thinks that he was at least *au fait* with the Philonic logos doctrine. Cf. T.H. Robinson, *The Epistle to the Hebrews* (MNTC; London: Hodder & Stoughton, 1933), p. xvi.

fundamental of all—that Hebrews is a Christian writing—Williamson
has demonstrated that where they do share common themes and ideas,[1]
the different treatment given to them is even more striking than their
commonality. Thus he asserts that Platonic language when employed
by Hebrews operates merely on the verbal rather than the conceptual
level, since our author has not abandoned the Jewish eschatological
concept of two ages in favour of the Platonic two coexistent spheres of
the Ideal and the copy.[2] In fact Williamson denies any evidence of
metaphysical dualism in Hebrews.[3] Graham Hughes is also of this
opinion. In *Hebrews and Hermeneutics* he states that the author's
dialectic of the past and present would rule out any suggestion that his
use of the Scriptures is in terms of their timeless ahistorical character.
For Hebrews the relationships between old and new covenants is an
historical one. Therefore there is more of an 'event quality' in
Hebrews' biblical exegesis than we find in Philo.[4] This can be seen in
their preferred exegetical tools; Philo employs allegory, whereas our
author has a typological approach.[5]

Perhaps the most striking way to see both the similarities and the
differences between Philo and Hebrews is to look at their respective
treatments of a passage which they have in common, that is, ὅρα
ποιήσεις κατὰ τὸν τύπον τὸν δεδειγμένον σοι ἐν τῷ ὄρει (LXX
Exod. 25.40). Philo's treatment of this text clearly reflects not only
the vocabulary but also the philosophical assumptions of Middle
Platonism. Hence his treatment of creation implies an acceptance of an
Idealist cosmology, according to which there is an immaterial world

---

1. Williamson, *Philo and Hebrews*, pp. 137-495.
2. Williamson, *Philo and Hebrews*, pp. 142-49. Cf. C.K. Barrett, 'The
Eschatology of the Epistle to the Hebrews', in *The Background of the New
Testament and its Eschatology* (ed. W.D. Davies and D. Daube; Cambridge:
Cambridge University Press, 1956), pp. 363-93.
3. Williamson, *Philo and Hebrews*, pp. 268-76, *contra* Thompson, *Beginnings*,
passim.
4. G. Hughes, *Hebrews*, especially p. 63.
5. See Williamson, *Philo and Hebrews*, pp. 496-580, who also stresses the
respective authors' predilections for different Old Testament passages, as well as
differences in their exegetical method. Cf. G.B. Caird, 'The Exegetical Method of
the Epistle to the Hebrews', *CJT* 5 (1959), p. 45. Yet note that Caird seems to
equate Alexandrian exegesis with the 'fantastic'—an epithet he is anxious not to
apply to Hebrews!

of ideal 'forms' upon which the material was patterned. These 'ideas' provided the copy or plan as a model for the substantial world. According to this philosophy, although there is some degree of correspondence between the plan and its execution, the latter is always inferior. The copy can never adequately duplicate the original. Behind this cosmology lies an attempt to maintain a qualitative difference between the divine, transcendent, non-material world, and the transient, flawed nature of the created order—while not entirely abandoning a relationship between the two.

Philo's discussion of God's plan for the wilderness sanctuary is also concerned with the relationship between the phenomenal and Ideal world. It occurs in a section (*Leg. All.* 3.95-105) in which his primary purpose is to uphold the supremacy of Moses. His intent is to demonstrate that it is to Moses alone that God speaks directly, without the mediation of the world of sense perception. So Philo discloses his main purpose in citing various biblical texts (including Exod. 25.40) when he concludes:

> 'If a prophet be raised up unto the Lord, God shall be known unto him in a vision' and in a shadow, not manifestly; but with Moses, the man who is 'faithful in all His house, He will speak mouth to mouth in manifest form and not through dark speeches' (Num. 12.6-8).[1]

Philo, accepting the Platonic premise of the inferiority of the copy (μίμημα), which he designates image (εἰκών), or shadow (σκία)[2] over against the Ideal—the pattern (παράδειγμα)—wishes nonetheless to maintain that the plan given to Moses belonged to the first-order world of the Ideal. In order to do this, he resorts to an appeal to creation itself. So he argues that Bezalel, the chief craftsman in the construction of the tabernacle (Exod. 31.2-6), was the instrument of its creation, just as the λόγος was God's artificer in all creation. (Here Philo allegorizes the tabernacle so that it becomes a symbol of the human soul.) The tabernacle, as indeed the whole of the created order, is impressed or stamped by the image or shadow of God. Thus God's original pattern (παράδειγμα) becomes the archetype for all future material creation. This is what Gen. 1.27 means by 'God made man

---

1. *Leg. All.* 3.103. (Throughout, the works of Philo are cited from the Loeb Classical Library edition, 10 vols.; London: Heinemann/Cambridge, MA: Harvard University Press, 1928–62.)

2. *Leg. All.* 3.102. Cf. 94-96.

after the image of God'. The image/shadow is not therefore God himself, but his instrument or agent in creation. Similarly, Bezalel (the etymology of whose name Philo gives as 'in the shadow') is Moses' agent in the construction of the tabernacle.

There are those whose knowledge of God is gained by inference from the material world. These are those who discern 'the artificer by means of His works' (*Leg. All.* 3.99). The one who needs no such mediated vision, who 'gains (his) knowledge of the First Cause not from created things', but 'obtains a clear vision of the Uncreated One' (*Leg. All.* 3.100) is Moses. Unlike Bezalel who is merely the copier of the archetype, Moses is the one who has had the ground plans direct from God. He has been given the pattern (παράδειγμα)[1] direct from God, whereas Bezalel's instructions have had to be mediated by Moses.

A comparison of this approach to the text of Exod. 25.40 with the way Hebrews (8.1-6) employs it is very instructive. The most obvious difference is that Philo uses it to maintain the superiority of Moses and to show that, following the dictates of Platonism, the plan for the tabernacle given by God to Moses was not itself a copy but genuinely part of the first order. Hebrews, on the other hand, is concerned to demonstrate the supremacy of Jesus, together with the heavenly sanctuary which he entered. So Hebrews 8 opens with the affirmation that Jesus (established as the Melchizedekian high priest in the preceding chapter) is now enthroned in heaven 'as a minister in the sanctuary (τὰ ἅγια) and the true tent (ἡ σκηνὴ ἡ ἀληθινή),[2] which is set up not by man but by the Lord' (8.2). Since our author's priestly model of Jesus was not Aaronic (indeed, he concedes that Christ, since he

---

1. The LXX of Exod. 25.40 reads τύπος rather than Philo's παράδειγμα. Heb. 8.5b also reads τύπος, but interprets it in 8.5a as ὑπόδειγμα καὶ σκία (probably a hendiadys).

2. Hebrews does not seem to keep σκηνή for the Mosaic tabernacle, and ἅγια for the heavenly sanctuary in which Jesus now intercedes. In Heb. 8.5 σκηνή refers to the inferior, wilderness tabernacle, in contrast to ἅγια, the heavenly one. Elsewhere, however, ἅγια can be used of the earthly, inferior sanctuary (see 9.1 τὸ ἅγιον κοσμικόν; cf. 9.24 for the ἅγια made with hands, the ἀντίτυπος of the true one; in 8.5 this is expressed as the ὑπόδειγμα/σκία of the heavenly sanctuary) and σκηνή becomes the 'true' one (8.2; 9.11). See P.E. Hughes, *Hebrews*, pp. 283-90. Hughes is probably correct in his assertion (p. 289) that 'the sanctuary and the true tent' of 8.2 was intended as a hendiadys.

was not of the tribe of Levi, would not be qualified to exercise a priestly role according to the Torah[1]), he goes on to claim that neither is the sanctuary in which he now officiates of the Mosaic order. At this juncture Hebrews uses Exod. 25.40 to demonstrate that the tabernacle created by Moses was based on what was merely an imitation (ὑπόδειγμα) and shadow (σκία) of the heavenly sanctuary. On the basis of his superior priestly order, exercised in a superior, heavenly cult place, Jesus has therefore 'obtained a ministry which is as much more excellent than the old as the covenant he mediates is better, since it is enacted on better promises' (8.6).

Similar language of the 'real' versus the 'copy' is used elsewhere in Hebrews. In 9.23-24 our author contrasts the copies of the heavenly things (τὰ ὑποδείγματα), that is, the Mosaic tabernacle and its paraphernalia which could be cleansed by the Levitical cult, with the heavenly things themselves (αὐτὰ τὰ ἐπουράνια) which require a better sacrifice. The former were merely ἀντίτυπα—antitypes of the purification required for entry into the 'greater and more perfect tent, not made with hands, that is not of this creation' (9.11). The Law on which the Levitical cult was based has only a shadow (σκία) of the good things to come instead of the true form (εἰκών) of these realities (10.1). Those invisible, unseen realities[2] are appealed to as the basis of Christian faith in ch. 11.

Although both Philo and the author of Hebrews, in the service of extolling their respective cult figures, use a common language which presupposes Platonic metaphysics, it would be unjust to both to fail to point out the considerable differences between them. Only someone who has not read Philo at first hand would miss the difference in 'feel' between him and the author of Hebrews. It is not simply that in dealing with this passage he employs his favourite method of allegorizing the biblical text; it is that the whole tenor of the argument is more dense. Principally, unlike our author, Philo seems positively concerned to employ the various philosophical systems of his time, utilizing not only Middle Platonic notions, but also drawing upon Stoic and neo-Pythagorean ideas when they serve his purpose of expounding the Scriptures. For the author of Hebrews, however, metaphysical con-

---

1. Heb. 8.4; cf. 7.14.
2. See Thompson, *Beginnings*, p. 71, for an understanding of ὑπόστασις in Heb. 11.1 as the unseen, 'real' world.

cerns are not nearly as important (which is not to say that Philo is to be viewed principally as a philosopher rather than a theologian). This is evident when we contrast Philo's atemporal treatment of the Mosaic tabernacle with Hebrews. By comparing the unmediated transmission of its plan to Moses with the creation of the antecedent, immaterial world, Philo has taken Exodus 25 and downplayed its event character. Hebrews, on the other hand, has retained the primitive Christian pattern of promise and fulfilment, seeing the wilderness tabernacle together with the Levitical priesthood, God's covenant with Israel and the sacrificial rites of the Day of Atonement as not merely examples of the phenomenological world, which are inferior to their spiritual, heavenly archetypes, but as features of a prior age, which were to be superseded by the 'good things to come' (10.1).

Our author's use of spatial categories of 'here' and 'there' is a striking feature of his eschatology. Thus he speaks of salvation in terms of entering into the promised land (interpreted as entering into God's rest) (3.7–4.11); going into the sanctuary (6.2–10.18); coming to Mount Zion (12.18-24). In its presentation of the exaltation of Jesus to the right hand of God (Ps. 110.1 which the author frequently cites[1]) Hebrews also, perhaps more naturally, resorts to spatial metaphor: 'Having then a great high priest who has passed through the heavens' (4.14). We shall see later how our author uses this spatial imagery to convey a theology of access.

For the purpose of placing him within the thought world of his own day, it is important to decide whether this spatial language is an indication of 'Platonic dualism' in Hebrews. The evidence seems to require a more nuanced conclusion than a simple 'yes' or 'no' answer.

J.W. Thompson believes that the contrast drawn between the earthly Sinai and the heavenly Zion in Heb. 12.18-29 essentially reflects a Platonic, cosmological dualism between the unstable inferior world of sense perception and the unshakeable, changeless, superior immaterial world of heaven. He maintains that this passage shows a greater concern with Greek metaphysics than with the end time of Jewish apocalyptic writings.[2] Personally I am not convinced that what we find here is any other than the employment of a typology of contrast typical of this Epistle. Our author certainly does not portray any antipathy

---

1. Heb. 1.3, 13; 8.1; 10.13; 12.2.
2. Thompson, *Beginnings*, pp. 44-52.

between spirit (or soul) and flesh, which we might expect had he been imbued with metaphysical dualism. On the contrary, in 2.14 he stresses that Jesus shared our common human nature of 'flesh and blood', and in 10.5-7, 10 emphasizes the bodily nature of his sacrifice. This surely is how 10.19-20 is also to be interpreted:

> Therefore, brethren, since we have confidence to enter the sanctuary by the blood of Jesus, by the new and living way which he opened for us through the curtain, that is through his flesh. . .

Here we have an allegorization of the veil which separated off the Holy of Holies in the tabernacle, so that it is seen as representing the flesh of Jesus which had to be rent if he and his subsequent followers were to enter the inner sanctum, that is, heaven.[1] This is to interpret σάρξ not as specifically a reference to the material nature of Christ's incarnation, and certainly not in terms of any Gnostic understanding of Christ as having escaped the alienation of corporality through his ascension,[2] but as a depiction of the death of Jesus as the means whereby his session was achieved. It is Jesus' participation in, rather than his escape from, human nature in all its finitude, including the experience of suffering and death, which makes him superior to the angelic inhabitants of the heavenly realm (2.9-18). Neither does Hebrews suggest any body/spirit dualism vis-à-vis Christians. 'Heart' and 'body' are purified by faith (10.22). Furthermore, not only does the Epistle's sanctification of marriage (13.4) imply no disparagement of bodily existence; the injunction to remember those in prison or otherwise suffering ill-treatment (presumably for their Christian faith) is explicitly based upon an appeal to common, physical existence—'since you also are in the body' (13.3). None of these suggests an anthropological or cosmological dualism between the material and the immaterial.

It is mostly in the area of eschatology that scholars have suggested the influence of Middle Platonism. Certainly here we find the employment of spatial language which could lend itself to an understanding of salvation as moving from one sphere (the earthly) to

---

1. So for, e.g., Moffatt, *Hebrews*, pp. 142-43.
2. *Contra* the Gnostic interpretation of Käsemann, *Wandering People*, pp. 209-10; E. Schweizer, 'σάρξ', *TDNT*, VII, pp. 98-151. Grässer ('Hebräerbrief', pp. 182-86) thinks that the Nag Hammadi findings basically support Käsemann's interpretation. Cf. also Theissen, *Hebräerbrief*.

another (the heavenly)—more as a timeless change of location rather than as a pilgrimage within history. Especially in proclaiming his conviction that Jesus, 'the same yesterday, today and forever' (13.8), is seated at the right hand of God, and in his reinterpretation of the promised land and the Holy of Holies as heaven itself, the horizontal of Israel's history gives way to the vertical of eternal verities. The same can be said of our author's depiction in spatial terms of the present experience of Jesus' followers. In 6.5 Christians are those,

> Who have tasted the heavenly gift, and become partakers of the Holy Spirit, and have tasted the goodness of the Word of God and the powers of the age to come.

Here we are firmly on the ground of traditional Jewish eschatology, whereby salvation belongs to a future age. The author of Hebrews, like other New Testament writers, believes that this age has broken into the present one. When emphasizing the present reality of this salvation, however, our author uses spatial language. Christians are exhorted in the present to follow Jesus in entering the sanctuary, that is, heaven (10.19-22):

> But you have come (προσεληλύθατε) to Mount Zion and the city of the living God, the heavenly Jerusalem, and to innumerable angels in festal gathering, and to the assembly of the first-born who are enrolled in heaven (12.22-23b).

As Robert Jewett has written, 'The perfect tense of the verb "you have approached" makes this one of the most dramatic and radical statements of realized eschatology in the N.T.'[1]

This is not to suggest that Hebrews does not believe that the consummation of God's purposes lies in the future. Our author thinks that we are living in the 'last days' (1.2), yet 'A sabbath rest remains for the people of God' (4.9). By this he does not simply mean that Christians are the true heirs of God's earlier promises of such a blessed state, but that they should strive to ensure that they enter into it in the future (4.11). The heroes of the faith in ch. 11 are those who rely confidently not merely on an unseen world but on God's future. Then Christ will return again to gather his elect (9.28). In the meantime, those promises which were intended to meet their fulfilment in Jesus still await their final consummation. In the light of this future

---

1. Jewett, *Hebrews*, p. 223.

dimension Hebrews exhorts its readers to ensure that they be not found wanting. Whereas our author can assure his readers that 'we who have believed enter that rest' (4.3), he also warns them that they, like Israel's wilderness generation, can fail to enter that rest (3.12–4.13).

Such a tension between inaugurated and future eschatology is not new in a New Testament writing. What is striking, however, is this particular mixture of spatial, timeless imagery with the linear language of history. The former may well owe something to the language of Platonic Idealism. Unlike some commentators, however, I see no evidence that in Hebrews it has subsumed the more traditional Judaeo-Christian concept of two ages.[1]

In this connection we cannot ignore the possibility that Jewish apocalypticists may throw some light on the conceptual world of Hebrews.[2] In *4 Ezra*,[3] for example, we find a similar combination of spatial and temporal language employed in the seer's description of the heavenly Jerusalem.[4] Here we have the descent of the heavenly city, ready-made, coming down from above:

---

1. *Contra* Thompson, *Beginnings*, p. 71.

2. W.D. Davies (*Paul and Rabbinic Judaism* [London: SPCK, 3rd edn, 1970], pp. 311-20) points out that in rabbinic Judaism the age to come (*hâ-ôlam ha-bâ*) connotes both a future event in time and an externally existent reality. Therefore, 'It both IS and COMES' (p. 316). He suggests this may lie behind Paul's juxtaposed statements of the 'now' (2 Cor. 5) and the 'not yet' (1 Cor. 15) of the resurrection body.

3. *4 Ezra* is usually dated c. 100 CE. See B.M. Metzger, 'The Fourth Book of Ezra', in *The Old Testament Pseudepigrapha*, I (ed. J.H. Charlesworth; London: Darton, Longman & Todd, 1983), p. 520.

4. See *4 Ezra* 9.26–10.59; 13.35-36. Cf. *2 Bar* 4.2-7; 6.9; 32.4; Gal. 4.26; Heb. 12.22; Rev. 3.12; 21.2, 10. A.T. Lincoln (*Paradise Now and Not Yet: Studies in the Role of the Heavenly Dimension in Paul's Thought with Special Reference to His Eschatology* [SNTSMS, 43; Cambridge: Cambridge University Press, 1981], pp. 9-32, 169-95) sees a similar combination of spatial and temporal imagery in Paul's use of 'heavenly Jerusalem' as an eschatological category. Paul, Jewish apocalypticists and Qumran writers alike thought of the heavenly Jerusalem as a present reality. Since it was not regarded as static, however, in all these writings it also has a future reference. Of Colossians and Ephesians Lincoln writes, 'We need not dismiss the emphasis on realized *eschatology which utilizes spatial terminology* as foreign to authentic Paul' (p. 184, my italics).

> For behold the days will come, and it shall be when the signs which I
> have foretold unto thee shall come to pass, then shall the city that now is
> invisible appear, and the land which is not concealed be seen (*4 Ezra*
> 7.26).

This suggests heaven and earth as parallel, contemporaneous worlds in
which salvation is already present in heaven. Such language may
reflect the influence of ancient Near Eastern cosmological mythology,
which worked within a framework of a correspondence between the
heavenly and the earthly order.[1] A similar interpretation could be
given to *2 Bar.* 4.2-4, where the plan for the new Jerusalem is spoken
of as engraved on the palms of God's hands and shown to Abraham
and Moses on Mount Sinai.[2] As Christopher Rowland says of this passage, however,

> It is not a question here of the Jerusalem of the new age actually existing
> as a physical entity in heaven. . . Rather we have reflected here the idea
> that all human history exists in the mind of God.[3]

So we have not merely the depiction of parallel worlds but also of
successive ages. It is true that Jewish apocalyptic literature can be
classified as 'dualistic' in that it presents a contrast between the divine
and the human, good and evil. To that dimension, however, must also
be added the contrast between the present and the future—and here
the language of successive ages rather than atemporal spheres is
employed. Ancient Near Eastern mythology of corresponding worlds
may have been incorporated into Jewish notions of temporal succes-
sion so that 'the contrast of present and future comes out as a spatial
contrast of above and below',[4] but in such a way as to suggest that
heaven is the earth's future. The dynamic of Jewish eschatology does
not become lost in the more static two-sphere model of reality.

---

1. See W.H. Schmidt, *The Faith of the Old Testament* (Oxford: Basil Blackwell,
1983), pp. 262-68.
2. *2 Baruch* is usually dated c. 70 CE. See C. Rowland, *The Open Heaven: A
Study of Apocalyptic in Judaism and Early Christianity* (London: SPCK, 1982),
p. 520. K.L. Schmidt ('Jerusalem als Urbild und Abbild', *Eranos Jahrbuch* 18
[1950], pp. 222-23) believes that all these 'heavenly Jerusalem' traditions have
developed from biblical texts (Isa. 54.10-13; 60–62; Ezek. 40–42; Zech. 2.1; 8.3;
9.14. [The LXX of Isa. 60.1 expressly mentions Jerusalem.]) For *2 Baruch* as a
Jewish response to the destruction of the Temple in 70 CE see F.J. Murphy, 'The
Temple in the Syriac Apocalypse of Baruch', *JBL* 106 (1987), pp. 671-83.
3. Rowland, *Open Heaven*, p. 56.
4. Schmidt, *Faith*, p. 265.

The Epistle to the Hebrews cannot, of course, be classified as an apocalypse. H.-M. Schenke's suggestion that it may owe something to the language of *Merkavah* mysticism[1] should not blind us to the fact that the mystical contemplation of the divine chariot/throne (*Merkavah*), which had its antecedents in the Bible (e.g. 1 Kgs 22.19; Isa. 6.1?; Ezek. 1; 3.22-24; 8.1?; 10) and was to develop in the *Hekhalot* (divine palaces) literature of the Talmudic age (200–700 CE), took the form of supernatural, heavenly vision. Hence it is to be seen, albeit in a less developed form, in Jewish Apocalypses such as *1 Enoch, 2 Enoch*, the *Apocalypse of Abraham*, and the *Ascension of Isaiah*.[2] Hebrews, however, lays no claim to heavenly vision. Yet in his eschatological thinking, especially in his combination of spatial and temporal images and his depiction of heaven as the future of the people of God, our author seems to be closer to the apocalypticists' world-view than to that of Greek metaphysicians. That is not to say that he, like the Jewish apocalypticists, did not live in a world where Middle Platonism was a pervading philosophy. No doubt some of its vocabulary has been adopted by Hebrews. But to understand *how* our author uses it we need to go beyond the 'either–or' approach of much of the debate in contemporary scholarship, and to see that the author of the Epistle inhabited an intellectual world in which 'both–and' could and did cohabit.

5. *A Preoccupation with Sacred Space*

It seem to me that the author of Hebrews' preoccupation is not that of the Hellenistic philosopher, that is, of the phenomenal versus the Ideal, but rather of the profane versus the holy. This was a common concern of all religion in the ancient world. It is frequently conveyed by the idea of 'sacred space', which the worshipper wishes to approach in order to gain access to the deity. Surrounding such space are all kinds of taboos and rituals. Standing as he does within the religious tradition

---

1. H.-M. Schenke, 'Erwägungen zum Rätsel des Hebräerbriefes', in *Neues Testament und christliche Existenz* (ed. H.D. Betz and L. Schottroff; Tübingen: Mohr [Paul Siebeck], 1973), pp. 421-37.
2. I. Gruenwald, *Apocalypticism and Merkavah Mysticism* (Leiden: Brill, 1980), pp. 29-72; G.G. Scholem, *Major Trends in Jewish Mysticism* (New York: Schocken Books, 3rd edn, 1955), pp. 40-79.

of Judaism, our author inherited notions of sacred space whereby it was identified with the land, Jerusalem, Zion and the sanctuary. He shares a priestly concern to guard the sacred and protect it from the profane; to regulate the means whereby the worshipper can approach the holy. From the stance of Israel's wilderness period, Hebrews' pre-occupation with sacred space is worked out in terms of both her entry into the promised land and entry into the inner sanctum of the desert tabernacle, together with the covenant and priesthood upon which these two means of access were based.

It seems unlikely that such a preoccupation was born *ex nihilo*. Our author seems to have faced some situation which would give rise to a need to return once more to the established theme of sacred space, and to reinterpret from a Christian viewpoint Judaism's beliefs about the God-given means of access to it. After the destruction of the Temple in 70 CE (and the end of the Jewish state in 135 CE) the Pharisaic-rabbinic response was to focus on Torah piety as the means whereby Israel, even without the Temple, could draw near to God. The priestly regulations of purity were now applied to the whole community, which saw itself as a kingdom of priests.[1] As Jacob Neusner puts it, 'The Temple altar in Jerusalem would be replicated at the table of all Israel'.[2]

Judaism's post 70 CE apocalyptic writers interpreted the fall of Jerusalem negatively; as God's punishment upon Israel for her sins.[3] Cosmological speculations of earlier apocalypses (e.g. *1 Enoch*) gave way to a greater interest in eschatology. Now the visionaries were concerned with the experience of ascent to the various heavens, categorized by Gruenwald as 'a kind of mystical escapism'.[4] He sees such mysticism as partly a response to the disastrous events of 70 CE:

> When the cultic centre of the nation was no longer available, some people adopted beliefs and cultivated experiences which in some sense could replace experiences which had once been connected with the now destroyed Temple and with the immanence of God it signified.[5]

1. See Neusner, *Early Rabbinic Judaism*, pp. 40-49.
2. Neusner, *Early Rabbinic Judaism*, p. 48.
3. Neusner, *Early Rabbinic Judaism*, pp. 36-39.
4. Gruenwald, *Apocalypticism*, p. 48.
5. Gruenwald, *Apocalypticism*, p. 47.

We have become accustomed to the idea that for the church, Christ came to replace Judaism's accepted means of access to God—not least due to the influence of the Epistle to the Hebrews. Whether such a displacement took place prior to the fall of Jerusalem and the destruction of the Temple, however, is far from certain. Our Epistle cannot be used as evidence since there is no compelling reason to date it either before or after 70 CE.

Jacob Neusner suggests that from the very beginning of the Christian church the death of Christ was seen to imply the end of the cult for his followers:

> Because of their faith in the crucified and risen Christ, Christians experienced the end of the old cult and the Old Temple *before it actually took place*, much like the Qumran sectarians. They had to work out the meaning of the sacrifice of Jesus on the cross, and *whether the essays on that central problem were done before or after 70 is of no consequence*. . . To them (i.e. Christians), the final sacrifice had already taken place; the perfect priest had offered up the perfect holocaust, his own body. So for the Christians, Christ on the cross completed the old sanctity and inaugurated the new.[1]

As a statement of the belief of the author of Hebrews this would be a fair summary, but how far it can be taken as typical of Christian theology of the first century—before or after 70 CE—is another matter.

It is true that Christ's death was early interpreted in sacrificial terms. The Synoptic Gospels' presentation of the Last Supper as a Passover meal,[2] together with Paul's employment of sacrificial language of the death of Christ as a covenant[3] or sin-offering[4] would suggest that a cultic model was soon adopted in Christian soteriology. But whether Christians were equally quick to infer from this that Christ had replaced the sacred space of the Jerusalem Temple is more problematic. Certainly the author of the Fourth Gospel does so when he reinterprets the accusation that Jesus threatened to destroy the Temple[5] as a reference to his own resurrection (Jn 2.18-22). In the

1. Neusner, *Early Rabbinic Judaism*, pp. 41-42 (my italics).
2. Mk 14.12, 14, 16 // Mt. 26.17, 18, 19 // Lk. 22.7, 8, 11, 13. See J. Jeremias, *The Eucharistic Words of Jesus* (London: SCM Press, 3rd rev. edn, 1966), pp. 41-88. Cf. 1 Cor. 5.7 for Christ as the paschal victim.
3. 1 Cor. 11.25.
4. 2 Cor. 5.21.
5. See Mk 14.58 // Mt. 26.61; Mk 15.29-30 // Mt. 27.39-40; Acts 6.13-14.

discourse with the Samaritan woman Jesus is portrayed as displacing
the temples of both Gerizim and Jerusalem:

> Woman, believe me, the hour is coming when neither on this mountain
> nor in Jerusalem will you worship the Father. . . But the hour is
> coming, and now is, when the true worshipper will worship the Father in
> spirit and truth, for such the Father seeks to worship him (Jn 4.21, 23).

John's Gospel was written towards the end of the first century,
however, and cannot be used in this instance as evidence of an early
conviction that in his cross Christ had replaced the Temple.[1]

Neusner, of course, is starting from the conclusion of Lloyd Gaston
that the Temple ceased to be regarded by Christians as a holy place
from the very beginning—and this because Jesus had been indifferent
to the cult.[2] More recently, E.P. Sanders has re-examined Gaston's
thesis and argued cogently against it.[3] For Sanders the 'cleansing' of
the Temple[4] and the sayings concerning Jesus' prediction of its
destruction together indicate that Jesus did in fact engage in controversy concerning the Temple.[5] This, however, was not an attack upon
the business transactions which would have been an inevitable part of
the operation of the sacrificial system, nor a protest against the external nature of the cult over against the inner virtues of repentance, etc.
Neither did Jesus attack the priesthood *per se*. His 'cleansing' of the
Temple is therefore a misnomer, which does not mean to say that he
was indifferent to it. Jesus' action was intended (and would have been
perceived by his contemporaries) as symbolic. It was an enacted prediction of the Temple's destruction and restoration in the eschaton.[6]
For Jesus, therefore, the Temple was not necessarily impure; it was

---

1. So L. Gaston (*No Stone on Another: Studies in the Significance of the Fall of
Jerusalem in the Synoptic Gospels* [Leiden: Brill, 1970], pp. 205-40, 242-44)
maintains, *contra* R.J. McKelvey (*The New Temple: The Church in the New
Testament* [Oxford: Oxford University Press, 1969], pp. 78-79) that the depiction of
Jesus as the new Temple was a late development, growing out of the idea of the
Christian community as the new Temple.
2. Gaston, *No Stone*, pp. 97-99, 102, 242-44. In order to maintain this position
he claims that Mk 14.58b reflects the church's later anti-Temple stance.
3. E.P. Sanders, *Jesus and Judaism* (London: SCM Press, 1985), pp. 61-90.
4. Mk 11.15-19 and parallels.
5. Sanders, *Jesus and Judaism*, p. 177.
6. Sanders, *Jesus and Judaism*, pp. 71, 75, 89 (following McKelvey, *New
Temple*, pp. 71-72).

his belief, however, that its days were numbered. This selfsame attitude is seen by Sanders to be shared by the early apostles, who are depicted in Acts (2.46; 3.1; 21.26) as continuing to worship in the Temple.[1] Certainly Jerusalem remained central to the early church until its destruction in 70 CE. After that date the need to replace its cult with Christian alternatives would become more urgent. Although the death of Christ, interpreted in sacrificial terms, would seem to be the beginning of the process, there is no evidence to suggest, as Neusner does, that it was all there in embryo from the time of the crucifixion.

It is our Epistle alone of all New Testament works which goes in the direction suggested by Neusner, at least in terms of Christ as 'the perfect priest' who 'had offered up the perfect holocaust, his own body'. Whereas in other New Testament traditions we see the presentation of the death of Jesus in sacrificial terms, only in Hebrews is this presented within the framework of the Day of Atonement. More importantly, whereas elsewhere we find either the person of Christ or the Christian community[2] depicted in terms of the Temple—and indeed as its replacement—in our Epistle the earthly tabernacle, along with the holy land, is superseded by heaven itself. Although the book of Revelation uses the image of the Temple as the heavenly setting for the visions in chs. 4–20,[3] when we come to the descent of the holy city, the new Jerusalem, there there is no Temple. It has been displaced, since 'Its temple is the Lord God Almighty and the Lamb' (Rev. 21.22).[4]

Similarities between Stephen's speech in Acts (7.2-53), the Fourth Gospel and the Epistle to the Hebrews have long been noted,[5] espe-

1. Sanders, *Jesus and Judaism*, p. 76. According to Sanders, therefore, for Jesus neither Temple nor Torah were inviolate. They were but part of the present dispensation which was coming to an end (see pp. 251-52).

2. 1 Cor. 3.16; 6.15-20; 2 Cor. 6.14–7.1; Eph. 2.18-22; 1 Pet. 2.3-6. For the Qumran parallels to these texts see B. Gärtner, *The Temple and the Community in Qumran and the New Testament* (Cambridge: Cambridge University Press, 1965).

3. Rev. 6.9; 7.15; 8.3, 5; 9.13; 14.18; 17.7.

4. *Contra* Sanders, *Jesus and Judaism*, p. 86, who agrees with McKelvey, *New Temple*, p. 11 n. 2, that a new Zion necessarily implies a new Temple, and who regards this as a piece of Christian polemic against Jewish speculations concerning a new Temple.

5. For the similarities between Stephen's speech in Acts 7 and Hebrews see Manson, *Hebrews*, pp. 25-46. For affinities between Hebrews and the Fourth

cially in their common conviction that Judaism's 'sacred space' has now been replaced by Christ. We must not, however, neglect to notice the differences between them. For example, our author, since he is expounding biblical texts concerning the wilderness tabernacle, does not ostensibly have the Jerusalem Temple in mind. Unlike Stephen, moreover, he does not draw a contrast between the tent in the wilderness and the subsequent building of the Temple, which he dismisses as a mere 'house made with hands'[1] and in which God does not dwell (Acts 7.44-50). Whereas both Stephen and Hebrews see no place for the cult within Christianity, the former's speech is thoroughly polemical in its rejection of the Jerusalem Temple, depicting it together with its sacrifices (like Amos 5.25) as always inferior to Israel's wilderness tabernacle. Hebrews, on the other hand, seems to be working within a promise-fulfilment schema, whereby the cult has been displaced because the purposes for which it was ordained, the removal of the barrier of sin which precluded access to God, had now been fulfilled in the sacrifice of Christ, himself at once the perfect victim and priest.

In his depiction of the work of Christ in priestly terms the author of Hebrews has introduced something quite unique in the New Testament. 1 Peter (2.5) describes the church collectively as a priesthood[2] whose calling is to 'offer sacrifices acceptable to God through Jesus Christ', and our own author (echoing Ps. 50.23) exhorts his readers to 'continually offer a sacrifice of praise to God (13.15). Yet only in Hebrews is Jesus, rather than the Christian community, depicted in priestly terms.[3] Here he is not the Temple, but the victim and officiant who has entered heaven itself.

Gospel and Johannine Epistles see Spicq, *Hébreux*, I, pp. 103-38; C.J.A. Hickling, 'John and Hebrews: The Background of Hebrews 2.10-18', *NTS* 29 (1988), pp. 112-15. O. Cullman (*The Johannine Circle* [London: SCM Press, 1975], pp. 49-55) sees links between the Johannine circle, Hebrews, Stephen's speech and heterodox Judaism (including Samaritanism).

1. In Heb. 9.24 the ἄγια made with hands is the wilderness tabernacle, contrasted with the 'true' one, i.e. heaven itself. See p. 54 n. 2.

2. Cf. IQS 8.4-10. See also Rom. 15.16 where Paul describes his bringing the Gentiles to God as a 'priestly service' (ἱερουργοῦντα) of the Gospel.

3. The attempt (e.g. Spicq, *Hébreux*, I, pp. 122-25) to interpret Jesus' prayer in Jn 17 in specifically priestly terms is unconvincing. Its common designation as 'The High Priestly Prayer' remains a misnomer.

6. *Conclusions*

What situation would therefore be answered by a presentation of Jesus as the pioneer (ἀρχηγός, 2.10; 12.2) whose pilgrimage attained the true, promised land of heaven itself, and whose role as victim and priest enabled him to gain access to God where he is now seated at His[1] right hand? The most likely answer would be the destruction of Jerusalem and its Temple. A sense of loss, inevitably felt keenly by Jewish Christians, called forth from our author a reinterpretation of Judaism's established means of access to God, replacing them by Christ and relocating sacred space in heaven itself—understood as the presence of God.

Scholars have suggested that Hebrews was written to counteract ideas among some of its readers which might lead to the displacement of Christ. Yet Christology seems to be our author's answer rather than his question. It is the displacement felt by his addressees as a result of the actual loss of Jerusalem which seems to give rise to his need to present Jesus as making the necessity for such a place redundant. Hence, Jesus is shown to have gained access to the only sacred space worth having—heaven. That space is superior to any previously gained through entry into the promised land or into the inner sanctum of the cult place. Trusting in this, his readers should not hanker after the lost Jerusalem.

This reading presupposes that a specific historical situation gave rise to the theology which we find in Hebrews. Christians of Jewish origin, whether in Judaea or the Diaspora, especially those with a priestly frame of mind, would have mourned the loss of Jerusalem. It is this which is the most likely scenario for the composition of our Epistle. Its author did not start with questions of Christology or soteriology in the abstract. These emerge out of his attempt to reinterpret the Scriptures to meet the specific needs of his audience. The interpretative traditions and methods which he brings to bear in this enterprise cannot neatly be categorized, but seem to have their closest affinities with Hellenistic Judaism, since he draws upon both Jewish and Greek traditions. From this interaction Hebrews has created a new and powerful theology of access.

---

1. The capitalization of personal pronouns for God adopted throughout this work is intended to signal that God is above gender—*not* that the deity is male.

Chapter 2

PREVIOUS GOD-GIVEN MEANS OF ACCESS AND THEIR FAILURE

1. *Hebrews' Citation and Use of Scripture*

Nothing is more evident of the author of Hebrews' Jewish background than his citation and use of what the church has subsequently come to call 'the Old Testament'. Clearly it is this corpus of writings which constitutes his sacred Scriptures, to be appealed to and explicated—albeit in terms of his overtly Christian stance. Its inspiration is accepted as axiomatic. Hence, although sometimes quotations are introduced by an impersonal form, for example, 'It is said' (3.5; cf. 11.18), 'The exhortation which addresses you' (12.5), 'The order that was given' (12.20), or even 'It has been testified somewhere' (2.6)—as if the human ascription of a biblical book was a matter of complete indifference to our author, the divine origin of Scripture is affirmed by its ascription to the holy spirit. Thus Hebrews introduces Ps. 95.7-11 with, 'As the holy spirit says [λέγει]' (3.7),[1] and Jer. 31.33 (LXX 38.33) with, 'And the holy spirit also bears witness (μαρτυρεῖ)[2] to us' (10.15). The most frequent formula used to introduce citations from the Old Testament is 'He [i.e. God] said',[3] or 'says (λέγει)'.[4] From the use of the present tense it is evident that for the author of the Epistle to the Hebrews, Judaism's Scriptures are no dead letter, but a living word of God. The very opening words of his homily, 'In many and various ways God spoke of old to our fathers by the prophets' (1.1), testify to his belief that the Scriptures are from God. That was not at issue between the early church and the Judaism from

---

1. See also 9.8 where Hebrews' interpretation of Lev. 16 is prefaced by 'By this the holy spirit indicates' (δηλοῦντος).

2. Cf. 7.17.

3. For past tenses see 1.5, 13; 4.3, 4; 5.5; 6.14; 8.5; 10.30; 12.26; 13.5.

4. 1.6, 7; 5.6; 8.8.

which it sprang. What was disputed was how the Scriptures were to be interpreted. So as a Christian exegete our author accepted the inspiration of the past as genuine, valid and from God. Hence, wherever possible he appealed to the Old Testament to substantiate the claims he made for Christ. Nonetheless, it is his christological convictions which dominate and dictate his hermeneutical approach. This is clear from the prologue, which continues, 'But in these last days he has spoken to us by a son' (1.2a). That the Scriptures are God's word our author is convinced; but that they are God's *last* word he is not prepared to concede. To Jesus alone is given that position of eminence. He is God's final and definitive revelation.

This is not only spelled out in the opening of the Epistle; it is manifest in the way its author selects, cites and interprets Scripture throughout. Jesus becomes the exegetical norm, 'the canon within the canon'. Thus the inspiration of the Old Testament lies precisely in its witness to Jesus as the Christ, that is, in its amenity to such a christological interpretation. Where that is not possible, then one part is used to demonstrate the redundancy of other parts. We shall see this when we come to consider the shadowy figure, Melchizedek. Biblical texts concerning him are used to demonstrate the redundancy of those which speak of a Levitical priesthood. Similarly, Jeremiah's prophecy of a new covenant is set over against the Mosaic covenant and used as evidence of the latter's impermanence. In this way Hebrews finds within parts of the Old Testament seeds of the redundancy of other parts. Holding at one and the same time a belief in its inspiration and the finality of revelation in Jesus Christ who becomes the 'touchstone' of all biblical interpretation, the author of Hebrews has a dynamic rather than static view of tradition; a nuanced approach, not always appreciated by those in our own day who wish to appeal to him to uphold either a crude biblicism or a Marcionite repudiation of the Old Testament.

All who would follow Marcion in an attempt to sever the inextricable bond between the testaments will find no support in our author, who upholds a genuine correspondence between the 'then' of the Old Testament and the 'now' of the Christian era. Hebrews stands firmly within New Testament tradition which seeks to emphasize the continuity of God's word in the past with its expression in Jesus of Nazareth. Among New Testament writers we find three principal ways of doing this: (1) by an appeal to the fulfilment of prophecy; (2)

by interpreting Scripture allegorically; (3) by presenting events of the past as 'types' of the future. The first is perhaps the most straightforward. So, for example, in his Gospel Matthew regularly interrupts the narrative with the claim, 'For this has fulfilled the words spoken by the prophet'.[1] Prophetic utterance is understood as prediction of the future, finding its fulfilment in the person and life of Jesus. The interpretative approach which regards Scripture as allegory,[2] although more oblique, is equally an attempt to lay contemporary claim to an ancient text. It is to view the Scriptures as a story with a hidden meaning; ostensibly about one set of events, but actually—for those with eyes to see—about another. This use of allegory as a hermeneutical tool is not the same as the self-conscious employment of allegory as a literary *genre*, such as we find for example in Spenser's *Faërie Queene* or Bunyan's *Pilgrim's Progress*. These works are clearly intended by their authors to be understood as allegories, operating as extended metaphors and drawing upon implicit comparisons, which the readers are intended to make explicit for themselves. Allegorization, on the other hand, is essentially the result of subsequent interpretation. It treats the text as a cypher to be decoded. Augustine's treatment of the parable of the Good Samaritan[3] is perhaps one of the better known (and extreme) examples. Here the man in the story becomes Adam, travelling from mortality (= Jericho) to heaven (= Jerusalem). He is hindered on his journey by the devil and his minions (= the thieves). The Old Testament (= the priest and the Levite) does not save him. Only Christ (= the Samaritan) is able to do so. The flesh of Christ's incarnation (= the donkey) upholds the stricken Adam, bearing him in safety to the church (= the inn) where he is tended by the apostle Paul (= the doorkeeper). And so the story goes on, with every term of the original made to represent something else.

Inevitably this method raises the question, 'What constitutes valid as opposed to invalid interpretation?' This is not simply a problem invented by modern biblical criticism, as a result of its emphasis upon historical method and insistence upon the importance of original

---

1. Mt. 1.22; 2.15, 17, 23; 4.14; 8.17; 12.17; 13.35; 21.4; 26.56; 27.9.

2. See G.B. Caird, *The Language and Imagery of the Bible* (London: Duckworth, 1980), pp. 144-71.

3. Augustine, *De Gen.C.Man.* 2.10-13; *Enarr. in Ps.* 60.8. Cf. *Quest. Evangel.* 2.19.

context. I doubt whether Jewish exegetes of the apostle Paul's day would have accepted the validity of his allegorical interpretation of the Sarah/Hagar story, whereby the slave woman Hagar and her offspring Ishmael are made to represent the old covenant, over against Sarah and her son Isaac, who symbolize the new![1] Paul's contemporaries, however, would not have taken issue with the use of allegorization as an exegetical method. That had long been employed by Gentile and Jew alike to contemporize ancient, sacred texts. It had been applied by the Stoics to the Homeric epics in an attempt to make them philosophically and morally respectable, and by Alexandrian Jewry (notably Philo) to Jewish Scripture in order to make it more relevant to their *confrères*, as well as to commend Judaism to the pagan world. Thus, for example, Philo allegorizes the patriarchal narratives so that they represent Stoic virtues,[2] thereby claiming to find in Scripture the basic tenets of subsequent Hellenistic philosophy. Judaism had got there first!

The author of Hebrews, in his attempt to demonstrate a correspondence between past and present, does not resort to a simple appeal to prophetic oracle and its fulfilment in Christ, although he clearly regards the Scriptures as prophetic in the sense that they are about God's eschatological future.[3] While he does draw upon the prophetic canon (especially Isaiah and Jeremiah), it is the Pentateuch and the Psalter which provide the majority of texts for this particular homily.[4]

One of the major differences between Philo of Alexandria and the author of Hebrews is the former's predilection for allegorization. This

---

1. Gal. 4.21-29.

2. See Philo, *Abr.* 208-276 where Abraham represents the cardinal Stoic virtues of justice, courage, prudence and temperance.

3. See Caird, 'Exegetical Method', p. 47.

4. According to Longenecker (*Exegesis*, pp. 164-67) 12 out of 38 quotations and 41 out of 55 allusions are from the Pentateuch; 18 out of 38 quotations and two out of 55 allusions are to the Prophets. There is one allusion and one quotation from Proverbs, and only one quotation from a historical book, i.e., 2 Sam. 7.14 (Heb. 1.5). The incidents of 2 Macc. 6–7 are alluded to in Heb. 11.35ff., yet this does not necessarily indicate that our author regarded the work as Scripture. With regard to those listed in ch. 11, A. Hanson (*Living Utterances*, p. 112) reminds us, 'our author is reviewing the heroes of Israel's history, not a gallery of exclusively scriptural heroes'.

is frequently pointed out by contemporary scholars, and rightly so. It would be wrong, however, to assume from this that allegory is entirely absent from Hebrews. In the ancient world, so-called etymologies were often nothing more than allegorizations. Thus, when in Heb. 7.2 we read of Melchizedek, 'He is first, by translation of his name, king of righteousness, and then he is also king of Salem that is, king of peace', we are being presented with an allegorical interpretation of both his name and that of his city, Jerusalem. In neither method nor conclusion is Hebrews original. We find both etymologies in Philo,[1] and that for Jerusalem in Josephus.[2] Anthony Hanson[3] would add two further examples of allegory in Hebrews: (1) 'By the new and living way which he opened for us through the curtain, that is through his flesh' (10.20). Hanson would agree with those scholars who see here an allegorization of the veil which divided the holy of holies from the rest of the tabernacle, so that it becomes a hidden reference to the flesh of Christ which was rent, that is, the death he had to pass through in order to gain access to God.[4] (2) The 'camp' outside of which the carcasses of the sin-offering were to be taken and burned on the Day of Atonement (Lev. 16.27) in 13.12 is interpreted as the gate of Jerusalem outside of which Jesus was taken for execution. Personally, I would not categorize this second example cited by Hanson as a piece of allegory, but more a claim, via a simple comparison, to the fulfilment of Scripture. The 'camp' of the wilderness generation and the regulations ostensibly designed for the tabernacle had long since been re-located in Jerusalem and its Temple. The shift between 'camp' and 'gate' had already taken place and would, therefore, hardly constitute a hidden meaning in the first century CE.

1. Philo, *Leg. All.* 3.79, 82.

2. Josephus, *Ant.* 2.10.2.

3. Hanson, *Living Utterances*, pp. 109-11.

4. E.g. Moffatt, *Hebrews*, pp. 143-44, more recently upheld by N.H. Young, 'τουτ' ἔστιν τῆς σαρκὸς αὐτοῦ (Heb X:20): Apposition, Dependent or Explicative?', *NTS* 20 (1973), pp. 100-104; *contra* N.A. Dahl, 'A New and Living Way: The Approach to God according to Heb. 10.19-25', *Int* 5 (1951), pp. 401-12, who interprets the curtain as a reference to the frontier between this world and the future heavenly one. Not least on grammatical grounds, Young refutes Dahl's suggested chiasm which would make τουτ' ἔστιν τῆς σαρκὸς αὐτοῦ a description of the way, and argues instead that, as it stands, it is explicative of the veil. See also Wilson, *Hebrews*, pp. 187-90.

Yet, while we do encounter some allegorizing on the part of the author of Hebrews, it would be wrong to suggest that is is his principal exegetical tool. Typology plays that role. The vocabulary of 'type'[1] is used only twice in the Epistle. In 8.5 it is part of the citation from Exod. 25.40 (LXX) concerning God's instructions for the erection and furnishing of the tabernacle. 'See that you make everything according to the pattern (κατὰ τὸν τύπον) which was shown you on the mountain.' As we have already seen (pp. 52-56) here Hebrews is clearly using τύπος in the sense of an inferior copy rather than the real thing (which is heaven itself). From this he goes on to argue (8.6–9.24) for the superiority of the new covenant, inaugurated by Christ, over against that of the Mosaic Torah:

> For Christ has entered, not into a sanctuary made with hands, a copy of the true one (ἀντίτυπα τῶν ἀληθινῶν) but into heaven itself (9.24).

In secular Greek both τύπος and ἀντίτυπος can refer either to the mould from which something (a coin, perhaps) is struck—in which case it is the prototype, pattern, exemplar and model—or to the copy which is produced from the mould—derivative and inferior. From our author's point of view, Mosaic Torah was to be understood in the second rather than the first sense. At first glance this might seem to fuel Marcionite fires, but only if we forget that the language of type and antitype is that of correspondence rather than disjuncture. Hebrews certainly wishes to claim for Christ a superiority to all that has gone before, but it is not thereby perpetrating a doctrine of discontinuity. As Hanson has rightly stated, 'Typology only makes sense in the context of an ongoing history of God's saving acts'.[2]

The way our author employs typology, moreover, goes far beyond his rare use of the vocabulary of type and antitype. It is his dominant hermeneutical principle, a way of portraying the relationship between Jewish Scripture and Christian insight. Once Israel's past is viewed as an anticipation of the church's present, the organic connection between the two becomes clear. This is to go beyond viewing Old

---

1. For other instances of the language of 'type' in the New Testament see Paul, for whom Adam is 'the type of the one who was to come' (Rom. 5.14). The apostle can also refer to his own good example as a τύπος (Phil. 3.17). Negatively, Israel's disobedience in the wilderness is a 'type' (1 Cor. 10.6). 1 Pet. 3.21 describes Christian baptism as an antitype of Noah's salvation through the flood.
2. Hanson, *Living Utterances*, p. 106.

Testament prophecies as predictions of the future; past events themselves are seen as a trailer or preview of what is to come. Since the
past is an anticipation of the future there is a genuine correspondence
between then and now. So the high priesthood of Melchizedek is an
anticipatory type of that of Christ; Israel's pilgrimage in the wilderness corresponds to that later to be faced by the Christian community.
As much as the more obvious appeal to the fulfilment of prophecy,
typological exegesis is dependent upon a belief in inaugurated eschatology, that is, a conviction that something decisive has happened of
which the events of the past spoke. It is, therefore, another kind of
argument for fulfilment.

   In the Old Testament itself we can see the anonymous prophet of the
exile viewing the present and future in terms of the past. So Isaiah 51
(vv. 3, 9, 10) speaks of the fulfilment of God's purposes in the future
in terms of the creation of the past; he describes paradise in terms of
Eden, and thereby sees a correspondence between the end time and the
beginning of time. In its annual celebration of Passover today, the
Jewish community, at one and the same time, looks back to the events
of the exodus and forward to 'next year in Jerusalem'. The exodus is a
type of the salvation yet to come. For the author of Hebrews, however, events of the past are principally types of the salvation which has
already occurred in Jesus. This is not to say that his eschatology is
wholly realized.[1] Especially in the paraenetic sections, he reminds his
readers that the consummation of God's purposes has not yet come
about, and that they should beware lest they be excluded when it does
(cf. 4.1).

   Yet if it is true that typology only works on the basis of a measure
of symmetry between type and antitype, it is also evident that in
Hebrews we find largely a typology of contrast rather than fulfilment.
So Israel's wilderness wanderings, the Aaronic high priesthood and
Mosaic covenant are anticipatory but inferior. The argument *a minori
ad maius* recurs frequently throughout the Epistle. Jesus is better
(κρείττων) than angels (1.4), and the Mosaic covenant (7.22; 8.6); he
introduces a better hope (7.19), and is a better sacrifice (9.23) which
speaks better than the blood of Abel (12.24). He entered a greater
(μείζων) tabernacle, that is, heaven itself (9.11). The Christian's
inheritance is therefore better, since it is an abiding one (10.34). Like

---

1. See Barrett, 'Eschatology', pp. 363-93.

the faithful heroes of the past, he or she aspires to a better country (11.16).

Only in the case of Melchizedekian high priesthood is there a genuine typology of fulfilment in Hebrews. In ch. 7 Jesus is depicted as a priest 'in the likeness of Melchizedek' (v. 16). Even here, however, our author is so dominated by his conviction that Christ is superior that in v. 3 he makes Melchizedek resemble him rather than vice versa:

> He [i.e. Melchizedek] is without father or mother or genealogy, and has neither beginning of days nor end of life, but *resembling the Son of God* he continues a priest forever.[1]

The Epistle to the Hebrews employs events (and in this case a figure) from the past as types of Jesus, but it is in no doubt that the antitype is to be preferred; the later has superseded the earlier. The warrant for this assertion is to be found in Scripture itself. Thus, if the radical discontinuities of Marcionitism find no home in this particular New Testament book, equally a biblical fundamentalism, which would understand 'All scripture is inspired by God and profitable for teaching' (2 Tim. 3.16) to mean that every text of Scripture has equal claim upon Christian obedience, should be discomfited by it. For our author some biblical institutions and injunctions have been made obsolete by Christ.[2]

It is not only *how* he approaches Scripture which reveals his theological stance; it is *what* texts he chooses and expounds. These emerge from the cultic preoccupation of his audience which he is at pains to re-direct. I suggested in Chapter 1 that it was the fall of Jerusalem in 70 CE which gave rise to this particular crisis of faith. Be that as it

1. See M.R. D'Angelo, *Moses in the Letter to the Hebrews* (Missoula, MT: Scholars Press, 1979), p. 11, who points out that for Hebrews not only Moses, but Melchizedek, the high priest, and Isaac also are made to resemble the son of God, rather than vice versa.

2. A similar appeal is made by contemporary feminist theologians such as R.R. Ruether, *Sexism and God Talk: Toward a Feminist Theology* (Boston: Beacon Press, 1983); E.S. Fiorenza, *In Memory of Her: A Feminist Theological Reconstruction of Christian Origins* (New York: Crossroad, 1983); and *idem*, *Bread Not Stone: The Challenge of Feminist Biblical Interpretation* (Boston: Beacon Press, 1984). They maintain that not only the Old Testament but passages in the New Testament which promulgate an inferior, subordinate status for women should be regarded as redundant in the light of Jesus' gospel of human liberation.

may, nothing could be more misleading than to interpret the situation which led to the writing of Hebrews as though it were the same as that which called forth the letters of Paul. Much of the apostle's theological writing was preoccupied with issues raised by his mission to the Gentiles. This is not so for Hebrews. Unlike Paul, our author has no need to discuss how God could work outside the Mosaic covenant and thus hold Gentiles as well as Jews culpable.[1] In fact, nowhere in Hebrews is there a discussion of 'us' and 'them' in terms of Jew and Gentile. Rather, the author distinguishes between those who were faithful and those who were faithless in both the past and the present. Both categories can be found then and now. Thus, at one and the same time he cites Israel in the wilderness as a warning paradigm of infidelity, and a whole list of Old Testament characters, stretching from Abel (11.4) to the martyrs of the Maccabaean revolt (11.35-37), as precursors of faith which culminates in Jesus himself, 'the pioneer and perfector of our faith' (12.2).

For Hebrews' author, Judaism's cult did not constitute a threat to Christian faith. Indeed, if my suggestion as to the occasion of the Epistle is right, it was not operative at the time. For Paul, however, in his situation, Mosaic Torah did pose a threat to his understanding of the gospel. Its imposition upon his Gentile converts (especially circumcision and kosher food laws) constituted a fundamental assault upon his conviction that salvation was located wholly and exclusively in Christ.[2] This can lead him on occasion to write as if there was a radical discontinuity between Law and gospel.[3]

The author of our Epistle is also aware of a discontinuity between past and present inherent in the claims he makes for Christ. If the Levitical priesthood under which the Law was received (7.11) has been superseded, he argues, then of logical necessity (ἐξ ἀνάγκης) that Law will not remain unchanged:

> For when there is a change in priesthood, there is necessarily a change in the law as well (7.12).

---

1. See Rom. 1.16–3.26.

2. See E.P. Sanders, *Paul and Palestinian Judaism* (London: SCM Press, 1977), pp. 442-97.

3. See Gal. 2.16, 19, 21; 3.15-18, 24-25. Paul has a more positive view of the Law in Romans (see Rom. 7.7-12). Yet, if with E. Käsemann (*Commentary on Romans*, pp. 280-83) *et al.*, τέλος in Rom. 10.4 is understood as 'end' rather than 'goal', then the note of discontinuity is found even in this epistle.

The more usual premiss would be that priesthood was inaugurated by Mosaic Torah. As W. Horbury has pointed out,[1] however, our author shares with other first-century CE Jewish writers such as Philo and Josephus a penchant for the polity of the priestly strand of the Pentateuch, whereby the theocracy of the sons of Aaron was thought to mediate divine rule. This stressed the interdependence of Law and priesthood, but on occasion, like Hebrews, could take the view that the former was dependent upon the latter.[2] For our author, both Aaronic priesthood and Law have found their successor in Christ. As the sanctuary in which that priesthood officiated was but a shadow (σκία) of the true, heavenly sanctuary (8.5), so 'the law was but a shadow of the good things to come' (10.1).

Unlike Stephen's speech in Acts 7, however, the author of Hebrews is not so much at pains to overthrow Judaism's established means of access to God as to reinterpret them in such a way as to demonstrate their fulfilment in Jesus. He shares with his readers a belief in the necessity for sacred space—an area in which God and humanity can meet. Hence, it is precisely those biblical texts which speak of sacred territory, that is, the land, Jerusalem, Mount Zion, the cult place and its inner sanctum, which he selects for explication. As with a series of Russian dolls, one encased within the other, we are led ever closer to the most sacred—into the very presence of God. Ostensibly these passages are set in the period prior to Israel's occupation of any of this territory, while she was in the wilderness, without settled land or cult place. Yet from the very way Hebrews explores the theme of access to God it is clear that the author is writing *post eventum* in two senses: (1) from the perspective of those future generations which did in fact go on to inherit the land, establish themselves in the city of Jerusalem and erect the Temple on Mount Zion; and (2) from the point of view of a generation which had now lost that sacred shrine and, in this sense, was once more back in the wilderness situation. This is surely the reason why our author confines his discussion of sacred space to the pre-settlement period of Israel's history—not because the Jerusalem Temple was still flourishing. To a group feeling bereft of

---

1. Horbury, 'Aaronic Priesthood', pp. 45, 55-58. Cf. S.N. Mason, 'Priesthood in Josephus and the "Pharisaic Revolution"', *JBL* 107 (1988), pp. 657-61.

2. Horbury ('Aaronic Priesthood', pp. 55-59) cites *Jubilees*, Josephus and *T. Levi*.

one of the major means of drawing near to God, he offers the consoling thought that Jesus has now opened for them a new and better way.
To understand the biblical texts aright is to see that precisely those
which promised the land and instituted the cult were never intended
by God to be His last word. That has been spoken to us in these last
days by a son (1.1).

2. *The Promised Land and God's Rest*

However divided biblical scholars are as to the historical origins of
the land-promises made to Israel which we find in the Old Testament,[1]
what is indisputable is how deeply they are embedded in Jewish consciousness. Even after the expulsion of the Jews by the Romans in 135
CE, a conviction that God had promised them the land remained a
major tenet of their belief:

> It has been taught: R. Simeon b. Yohai says: 'The Holy One, blessed be
> He, gave Israel three precious gifts, and all of them were given through
> sufferings. These are: The Torah, the land of Israel, and the World to
> Come (*b. Ber.* 5a).[2]

True to this tradition, the author of Hebrews also starts with the premiss that the land is not merely a political but a religious heritage. By
concentrating on those biblical narratives which tell of the wilderness
generation's failure to enter Canaan (and especially the psalmist's
comment upon them) he stresses the previously unfulfilled nature of
the land promises.

This is the dominant theme of Heb. 3.7–4.13.[3] A comparison of

---

1. See W.D. Davies, *The Gospel and the Land: Early Christianity and Jewish
Territorial Doctrine* (Berkeley: University of California Press, 1974), pp. 1-160 for
a résumé of the principal Jewish sources concerning the place of the land in Israel's
faith. Major contemporary scholarship on the topic is also discussed.
2. Cited by Davies, *Gospel and Land*, p. 56, who also points out that a third of
the Mishnah is concerned with the land.
3. Scholars are divided as to where this section begins and ends. A. Vanhoye
(*L'épître aux Hébreux texte grec: structure* [Rome: Pontifical Biblical Institute,
1967], pp. 11-14) suggests 3.1–4.14 with ἀρχιερεύς constituting an *inclusio*;
Buchanan (*Hebrews*, p. 60) extends the section to v. 16 to complete the sense of
the unit; O. Michel (*Der Brief an die Hebräer* [Göttingen: Vandenhoeck & Ruprecht,
12th edn, 1966], p. 100), Braun, (*Hebräer*, p. 88) *et al.* take 3.7–4.13 as a unit.

Jesus with Moses in the preceding verses (3.1-6) has already paved the way for a discussion of the wilderness generation. The faithfulness (πιστός) of Moses (an allusion to Num. 12.7[1]) is not only shared by Jesus—'He was faithful to him who appointed him, just as Moses also was faithful in God's house' (3.2)—it is excelled by him, since his was the fidelity of a son rather than a servant (3.3-6). The faithfulness of Moses, however, is in stark contrast to the lack of faith on the part of those whom he led. Thus our author cites Psalm 94(MT 95).7-11 (Heb. 3.7-11), a psalm which refers to God's threat to disinherit Israel for her lack of trust and her desire to return to a place of bondage rather than go forward to the land of promise (cf. Num. 14.1-35):

> As I swore in my wrath,
> They shall never enter my rest (τὴν κατάπαυσίν μου)
> (3.11 = LXX Ps. 94.11).

Like the psalmist, he does not mention that Numbers goes on to recount Moses' intercession, which results in God relenting of His first intention to disinherit the whole of Israel. Caleb and Joshua (cf. Deut. 1.34-39) and all those under the age of 20 were exempted (Num. 14.29-30). The author of Hebrews knows full well that under the leadership of Joshua, Israel did enter Canaan (4.8). First of all, however, he concentrates upon those who did not. 'So we see that they were unable to enter because of unbelief' (3.19).

A further example of unfaithfulness is alluded to in the psalm used by our author, that is, Israel's complaint at the lack of water (see Num. 20.2-13; Exod. 17.1-7). In Old Testament tradition this was interpreted as putting God to the test. Hence the place at which it occurred was named Meribah (contention/testing) and Massah (proof). Hebrews, following the LXX of the psalm, rather than transliterating the Hebrew place names, translates them, 'as in the rebellion' (ἐν τῷ παραπικρασμῷ) and 'on the day of testing' (κατὰ τὴν ἡμέραν τοῦ πειρασμοῦ) (3.8). The rebellious nature of the wilderness generation is heightened even more by Hebrews than the LXX, moreover, in 3.10,

---

Clearly this is closely linked to 3.1-6, which introduces the theme of Moses and the wilderness generation.

1. It is possible that this is also an echo of the oracle in 1 Sam. 2.35 which predicts the appointment of a faithful priest. (LXX 1 Kgdms 2.35 καὶ ἀναστήσω ἐμαυτῷ ἱερέα πιστόν; cf. Heb. 2.17 πιστὸς ἀρχιερεὺς.)

where our author, by altering the punctuation and introducing 'therefore' (διό), takes the 40 years to refer to the preceding verse, that is, to the length of time during which Israel saw God's mighty works, rather than to the succeeding verse, as a reference to the duration of God's wrath. In 3.17 the author of Hebrews reverts to the more usual reading, but at this earlier stage in his exposition it enables him to draw a dramatic contrast between the faithfulness of Israel in the desert and the faithfulness and perseverance to which he is calling his readers:

> Take care, brethren, lest there be in any of you an evil, unbelieving heart,
> leading you to fall away from the living God (3.12).

This is no simple antithesis between Judaism and Christianity. This is a contrast between generations in the on-going history of the people of God. Hence in 3.2-6 we are not presented with two 'houses', that of Moses over against that of Christ, but one—the house of God. It is unlikely that Hebrews is interpreting the 'house' of Num. 12.7 as the shrine or cult place,[1] since we have already noted that, unlike Paul, 1 Peter or the Qumran writings, the Epistle does not present the community itself as the replacement of either the Temple or the priesthood. Rather our author understands God's house as a household or family.[2] To his Christian community he says:

> And we are his house if we hold fast our confidence (παρρησίαν) and
> pride in our hope (3.6).

But:

> We become Christ's partners (μέτοχοι τοῦ Χριστοῦ)[3] only if we hold
> our first confidence (τὴν ἀρχὴν τῆς ὑποστάσεως) firm to the end
> (3.14).[4]

Thus, like Deuteronomy,[5] Hebrews addresses its readers as a generation standing on the brink of entry into the promised land.

---

1. *Contra* Buchanan, *Hebrews*, p. 60.
2. As in *Targ. Num.* 12.17 'my people' (*'ammî*).
3. See Montefiore, *Hebrews*, pp. 78-79; Bruce, *Hebrews*, pp. 67-68.
4. In 1 Cor. 10.1-13 Paul also cites the wilderness generation as an exemplary warning for Christians. He, however, uses the incidents of the miraculous provision of manna and water as warnings against assuming that supernatural food and drink necessarily saved that generation from God's displeasure, since they subsequently committed idolatry.
5. See Deut. 12.9, 'For you have not as yet come to the rest and to the inheritance which the Lord your God gives you'.

Theirs is the 'today' of the psalm (3.13). They are challenged with either siding with the past generation's rebellion and its resultant failure to participate in God's promises, or with responding and continuing in faith and thereby becoming the heirs of those promises.

'So then (ἄρα), there remains a sabbath rest for the people of God' (4.9). This is the conclusion to which our author's exposition of Ps. 94.7-11 (LXX) has been leading from 3.7. The route by which he arrives there, together with what he is claiming by this assertion, is instructive if we would understand his theology of access. Neither can be appreciated unless we read Hebrews against the Jewish tradition in which it stands.

In Old Testament tradition Canaan is not only important since it provided a home for the homeless, a 'rest' for wandering people.[1] It is also seen as a place of safety for Israel from her enemies:[2]

> But when you go over the Jordan, and live in the land which the Lord your God gives you to inherit, and when he gives you rest (LXX κατα-παύσει)[3] from all your enemies round about, so that you live in safety. . . (Deut. 12.10).

Commenting on Deuteronomy's attitude to the land, G. von Rad writes:

> In this work the land is undeniably the most important factor in the state of redemption to which Israel has been brought and on this basis the nation is to expect an additional gift from Yahweh—'rest from all enemies round about'.[4]

Von Rad's plea that this state of salvation should not be divorced from its physical locality and thereby 'spiritualized'[5] is taken up by W.D.

---

1. See Deut. 3.20; Josh. 1.13. For a résumé of 'rest' in the Old Testament, see Spicq, *Hébreux*, II, pp. 95-104.

2. Deut. 25.19; Josh. 11.23; 21.44; 22.4; 23.1.

3. In the LXX καταπαύειν/κατάπαυσις and ἀναπαύειν/ἀνάπαυσις can be used interchangeably. See Exod. 20.11 (cf. 23.23); Lev. 23.3, 24, 29 (cf. Lev. 25.28). In Exod. 35.2 both occur in the same sentence.

4. G. von Rad, *The Problem of the Hexateuch and other Essays* (Edinburgh: Oliver & Boyd, 1966), p. 95; *idem*, *Deuteronomy* (London: SCM Press, 1966), p. 93: 'Deuteronomy has spoken of this land of Canaan almost as if it were paradise'.

5. Von Rad, *Hexateuch*, p. 95. See also Braun, *Hebräer*, p. 91, who points out that in Judaism, locality and condition are not separated.

Davies in terms of what he sees as a Christian tendency to
'intellectualize' both its own tradition and that of Judaism:

> Christians have usually understood Judaism in too theological and, there-
> fore, intellectual terms. And they have also usually looked at their own
> foundation document, the New Testament, in the same way.[1]

He goes on to say, apropos of the land, that, since in Christian tradition this results in a preoccupation with the transference of hope from
the earthly to a heavenly Jerusalem, he has excluded the Epistle to the
Hebrews from his study, *The Gospel and the Land*—presumably
because it displays this tendency.[2] In my opinion this is to be
regretted—not only because Hebrews builds upon the premiss that
locality and condition, land and salvation are inextricable, but because
our author's exploration of the theme of sacred space deserves more
than a dismissal. For all the problems involved in accepting G.W.
Buchanan's reading of Hebrews as simply a restatement of Judaism's
traditional belief in the earthly restoration of the land under a Davidic
ruler,[3] at least he takes the theme of the land in Hebrews seriously.
What he misses, however, is that in consoling his readers for its loss,
our author urges them to move beyond an understanding of sacred
territory as located geographically on earth to an appreciation of its
re-location as a beatific state in heaven.

It is with re-location that Hebrews is principally concerned.
Working within a traditional Jewish framework of space, the author is
not attempting to dispense with all ideas of associating the holy with
locality; he is re-locating the holy. His message is that the promised
land and its rest is no longer to be understood as the land of Israel in
which God makes His name to dwell. Settlement in Canaan is not to be
equated with salvation. Accepting the traditional, Davidic authorship
of the Psalms, Hebrews is able to claim that the 'today' of Psalm 94
(MT 95) is addressed to a generation later than that of the wilderness

---

1. Davies, *Gospel and Land*, p. 161.
2. Davies, *Gospel and Land*, p. 162 and n. 3.
3. Buchanan, *Hebrews*, p. 65: 'the author expected the promised heritage of the
land of Canaan under the rule of the messiah to be fulfilled for Jesus and his
followers'. Cf. pp. 73-74 where he takes issue with those scholars who interpret the
heavenly Jerusalem as a wholly other-worldly domain, and therefore not to be
located on earth.

(4.7), 'For if Joshua[1] had given them rest, God would not speak later of another day' (4.8). The oath of the psalm, 'They shall never enter my rest (κατάπαυσιν)', is extended by our author to include subsequent generations.[2] This is possible because Hebrews includes in God's 'rest' far more than simply a notion of entry into the land. It is to be in the very presence of God—and hence located in heaven.

The interpretation of 'rest' in terms of the presence of God was not the invention of the Epistle to the Hebrews. In Exod. 33.14 God promises Moses, 'My presence will go with you and I will give you rest (LXX καταπαύσω[3]). Deuteronomy is more specific as to where God makes His name dwell (Deut. 12.11[4])—in the one, true cult place, the Jerusalem Temple. As the symbol of the presence of God, in Num. 10.33 the ark goes before Israel, seeking a place of rest (LXX ἀνάπαυσις) for the nation. According to 1 Chron. 6.31 (LXX 1 Par. 6.16) it rested in the tabernacle. Psalm 131(MT 132).14 extols Zion as God's resting place (ἡ κατάπαυσίς μου) for ever. An understanding of God's 'rest' as His abiding presence, located in the Temple, is evident in Isa. 66.1, which inveighs against any such earthly limitation of God:

> Thus says the Lord: 'Heaven is my throne and the earth my footstool;
> What is the house which you have built for me, or what is the place of my
> rest?' (LXX τόπος τῆς καταπαυσεώς μου).

Unlike Stephen's speech in Acts (7.49-50), the author of Hebrews makes no overt use of this passage. He seems, however, to understand the κατάπαυσις μου of Psalm 94 (MT 95) similarly, in terms of the

---

1. Bruce (*Hebrews*, p. 71) thinks that a Joshua–Jesus typology 'could scarcely have been absent from our author's mind'. Yet, although this typology is to be found in the *Epistle of Barnabas* and Justin, there is no evidence (as Bruce is forced to admit) that this is developed in Hebrews. On the evidence cited it is impossible to prove that it is present 'in our author's mind'—merely that it could have been.

2. *Contra* Josh. 21.44; 22.4; 23.1 where it is inherited by Joshua. In 2 Sam. (LXX 2 Kgdms) 7.1 David is given rest from his enemies and in 1 Chron. (LXX Par.) 22.9 Solomon is ἀνήρ ἀναπαύσεως, a man of peace, i.e., one who has defeated his enemies.

3. Cf. also the LXX of Deut. 33.12 which reads, 'He has taken up his rest in the midst of them' (ἀνὰ μέσον τῶν ὑμῶν αὐτοῦ κατέπαυσεν) rather than the MT, 'makes his dwelling between his [i.e. Benjamin's] shoulders'.

4. *Contra* the MT, LXX Deut. 12.11 refers to the place where God's name is called upon (ἐπιληθῆναι τὸ ὄνομα αὐτοῦ) rather than where it dwells.

presence of God. In postexilic Judaism there was a general tendency for the focus to shift from the land to the city of Jerusalem and its cult place.[1] Our author inherits this tradition whereby Jerusalem becomes the quintessence of the land, and the Temple the quintessence of Jerusalem.

In 3.7–4.11, however, he concentrates upon the land, interpreting its entry as entering into the very 'rest' which God Himself enjoyed on the seventh day of creation (4.4). Exegetically this shift in interpretation is made possible by associating the noun κατάπαυσις in Psalm 94 with its cognate verb καταπαύειν in Gen. 2.2 (LXX), 'And God rested (κατέπαυσεν) on the seventh day'. Our author coins the term σαββατισμός[2] (4.9) to characterize this rest as one which had existed from creation, and yet which had not been achieved by Israel in the past. Its promise, therefore, remains outstanding. 'A sabbath rest remains for the people of God' (4.9).

The sabbath[3] and the jubilee year[4] are well established as times of rest in biblical tradition. According to G. von Rad, however, God's rest in Gen. 2.2 is entirely different from that enjoined upon Israel in her sabbath practice. Hence he claims that the sabbath, as a cultic institution, lies entirely outside the purview of the passage. It was the Epistle to the Hebrews which united what had previously been entirely different concepts.[5] In his later commentary on Genesis, von Rad allows for a closer relationship in the thought of the priestly writer between creation and redemption in the purposes of God:

> This rest means that P does not consider it as something for God alone but as a concern of the world, almost a third something that exists between God and the world. . . Thus Gen. 2.1ff. speaks about the preparation of an exalted saving good for the world and man, of a rest 'before which millennia pass away as a thunderstorm' (Novalis). It is as tangibly 'existent' protologically as it is expected eschatologically in Hebrews.[6]

1. See Davies, *Gospel and Land*, pp. 130, 150.
2. Spicq, *Hébreux*, II, pp. 83-84. *Contra* P.E. Hughes, *Hebrews*, p. 160 n. 7, who suggests that it was probably coined from the LXX verb σαββατίζειν, and current in Jewish and Jewish Christian circles prior to, or contemporary with, Hebrews.
3. Exod. 20.11; 23.12; 35.2; Lev. 23.3; 2 Macc. 15.1; etc.
4. Lev. 25.28.
5. Von Rad, *Hexateuch*, p. 101.
6. G. von Rad, *Genesis: A Commentary* (London: SCM Press, 2nd edn, 1972), pp. 62-63.

In Jewish apocalyptic and rabbinic writings we find evidence of specu-lation which brings together the idea of God's heavenly rest, the sab-bath, and the rest promised in the age to come.[1] O. Hofius[2] has drawn our attention especially to *4 Ezra* (another post 70 CE response to the fall of Jerusalem), which depicts the place of rest, the paradise of delight, as the fate of the righteous, over against the furnace of hell which awaits the wicked (*4 Ezra* 7.36, 38). As the as yet unseen rest of God it remains in heaven, waiting to be realized on earth at the end time (*4 Ezra* 7.75-76).[3]

As a metaphor for salvation, 'rest' was not uncommon in the ancient world in both Jewish and non-Jewish circles. The content of the library discovered at Nag Hammadi has only confirmed what had already been known, that is, that we meet 'rest'[4] in Gnosticism as a designation of the highest aeon (sometimes identified as the sabbath[5]) from which the soul has fallen and to which it journeys on its pilgrim-age to salvation.[6] It is therefore both humanity's origin and destiny. Even before these Gnostic Coptic manuscripts had come to light, E. Käsemann had suggested an Alexandrian Gnostic conceptual back-ground for Hebrews' appeal to God's rest.[7] He pointed out that both

1. For evidence that the rabbis understood κατάπαυσις as the age to come (ζωὴ αἰώνιος) see H.L. Strack and P. Billerbeck, *Kommentar zum Neuen Testament aus Talmud und Midrasch*, III (Munich: Beck, 1926), p. 687. For citations of Jewish apocalyptic material see O. Hofius, *Katapausis: Die Vorstellung von endzeitlichen Ruheort im Hebräerbrief* (WUNT, 2; Tübingen: Mohr [Paul Siebeck], 1970), pp. 59-74.

2. Hofius, *Katapausis*, pp. 60-63, 69-70, 95-97.

3. Cf. also *1 En.* 45.5-6; *2 Bar.* 4.1-7.

4. Gnostic sources prefer to use ἀνάπαυσις. Any particular significance in Hebrews' preference for κατάπαυσις, however, cannot be inferred, since the source common to both, i.e., the LXX, can use either interchangeably. See Thompson, *Beginnings*, pp. 88-102.

5. Thompson (*Beginnings*, pp. 81-102) thinks that here Hebrews is closer to the cosmological and metaphysical speculations of Philo, who links the aeon with rest and uses it to designate the stability and unchangeableness of God.

6. For a study of the concept of rest in Gnosticism see J. Helderman, *Die Anapausis in Evangelium Veritatis* (Leiden: Brill, 1984).

7. E. Käsemann, *Wandering People*, pp. 68-76. *Contra*, see Hofius, *Katapausis*, pp. 1-21.

for Gnosticism and the Epistle, 'rest' is purely a heavenly blessing.
Thus in Hebrews Canaan is only a way station *en route* to the heavenly
Jerusalem.[1] This is noticeably different from Jewish apocalyptic
writings[2] which look forward to a heavenly renewal of the earth. In
spite of G. Buchanan's reading to the contrary, Hebrews does not
speak of a restoration of sacred space on earth but of its re-location in
heaven. On the other hand any 'dualism' between heaven and earth
which we find in Hebrews is more nuanced than that found in Gnostic
sources, which display an antipathy towards the material world *per
se*.[3] Our author's combination of the linear (future) with the spatial
(heaven) is at once similar to, and dissimilar from, Jewish tradition.
In both heaven can be depicted as the goal of the future,[4] but in
Judaism that future finds its locale on earth. It is only a 'heavenly'
Jerusalem, in as far as it is God's plan, which awaits territorial actual-
ization. The recipients of Hebrews, however, are exhorted not simply
to look forward but to look elsewhere if they would find the presence
of God. He is not to be found in the holy city but in heaven.

Thus the land of promise was not Abraham's settled abode; his resi-
dence there was merely temporary (παρῴκησεν) as in a foreign land
(11.9; cf. Gen. 23.4). For Hebrews, Abraham, Isaac and Jacob were
heirs of a different promise from that of the land of Canaan. Their
goal was 'the city which has foundations whose builder and maker is
God' (11.10). Their desire was a 'better country, that is a heavenly
one' (11.16). The city which God has prepared for them is not merely
to be located on the earthly Mount Zion, but is the city of 'the living
God, the heavenly Jerusalem' (12.22). The patriarchs were granted
but a vision of this homeland:

> These all died in faith, not having received what was promised but having
> seen it and greeted it from afar and having acknowledged that they were
> strangers and exiles (ξένοι καὶ παρεπίδημοι[5]) on earth (11.13).

By interpreting the biblical promises of a holy land and a sacred city
as promises to be realized not on earth but in heaven, our author

1. Käsemann, *Wandering People*, p. 68; cf. *Barn.* 16.2.
2. E.g. *4 Ezra* 7.26-44; cf. Rev. 21.1-2. See Braun, *Hebräer*, p. 92.
3. See pp. 56-57; Braun, *Hebräer*, p. 92.
4. See pp. 60-61.
5. Cf. Gen. 23.4; 47.9; 1 Chron. 29.15; Ps. 39.12. 1 Pet. 2.11 exhorts
Christians 'as aliens and exiles' (ὡς παροίκους καὶ παρεπιδήμους).

shows that they were achieved neither by the patriarchs nor the wilderness generation nor indeed by any generation of the past, since they only met their fulfilment in Jesus, who is now seated at the right hand of God, enthroned in heaven. (As we shall see later, the session of Christ forms both this sermon's starting point and conclusion.) The faithful of the past have not thereby been excluded from a share in the inheritance, but, since the promises were not made good until Jesus' death and enthronement in heaven, 'apart from us they should not be made perfect' (μὴ χωρὶς ὑμῶν τελειωθῶσεν, 11.40), that is, those who had looked forward to those promises did not see their fulfilment prior to the Christian generation.

This is not to suggest that the present generation has fully entered into the salvific state. In the paraenetic sections our author constantly exhorts his readers, as those living in the last days (1.2), to 'strive to enter that rest' (2.11), to follow Jesus the pioneer (ἀρχηγός, 2.10), and to look to the consummation of God's purposes in the future.[1] Hence, even in the culminating exhortation with which he concludes his sermon (12.18-28) and in which he contrasts the access gained by the new covenant of Jesus with the distance imposed upon the people by the awesomeness of the Sinai covenant (cf. Exod. 19.17; 20.21; Deut. 4.11-12; 5.23-27), he uses the language of approach (see προσέρχομαι in vv. 18, 22) rather than final attainment of Mount Zion, the heavenly Jerusalem. Like the faithful generations of the past (cited in ch. 11), Hebrews' present audience also has to look to the future for that. 'For here we have no lasting city (μένουσιν πόλιν) but we seek the city which is to come (μέλλουσαν)' (13.14).

Our author pictures that heavenly city peopled not only by angels, but as a festal gathering of the ultimate, completed company of the

---

1. W.G. Johnson ('The Pilgrimage Motif in the Book of Hebrews', *JBL* 97 [1978], pp. 239-51) applies a phenomenological model of pilgrimage to Hebrews. He finds it implicit in 3.7–4.11 and explicit in chs. 11 and 12, although in both sections it is mostly confined to the paraenetic sections. The doctrinal sections only deal with the first phenomenon of pilgrimage, i.e., separation. The other three ([1] journeying to a sacred place; [2] with a fixed purpose; and [3] having to endure difficulties en route) lend themselves more naturally to our author's exhortation, and become vehicles of the future eschatology which predominates in these paraenetic sections.

people of God—the righteous of all ages who are perfected through the work of Christ (12.22).[1] This, however, is to view salvation proleptically. In the meantime, alone of all humanity, Jesus has entered into the presence of God. From there he beckons the faithful to follow where he has led. Thus Hebrews has not so much altered the future perspective of salvation, dominant in Judaism and early Christianity alike, as shifted the focus of its realization from earth to heaven. As we have already noted, both the metaphysical speculations of Hellenistic philosophy and the dualistic cosmology of Gnosticism have been postulated as the source upon which the author of Hebrews drew for this aspect of his thought. While not discounting the possible influence of Middle Platonism upon some of the language of our Epistle, in other respects it is those Jewish apocalypticists who responded to the fall of Jerusalem by projecting their aspirations for Israel's future into the heavenly realm who are closer to Hebrews. Both direct their readers away from this world. Unlike the apocalyptic writers, however, our author does not look for a restored earthly city based upon a heavenly model. His solution to the loss of the traditional venue of the divine presence is to ask his readers to see in Christ the one through whose death God's promises of a land, a city and a shrine where He will dwell with His people, have been fulfilled. In entering heaven itself, Jesus has achieved that goal. His followers, therefore, should not be despondent at the fate of Jerusalem, nor should they be looking to its earthly restoration. Scripture itself shows that it was never to be understood as other than partial and transient. Heaven is the true goal of the people of God. 'Therefore let us be grateful for receiving a kingdom which cannot be shaken (βασιλείαν ἀσάλευτον)' (12.28a).

3. *Temple Cult and Aaronic Priesthood*

Although modern scholars may attempt to do so, the Old Testament puts forward no rationale for Israel's sacrificial system. It is simply presented as the God-given means of maintaining that purity which is the essential condition of and for the divine presence. The cult place,

---

1. So D. Peterson, *Hebrews and Perfection: An Examination of the Concept of Perfection in the Epistle to the Hebrews* (SNTSMS, 47; Cambridge: Cambridge University Press, 1982), pp. 160-66.

whether in the desert or Jerusalem, was intended as a place of rendezvous between God and people. Thus the desert tabernacle is called
the 'tent of meeting' (*'ohel mô'ed*). The P tradition prefers the more
permanent 'abode' (*mishkan*; cf. Num. 24.5) and has the cloud, the
symbol of the presence of God,[1] cover the tent immediately upon its
erection (Exod. 40.34-35), thereby indicating that He has taken possession of it.[2]

Since purity is the *sine qua non* of that presence, however, the
sanctuary must be set apart from profane use. Furthermore, since the
priestly system worked on the assumption that nothing can prevent its
human pollution, many of its activities were designed to rid its sacred
space of all contamination. This lies at the heart of Israel's sacrificial
system. It was the means whereby both place and people could be
decontaminated and re-sacralized. In describing Israel's sanctuary as
'the Picture of Dorian Gray', Jacob Milstrom has drawn our attention
to the close connection in priestly thought between the sanctity (or
otherwise) of the people and that of the cult place:

> On the analogy of Oscar Wilde's novel, the priestly writers would claim:
> sin may not leave its mark on the face of the sinner, but it is certain to
> mark the face of the sanctuary, and unless it is quickly expunged, God's
> presence will depart.[3]

Since the defilement of the one is the mirror of the other, sanctuary
and people alike stand in need of purification. Thus in the Day of
Atonement ceremonies there are two goats: (1) that which is killed as
a purification offering (*hattā't*) for the cult place (Lev. 16.16); and (2)
'the goat for Azazel' which is sent out live into the desert, and upon
whose head the sins of the people have been transferred. This second
goat is for the purification of the people (Lev. 16.21).[4]

In drawing upon a cultic model for his presentation of the work of
Christ, the author of Hebrews makes the Day of Atonement

---

1. Later taken up in Jewish tradition in terms of the divine *Shekhinah*. See J. Dan,
'Shekhinah', *EncJud*, XIV, pp. 1349-54.

2. See R. de Vaux, *Ancient Israel: Its Life and Institutions* (London: Darton,
Longman & Todd, 1961), pp. 294-97.

3. J. Milstrom, 'Israel's Sanctuary: The Priestly "Picture of Dorian Gray"', *RB*
83 (1976), pp. 390-99. For the departure of the presence of God from the sanctuary
see Ezek. 11.22.

4. Milstrom, 'Israel's Sanctuary', pp. 396-97.

ceremonies and the high priest's role in them the centrepiece of his exposition. At first glance it might seem as if he waits until 9.7 to do so. Certainly this is the first explicit reference to the annual occasion upon which the high priest, having sacrificed a bull for the sins of himself and his household, and having sacrificed a goat on behalf of the people, enters the inner sanctum with the blood of the two victims and sprinkles it upon the mercy seat[1] which covered the ark. Yet in 4.14-16 (a section which forms a transition from the theme of access to God explored in terms of entry into the promised land to its interpretation in terms of the cult) it has already been introduced.[2] Jesus is the 'great high priest who has passed through the heavens'. This image may reflect a Jewish cosmological belief in seven heavens interposed between God and the earth.[3] Yet it is not the notion of a heavenly journey, found in such apocalypses as the *Ascension of Isaiah* and *2 Baruch*, which we meet in Hebrews. For our author it is the conviction that Jesus is now in heaven which is paramount, and an enthronement psalm (Psalm 109[MT 110].1: 'Sit at my right hand, till I make of thy enemies a stool for thy feet') which is the principal influence on his treatment of the theme of Christ's sovereignty.[4] It is because he has entered heaven that the readers are exhorted:

> Let us then with confidence draw near to the throne of grace, that we might receive mercy and find grace to help in time of need (προσερχώμεθα οὖν μετὰ παρρησίας τῷ θρόνῳ τῆς χάριτος ἵνα λάβωμεν ἔλεος καὶ χάριν εὕρωμεν εἰς εὔκαιρον βοήθειαν, 4.16).

Albeit elliptically, heaven is here depicted as the superior 'holy of holies' into which Jesus has entered and from which he bids Christians draw near to God, not with fear but with bold confidence (παρρησία;

---

1. 'Mercy seat' = Hebrew *Kapporeth* (LXX ἱλαστήριον), refers to the covering or lid of the ark. In view of its place in the expiatory rites of the Day of Atonement many scholars suggest that it is related to the verb *kipper*, which in the pi'el means 'to make expiation or atonement'.

2. The theme of Jesus as high priest occurs even earlier, i.e. at Heb. 2.17. Cf. also 1.3 where it is implied.

3. Cf. 2 Cor. 12.2-4. See Spicq, *Hébreux*, II, p. 91.

4. See Heb. 1.3, 13; 8.1; 10.12-13; 12.2 for the citation of or allusion to Ps. 110(LXX 109).1. This verse is much used by other New Testament authors. See Mt. 22.41-46 // Mk 12.35-37 // Lk. 20.41-44; Mt. 26.64 // Mk 14.62 // Lk. 22.69; Mk 16.19; Acts 2.33-35; 5.31; 7.55-56; Rom. 8.34; 1 Cor. 15.25; Eph. 1.20; 2.6; Col. 3.1; 1 Pet. 3.22; Rev. 3.21.

cf. 3.6; 10.19). Chapter 6 also ends with a similar allusion to Jesus having gone behind the veil into the inner shrine, thereby acting as a forerunner (πρόδρομος, 6.20) for others to follow.

At 9.5 the mercy seat (ἱλαστήριον) of the earthly tabernacle is explicitly referred to, by which time it has become clear that for our author the 'throne of grace' where we may receive 'mercy' (4.16) is the heavenly antitype of the ark and its 'mercy seat'. Yet whereas for Josephus the holy of holies is like heaven,[1] for the author of Hebrews it has to be the other way round, since he believes that the earthly tabernacle was but an inferior copy of the true, heavenly one (8.1-6. See pp. 52-55).

This is not to suggest that the two are wholly dissimilar. Indeed we have seen that a typological approach to exegesis is only meaningful on the basis of some degree of correspondence. So our author appeals both to comparison and contrast in using Israel's Day of Atonement ceremonies in particular and its sacrificial system in general[2] as a model for a Christian soteriology. Above all it is important to appreciate that he is working wholly within the framework of Jewish cultic presuppositions.

Principal among these is that the sacrificial system was intended to remove the barrier of sin which hinders the worshipper's approach to God. To that end expiatory sacrifices were made and the blood of their victims offered:

> Indeed, under the law almost everything (σχεδὸν πάντα) is purified with blood, and without the shedding of blood there is no forgiveness of sins (9.22).

That Hebrews says 'almost' (σχεδόν) should prevent us from accusing its author of ignorance of those expiatory media, other than blood, which may be found in the Old Testament.[3] In the Law, provision was even made for the impoverished, who could not afford an animal, to present a cereal offering instead (Lev. 5.11). Our author, however, is making a general statement about expiatory rites. F.F. Bruce, on the evidence of similar statements found in rabbinic writings, suggests

---

1. Josephus, *Ant.* 3.123.
2. See 7.27 which mentions daily sacrifices.
3. E.g. incense (Num. 16.46), water (Lev. 15), water mixed with the ashes of the red heifer (Num. 19), and fire (Num. 31.22-23) are all means of expiation.

that Hebrews may be citing a well-known proverb.[1] Be that as it may, the author of Hebrews shares with his Jewish contemporaries a belief in sacrifice as the divinely appointed means of dealing with sin. Even when he cites Ps. 39.5-7 (MT 40.6-8), unlike the psalmist it is not to insist upon obedience as the essential accompaniment to sacrifice, nor is it to contrast the two. Hebrews (10.5-7) uses the psalm to contrast the superiority of Christ's self-offering over against the fact that animals had no option. They were passive victims, whereas Jesus actively offered himself. So it is not sacrifice *per se* that the author of Hebrews attacks. To do so would hardly enable him to present the death of Christ as the sacrifice to end all sacrifices! Rather he works within the system, both affirming and transforming it.

His basic criticism of Israel's cult is that it did not really achieve its intended goal—the removal of the barrier of sin. Had it done so there would have been no need for sacrifice to be constantly repeated (10.4, 11). This particular allegation gives us an insight into the author of Hebrews' true purpose; to move his readers away from an understanding of the sacrificial system as an essential part of maintaining contact with God, to an acceptance of the death and ascension of Christ as its replacement. Thus against the repetitive (πολλάκις) nature of the one he contrasts the 'once' (ἅπαξ), 'once for all time' (ἐφάπαξ),[2] definitive character of the other:

> Nor was it to offer himself repeatedly (πολλάκις), as the high priest enters the Holy Place yearly with blood not his own; for then he would have had to suffer repeatedly (πολλάκις) since the foundation of the world. But as it is, he has appeared once for all (ἅπαξ) at the end of the age to put away sin by the sacrifice of himself (9.25-26).

Therefore, by the very logic of the argument, our author cannot admit the possibility of the re-admission of an apostate. It is significant that the two paraenetic passages which remind the audience of this (6.4-6; 10.26-31) come within the context of his exposition of Jesus as the antitype both of the high priest and victim on the Day of Atonement, and of the sacrifice which accompanied the inauguration of the Sinai covenant.

Chapter 6 forms a paraenetic interlude in a section which deals with Christ's priesthood finding its type in Melchizedek rather than Levi

---

1. Bruce, *Hebrews*, p. 217 n. 144.
2. See p. 21 nn. 3, 4.

(4.14–7.28). In chs. 3 and 4 he has reminded his readers of the failure of the wilderness generation to enter the promised land. Now, this time in cultic terms, he reminds them of what Christ's sacrifice *cannot* do. Already in 5.2, when discussing the function of the high priest, he has stated that his task was to deal with those who stray through ignorance (τοῖς ἀγνοοῦσιν καὶ πλανωμένοις[1]). Like Israel's sacrificial system, the sacrifice of Christ cannot deal with 'sin done with a high hand'. The Torah states:

> But the person who does anything with a high hand, whether he is native or sojourner, reviles the Lord, and that person shall be cut off from among his people. Because he has despised the word of the Lord, and has broken his commandments, that person shall be utterly cut off; his iniquity shall be upon him (Num. 15.30-31).

This seems to lie behind Hebrews' insistence that it is possible for Christians to put themselves beyond the efficacy of the sacrifice of Christ:

> For it is impossible (ἀδύνατον) to restore again to repentance those who have once been enlightened. . . and have tasted the goodness of the word of God (θεοῦ ῥῆμα) if they then commit apostasy (παραπεσόντας) since they crucify (ἀνασταυροῦντας) the Son of God on their own account and hold him up to contempt (παραδειγματίζοντας) (6.4a, 6).

In view of our author's argument from the singularity of the death of Jesus to its supremacy over other sacrifices, it makes a nonsense to translate the compound verb ἀνασταυρόω as 'crucify again'. In non-biblical sources it is used simply as an emphatic form of σταυρόω. Hebrews employs it to emphasize the point that to abandon Christian discipleship is to ally oneself to the rejection which brought about Jesus' crucifixion. If 'holding up to contempt' is a deliberate echo of the public example (cf. LXX Num. 25.4, παραδειγματίζω) made of the instigators of apostasy to Ba'al of Pe'or in being left out in the sun (presumably to die), then he is also portraying as an irony the fact that Jesus should be so treated by those who are themselves the apostates! This may, however, be reading too much into the text.

What can be said with assurance is that the context in which the author of Hebrews introduces his warning on the impossibility (note

---

1. Understood as a hendiadys.

the emphatic position of ἀδύνατον at the beginning of 6.4) of a
second repentance is in the central section of the homily, in which he
draws comparisons and contrasts between the work of Christ and
Jewish cult and covenant. Furthermore, Hebrews is at one with Jewish
tradition, which did not expect the sacrificial system to expiate deliberate, witting sins, since they were tantamount to a refusal to accept
the sovereign commandments of God. Sin 'done with a high hand' was
nothing less than a unilateral declaration of independence, and to do
that was to place oneself outside the covenant community. The cult
was designed as a mechanism for maintaining the covenant. It could
not be expected to be effective for those who wilfully placed themselves outside the covenant it was there to service.

The author of Hebrews accepts this as axiomatic not only for the
Jewish cultus but for the sacrifice of Christ. So he reminds his congregation:

> For if we sin deliberately (ἑκουσίως) after receiving knowledge of the
> truth, there no longer remains a sacrifice for sins (10.26).

The consequences of apostasy from the community of the new
covenant are the same as those from the old. Members of the Qumran
community also saw themselves as the true 'sons of the covenant' and
in their *Community Rule* similarly distinguished between advertent
and inadvertent sins. A whole plethora of penalties are prescribed for
the latter. 'But as for him who has sinned deliberately, he shall never
return.'[1]

The seriousness of wilful sin is similarly emphasized by the author
of Hebrews in an allusion to Deut. 17.6:

> A man who has violated (ἀθετήσας) the law of Moses dies without
> mercy at the testimony of two or three witnesses (10.28).

The verb ἀθετέω is better understood here as 'reject' or 'put aside',
that is, 'ignore', rather than the RSV 'violate'. Certainly in its context
in Deuteronomy it concerns the death penalty, not for any or every
infringement of the Torah, but for idolatrous apostasy, which was
regarded as a denial of the very covenant relationship itself. Employing an *a fortiori* argument, our author moves from the fate of those
who have put themselves outside the Mosaic covenant to the worse one

---

1. 1QS 9.3; Vermes, *Dead Sea Scrolls in English*, p. 86. Cf. also 1QS 2.13-14
where a curse is placed upon those who leave the community.

which awaits those who have treated contemptuously (κατα-
πατήσας—literally 'trampled under foot') the Son of God and treated
his Passion as if it were a common (κοινόν) death rather than a sacred
sacrifice. Thereby they insult (ἐνυβρίσας) the gracious spirit (τὸ
πνεῦμα τῆς χάριτος) of God[1] (10.29).

Once this is placed within the context in which our author deals
with it, that is, of Judaism's self-acknowledged limitations of the cult,
we see that much of the debate to which his Epistle subsequently gave
rise falls wholly outside its author's purview. For Hebrews it is the
repudiation of the new covenant (and thereby the sacrifice of Jesus
which inaugurated it) having once joined its community, which constitutes that sin for which no second repentance is possible. Christ's
sacrifice, viewed as an antitype of the expiatory rite of the Day of
Atonement, can no more deal with 'sin done with a high hand' than
could its type. Perhaps even more importantly, for the equation of the
death of Jesus with the expiatory sacrifice to work at all, our author
cannot allow for more than one sacrifice. Since that has taken place
within time, it cannot be repeated. Understood as the natural outcome
of the typological method he employs in drawing out (in this instance)
the correspondence between the death of Jesus and the Jewish cult, the
author of Hebrews can be called a 'rigorist'.

What he is not, however, is a 'perfectionist', in the sense of one who
believes that Christians, by definition, are no longer capable of sin.
That particular debate may well lie behind the circumstances which
led to the writing of 1 John,[2] but it would be misleading to read
Hebrews against the same background. As we shall see, in our Epistle,
'perfection' for the believer is a process and not simply a once-for-all
state. Unlike its subsequent Christian interpreters, here we find no
interest in drawing up a league table of sins ranging from the major
('mortal') to the minor ('venial'). Like Tertullian, no 'lapse' is
permissible according to the author of Hebrews. Yet clearly, unlike
Tertullian, what constitutes lapse is not sexual sin (adultery and

---

1. τὸ πνεῦμα τῆς χάριτος could be a reference to the gracious disposition either
of Christ or God. There seems no reason, however, to connect it with the 'sin
against the holy spirit' in Synoptic tradition (Mk 3.29 and parallels).

2. See 1 Jn 3.9; cf. 1.8-10. In 1 Jn 5.16 the sin which 'leads to death' (πρὸς
θάνατον) for which prayer is of no avail is probably apostasy, the 'sin done with a
high hand' of Num. 15.30.

fornication[1]), but deliberately placing oneself outside the new covenant by giving up Christian discipleship. This is not to claim that the stance of Hebrews, if divorced from the context in which it is discussed, does not raise problems for contemporary Christian understanding and pastoral practice. These are reflected for example in the attempts of many commentators to come to terms with a text which, in its presuppositions, is in many ways alien to us. So C. Spicq, drawing upon the use of ἀδύνατον in Philo of Alexandria, tries to soften the 'impossibility' of a second repentance by claiming that, for our author, that inability is wholly from the point of view of the apostate rather than God:

> Il s'agit d'une impossibilité subjective et relative, sous réserve de l'intervention divine, et c'est bien en ce sens que Hébr. conçoit l'impossibilité non point du pardon, mais de la conversion de l'aspostat.[2]

Spicq's concern is with the philosophical and theological implications which might be drawn from the Epistle. He seems anxious to absolve its author from any suggestion that there is any limitation to the power of God to pardon. F.F. Bruce's approach is more mundane. He sees Hebrews' teaching as a piece of experiential wisdom:

> he is stating a practical truth that has verified itself repeatedly in the experience of the visible church. Those who have shared the covenant privileges of the people of God, and then deliberately renounced them, are the most difficult persons of all to reclaim for the faith.[3]

In my opinion, the problem with such interpretations is that they do not take Hebrews' 'rigorism' sufficiently seriously—and that, because they have divorced it from the system from which it springs. Our author chose to adopt Judaism's sacrificial model for his soteriology. An integral part of the cultus was a recognition of its limitations. He makes use of that in exhorting his congregation not to relinquish their life of Christian discipleship. How far his 'rigorism' can be lifted out of this context is debatable. Perhaps we do well to remind ourselves that New Testament writers inevitably fail when judged as systematicians. Within the terms in which he chooses to conduct the debate, the author of Hebrews is singularly successful, however, and it is in those

---

1. Tertullian, *De Pudiata* 20.
2. Spicq, *Hébreux*, I, pp. 57-58.
3. Bruce, *Hebrews*, p. 118.

terms that he should be understood. The sacrificial model is not the only one for soteriology even within the New Testament itself, and we should beware of treating it as some sort of Platonic Ideal or expecting it to bear the burden of all our unresolved theological problems. In the case of 'no second repentance' it can be said to have contributed to them.

Working within his chosen model of sacrifice, he does not stop in his criticism of the Levitical cult simply with the allegation that the need for the constant repetition of its expiatory offerings was itself a sign of their inefficacy. He goes further.

> If the worshippers had once been cleansed they would no longer have any consciousness of sin (συνείδησιν ἁμαρτιῶν). But in these sacrifices there is a constant reminder (ἀνάμνησις) of sin year after year (10.2b-3).

It was, of course, part of the cult's function to remind Israel of her sins—but for our author a reminder is not enough. The inner sense of sin, the guilt of the worshipper, is not dealt with. That by συνείδησις an inner disposition is meant is evident both here and in the other four passages in the Epistle where the word is used. (1) In 9.9-10 the whole purificatory system of the cult, including not only animal sacrifices but also food offerings, wine libations[1] and ritual ablutions,[2] are relegated to the merely external or bodily (σάρξ) sphere. They are therefore unable to 'perfect the conscience', that is, the interior. (2) In 9.12-14 Hebrews claims that the expiatory blood of the Day of Atonement sacrifices, like the ashes of the red heifer[3] (used to expunge ritual pollution incurred by contact with a corpse) merely

---

1. See Exod. 29.40-41; 30.9; Lev. 23.13, 18, 37. Since Hebrews provides no evidence of an interest in Jewish food laws (which caused such problems for fellowship between Jews and Gentiles in the churches of Paul's mission), it is unlikely that here we have a reference to kosher food laws.

2. Given that its context is a discussion of the Day of Atonement, it is likely that the ablutions required of the high priest on that occasion (Lev. 16.4, 24) are in mind. Water as a medium of purification also occurs in other contexts in Judaism, e.g., Lev. 6.27; 14.8; Num. 8.7. It played an important role in John the Baptist's call to repentance (see *Ant.* 18.117), and, as symbolic of inner purity, ritual baths were part of the practice of the Qumran community (1QS 3.4-9). Cf. Heb. 6.2.

3. For regulations concerning the red heifer see Num. 19. At Heb. 9.19 our author seems to have incorporated some of the details of this rite (e.g. scarlet wool and hyssop) into his account of the Mosaic covenant sacrifice. See B.S. Childs, *Exodus* (London: SCM Press, 1974), pp. 509-11.

purifies the flesh (σάρξ). The blood of Christ, on the other hand, is far more efficacious since it cleanses the interior, the conscience. The contrast between 'dead bodies' and 'dead works' is not overtly drawn, although it could be implicit. What is explicitly stated, however, is that the sacrifice of Christ removes the inner barrier of guilt (i.e. purifies the conscience), freeing the worshipper from a way of life which leads to death (νεκρῶν ἔργων). Thereby the believer is enabled to serve the living God. (3) In accord with its predominant use in the popular parlance of his own day,[1] our author uses συνείδησις[2] not in the sense of some neutral moral geiger counter, registering both right and wrong, but as a negative indicator,[3] registering only what is reprehensible. It is, therefore, closer to our use of the word 'guilt', rather than the more open 'conscience'. Hence 10.22 speaks of 'an evil (πονηρά) conscience', that is, a consciousness of one's own evil deeds. It is not simply to be re-educated but done away with. For our author, the person without a conscience is not someone who is unprincipled, but one who has no inner accuser. His conviction is that that guilt, which formed a barrier to the worshipper's access to God, has itself been removed through the sacrifice of Christ. (4) Only in 13.18, 'Pray for us, for we are sure that we have a clear conscience' (καλήν συνείδησιν), do we find συνείδησις used in other than a negative sense. Even here it is far from certain that it is any more than an expression of the absence of guilt on the author's part, that he is unaware of any wrongdoing. This, of course, is in his direct address to his audience in the epistolary ending of the work. He is saying that his conduct towards them can stand up to scrutiny.[4] Here συνείδησις hardly carries the full weight of its previous usage in the earlier cultic sections.

In criticizing the Levitical cult for not dealing with a continuing inner awareness of wrongdoing, our author is drawing attention to what he sees as an inherent weakness in the system. There was in fact

1. C.A. Pierce (*Conscience in the New Testament* [SBT, 15; London: SCM Press, 1955], pp. 13-20) sees the background of this comparatively late, Hellenistic terminology to be popular parlance rather than philosophy.

2. ευνείδησις occurs only three times in the LXX (Eccl. 10.20; 42.18; Wis. Sol. 17.11) where it indicates wickedness condemned from within.

3. Philo prefers to use συνειδός. For him it is the God-given faculty of self accusation. See Isaacs, *Concept of Spirit*, pp. 41-42.

4. Cf. Acts 23.1; 24.16; Rom. 9.1; 2 Cor. 1.12.

no legislation within the cult which provided for a guilty conscience. Although we can find one or two particular offences[1] covered by the expiatory offering (*ḥaṭṭā't*) which can hardly be classified as inadvertent, nonetheless, this sacrifice was largely for unwitting sin. The same can be said of the 'guilt offering' (*'āšām*).[2] The translation of *'āšām* as 'guilt' is misleading, not only because this Hebrew word simply means 'offence', but because to our twentieth-century minds it introduces a notion of conscience not found in the legislation. Roland de Vaux prefers 'reparation', since sometimes the payment of a compensatory fine accompanied the *'āšām*.[3] He also reminds us that in the final edition of the Torah which we have, it is impossible to distinguish clearly between the *ḥaṭṭā't* and the *'āšām* in terms of the offences for which they legislate.[4] More importantly for our discussion, there is no evidence that at any stage in the development of Israel's cult they were intended to expiate a guilty conscience.

This is not to suggest that ancient Judaism had no moral sense or lacked an interior spirituality. Such indeed existed and had been linked with the cult by a prophetic tradition which insisted that the sacrificial system should itself be an expression of Israel's moral obedience to God.[5] Although later the Qumran covenanters in their repudiation of the Jerusalem Temple went much further than this prophetic tradition, unlike the Epistle to the Hebrews they looked forward to its future restoration rather than its abolition. Since they did not recognize the incumbents of the high priestly office as of the legitimate line of descent, they refused to take part in the sacrificial system until such time as a true high priest would be installed.[6] Meanwhile they appropriated the language, if not the rites of the cult, in their understanding of worship:

> They shall atone for guilty rebellion and for sins of unfaithfulness that
> they may obtain loving kindness for the land without the flesh of

1. E.g. the refusal of a witness to testify in court (Lev. 5.1).
2. Although predominantly for inadvertent sin, the *'āšām* is the prescribed penalty for fraudulent behaviour (Lev. 5.21-22).
3. De Vaux, *Ancient Israel*, p. 420. Cf. also H. Ringgren, *Israelite Religion* (London: SPCK, 1969), pp. 171-73.
4. De Vaux, *Ancient Israel*, p. 421.
5. E.g. Amos 5.21-24; Mic. 6.6; Isa. 1.10-17; cf. Ps. 50.7-15.
6. For Qumran's religious rites and practices, see G. Vermes, *The Dead Sea Scrolls: Qumran in Perspective* (London: SCM Press, 1977), pp. 175-82.

holocausts and the fat of sacrifice. And prayer rightly offered shall be an acceptable fragrance of righteousness, and perfection of way as a delectable free-will offering.[1]

We find a similar sentiment in Philo:

And indeed, though the worshippers bring nothing else, in bringing themselves they offer the best sacrifices, the full and truly perfect oblation of noble living, honouring God their benefactor and saviour, with hymns and thanksgivings.[2]

Philo, of course, did not repudiate the Jerusalem cult. Like most Diaspora Jews he made pilgrimages to its sacred site[3] and would have contributed, through the annual levy on all adult males, to the upkeep of its services. For those Jews who lived outside Judaea, however, it would inevitably have been a more distanced affair, and one can detect among their ranks, even before the destruction of the Temple in 70 CE, an increasing focus upon meditation on the Torah and prayer as constituting the heart of piety. In the process, sacrificial language became appropriated as an expression of a truly righteous, God-wardly directed way of life. It is possible that sacrifice continued to be offered amidst the ruins of the Jerusalem shrine even after its destruction by the Romans.[4] Even if that were the case it could not have continued beyond the defeat of the Bar Kochba uprising in 135 CE. With the erection of a pagan shrine on the site, sacrifice became impossible for mainstream Judaism, which had long insisted on the one, true cult place, located in Jerusalem.[5] Whether Christianity had

1. 1QS 9.4-5. Vermes, *Dead Sea Scrolls in English*, p. 87.
2. *Spec. Leg.* 1.272 (LCL); cf. *Aristeas* 234.
3. *Prov.* 2.64 (Eusebius, *Praep. Ev.* 8.14.389b).
4. See Clark, 'Worship', pp. 269-80.
5. We have evidence of the existence of two Jewish temples other than that at Jerusalem. Both were situated in Egypt: (1) that at Elephantiné in Upper Egypt, erected in the sixth century BCE by Jewish mercenaries in the employ of the Persian rulers of that land. With the demise of Persian control, the temple was destroyed in 411 BCE by Egyptian priests. See *EncJud*, VI, pp. 603-10. (2) That at Leontopolis, near Memphis, was also built by and for a settlement of Jewish mercenaries, only in the second century BCE, and at the instigation either of the deposed Jerusalem high priest Onias III or his son Onias IV. It was closed by the Romans after the Jewish War in 73 CE. See V. Tcherikover, *Hellenistic Civilization and the Jews* (Philadelphia: Hebrew University Press/Jerusalem: Jewish Publication Society of America, 1959), pp. 275-81.

anticipated Judaism or not by dispensing with the cult, after 70 CE both communities of faith survived as religions without a sacrificial system. In both, thereafter, the rites of the cult became 'spiritualized' and subsequently emerge wholly as religious metaphors.

Yet hindsight should not lead us to conclude that the sacrificial system was peripheral to first-century Judaism. Even for the Diaspora, the Temple cult played an important part, operating (albeit at a distance) on their behalf. Outside Judaea's borders the multiplicity of pagan shrines by which they were surrounded also stood as testimony to the centrality of sacrifice in all religions in the ancient world, Jewish and Gentile alike. C.F.D. Moule has rightly drawn our attention to the novelty of a religion without a sacrificial cult prior to 70 CE. He has suggested that our Epistle was written at a time when the Temple was still flourishing, to help Christians understand why theirs alone of all religions did not need sacrifice. I, on the other hand, would suggest the possibility that Hebrews was written as a Christian response to the destruction of the Temple, and that it should be seen alongside Judaism's own explanations of that event. Unlike them, however, our author looked to Jesus as the true fulfilment of the cult's purposes.

In claiming that Christ cleanses the conscience, unlike the cult which made no such provision, our author goes further. Jesus does far more than the Levitical system was ever intended to do. Does the same claim lie behind Hebrews' use of the language of perfection? Our answer will depend upon the interpretation we give to the Epistle's terminology of τελειοῦν and its cognates.

If the language of perfection is understood exclusively as cultic, drawn either from the septuagintal phrase τελειοῦν τὰς χεῖρας, to consecrate (literally 'to fill the hands of') a priest,[1] or (as is more likely) from notions of purity more generally applied to all worshippers who would draw near[2] to God, then our author is claiming that the cult was inadequate even within its own terms. It did not bring the worshippers to perfection, that is, that state of ritual purity essential before human and divine can meet. From the way Hebrews parallels 'to make perfect' (τελειοῦν) in 9.9 and 10.1 with 'to cleanse'

---

1. LXX Exod. 29.9. *Contra* Peterson, *Hebrews and Perfection*, pp. 46-47.

2. Note that in the LXX προσέρχομαι is frequently used as a technical term for approach via the cult (e.g. Exod. 16.9; Lev. 9.5, 7, 8; Num. 18.3).

(καθαρίζειν) in 9.14 and 10.2 and 'to sanctify' (ἁγιάζειν) in 9.14 and 10.14—both cultic terms—it would seem that what is meant by perfection by our author is that state of purity which makes contact between God and the worshipper possible, together with the processes by which that is achieved.

Yet in employing the language of perfection—and not simply cleansing—our author goes further than to claim that Jesus fulfilled (πληροῦν) the purposes for which the sacrificial system was ordained. The reason why perfection (τελείωσις) was not attainable under the Levitical priesthood (7.11)—why the Mosaic Torah, the basis of the cult, 'made nothing perfect' (οὐδὲν γὰρ ἐτελείωσεν 7.19)—is stated baldly at 10.1:

> For since the law has but a shadow of the good things to come instead of the true form of these realities, it can never, by the same sacrifices which are continually offered year after year, make perfect those who draw near (οὐδέποτε δύναται τοὺς προσερχομένους τελειῶσαι).

Here our author is no more denying access to God via the cult to previous generations than in his earlier chapters (3 and 4) he denied them the land of Canaan. In both cases, however, he directs his readers to a new understanding. The true land and cult place is heaven itself. Since the tabernacle was but a shadow of its superior, heavenly antitype, its cult could not bring the worshipper to his or her intended goal, which is nothing less than heaven itself. The language of 'to make perfect' (τελειοῦν), 'perfection' (τελείωσις[1]) and 'perfecter' (τελειωτής), therefore, looks beyond the earthly cult to its superior prototype. Amid the plethora of interpretations which scholars have given this terminology (e.g. cultic, moral, eschatological, metaphysical, vocational),[2] it is important not to lose sight of the formal meaning of τελειοῦν in Greek, which is to make perfect in the sense of complete, to bring something to its appointed end or goal (τέλος). And that 'end' for our author is nothing less than God's future, which he expresses as 'heaven' and which still remains to be attained by the people of God. In the meantime only Christ, through his death and

---

1. τελειότητος in 6.1 is probably best translated simply as 'maturity'. Cf. 5.13-14 where the adult (τέλειος) is contrasted with the infant (νήπιος).

2. For a résumé of contemporary interpretations, see Peterson, *Hebrews and Perfection*, pp. 3-20. He himself favours a 'vocational' interpretation. Attridge (*Hebrews*, pp. 83-87) comes to the same conclusion.

ascension, has entered into that realm. At first glance, 'by a single offering he has perfected (τετελείωκεν) for all time those who are sanctified (τοὺς ἁγιαζομένους)' (10.14) might seem to contradict this. Yet the present participle (ἁγιαζομένους) conveys the on-going sense of 'are now in the process of being sanctified', and should warn us against understanding the perfect (τετελείωκεν) 'he has perfected' as the present full attainment for the believer of perfection which is the future age.[1] For our author an event in the past, that is, the death of Christ, has made the realization of that perfection possible in the future. Meanwhile it can be experienced proleptically in the present. Thus in 12.23 we meet an equally proleptic vision of the future, of the heavenly Jerusalem peopled by 'the spirits of just men made perfect' (τετελειωμένων). In the present, however, perfection is yet to be attained.[2] Therefore, in their life of pilgrimage to this promised land, he exhorts his readers to look 'to Jesus the pioneer and perfecter (ἀρχηγὸν καὶ τελειωτήν) of faith' (12.2). The RSV, by inserting the possessive pronoun 'our', understands this to be the faith of the disciple. Yet this is not in the Greek text and it is therefore possible that it refers to faith in general, including that of Jesus himself,[3] which was not only there at the outset, but was brought to its destined goal of heaven through his suffering and death.

So far we have discussed the perfecting of the believer; but what of the perfecting of Jesus? In Hebrews he not only brings the faithful to perfection; he himself is perfected. For those who understand perfection in moral terms this poses problems. Does it imply that he lacked some virtue? In which case how is it that our author also describes Jesus as sinless? Was that sinlessness acquired as the final pinnacle of his life or was it a permanent condition throughout? The problem with these questions is that they not only reflect the concerns of later Christian theology, but they presuppose an understanding of both perfection and sinlessness not uppermost in our author's thinking.

1. See Peterson, *Hebrews and Perfection*, pp. 148-52, 167.
2. For a discussion of the tension between future and realized eschatology in Hebrews see Barrett, 'Eschatology'. Dey (*Intermediary World*), reading the Epistle wholly against a background of Philo and Hellenistic philosophy, on the other hand, underestimates the future, heavenly character of perfection. This leads her to state that Jesus 'has opened the way for others to participate in *perfection within this realm of creation and not outside it*' (p. 219, my italics).
3. See Peterson, *Hebrews and Perfection*, p. 173.

Earlier scholars, who believed in the 'myth' of a first-century CE
myth of a redeemed redeemer,[1] interpreted the perfecting of Christ as
well as the Christian as evidence of its Gnostic background. Yet the
Jewish cult seems the more natural context for understanding
Hebrews' notion both of perfection and sinlessness. We have no evidence in Gnosticism of a cultic interest, whereas our author, by his
choice of particular scriptural passages for explication, especially in
the central section of his homily, clearly draws upon the Jewish
sacrificial system as his model for the presentation of the work of
Christ.

In this analogy the perfecting of Jesus is his attainment of heaven,
his entry into the true holy of holies. Being made perfect, however, is
a process which involves the means by which that goal is reached. In
the case of the Levitical high priest on the Day of Atonement, the
offering of a sacrifice is the essential means of entry into the holy of
holies. Without that sacrifice having been made he is unable to go
behind the veil into the inner sanctum. It is therefore an integral part
of the process. Clearly, by analogy, in his death Christ plays the part
of both victim and priest. His Passion is therefore an essential part of
the path to perfection, without which he can no more enter heaven
than the Levitical high priest could enter the holy of holies without
sacrifice having first been made. Once understood in terms of this
analogy it becomes clear why Hebrews speaks of perfecting as a process which Jesus himself had to undergo:

> In the days of his flesh, Jesus offered up prayers and supplications, with
> loud cries and tears to him who was able to save him from death, and he
> was heard for his godly fear (καὶ εἰσακουσθεὶς ἀπὸ τῆς εὐλαβείας).
> Although he was a Son he learned obedience through what he suffered;
> and being made perfect (τελειωθείς) he became the source of eternal sal-
> vation to all who obey him, being designated by God a high priest after
> the order of Melchizedek (5.7-10).

---

1. *Contra* the History of Religions School (especially W. Bousset and
R. Reitzenstein) and R. Bultmann, many contemporary scholars do not accept the
existence of a fully-fledged myth of a redeemed redeemer in the first century CE. See
R.McL. Wilson, *Gnosis and the New Testament* (Oxford: Basil Blackwell, 1968),
p. 5; E. Yamauchi, *Pre-Christian Gnosticism* (London: Tyndale Press, 1973),
pp. 163-86. E. Käsemann came to modify his belief in the early existence of such a
myth and hence was reluctant to allow the reissue and English translation of his work
on Hebrews. See the preface to *Wandering People*.

This passage, especially v. 7, poses a number of difficulties for commentators.[1] (1) Is it an allusion to the Gethsemane tradition and if so has it come directly from a knowledge of the Synoptic Gospels (cf. Mt. 26.36-46; Mk 14.32-42; Lk. 22.40-46), or indirectly via common oral tradition? (2) Does it draw upon an earlier credal confession or confessions, and if so (3) was this credal affirmation itself based upon Psalm 114 (MT 116)?[2] (4) Is εὐλαβεία to be translated as 'anxiety' or as 'reverence', and does the preposition ἀπό mean 'from' or 'because of'? Since in both cases the alternative is linguistically possible, contextual factors have to determine the matter.

In this nexus the main problem is the first; whether v. 7 should be read as a reference to the Gethsemane tradition. If Jesus' prayer, 'Let this cup pass from me' is what is in mind, then how can our author say that God 'heard' it? Certainly not in the sense of saving him from death. This has led some commentators to amend the text by inserting οὐκ before εἰσακουσθείς—'and he was *not* heard!'[3] Others, linking the phrase with ἐκ θανατοῦ, have translated ἀπὸ τῆς εὐλαβείας as 'from fear'. The verse would then mean 'He was heard in such a way that he was delivered from fear of death by him who was able to save him'[4]—a sense which syntax alone would preclude.

These problems need not arise, however, if we read this verse in its wider context, that is, with reference to what comes before and after. Verses 6 and 10 set the scene for Jesus' prayer. It is that offered in his role as Melchizedekian high priest. In this light εὐλαβεία is the appropriate attitude of reverence (see Heb. 12.28) with which he approaches God in prayer, both on his own behalf and on behalf of others. Through the prayer which accompanies his sacrifice, he himself 'was made perfect' (v. 8), that is, entered heaven. His prayer, therefore, was not one of fearful entreaty, but of loud confidence. Psalm 116 certainly presents us, if not with a written source for this

1. See Montefiore, *Hebrews*, pp. 97-99; H.W. Attridge, '"Heard Because of His Reverence" (Heb. 5.7)', *JBL* 98 (1979), pp. 90-93.

2. So E. Brandenburg, 'Text Vorlagen von Hebr. V.7-10', *NovT* 11 (1969), pp. 190-224, followed by Buchanan, *Hebrews*, pp. 97-99.

3. A. von Harnack, 'Zwei alte dogmatische Korrekturen im Hebräerbrief', in *Studien zur Geschichte des NT und der alten Kirche* (Berlin: de Gruyter, 1931), pp. 245-47; R. Bultmann, 'εὐλαβής', *TDNT*, II, p. 753.

4. Montefiore, *Hebrews*, p. 98.

passage, at least with a parallel to the assurance at the outset that God will hear and answer the worshipper's prayer for deliverance:[1]

> I love the Lord, because he has heard
> my voice and my supplications.
> Because he has inclined his ear to me,
> therefore I will call on him as long as I live (Ps. 116.1-2).

Standing in this tradition Jesus can therefore speak of his prayer being answered. Furthermore we find, not only in the Psalms but also in Hellenistic Jewish traditions of prayer, tears and loud cries denoting the ideal characteristics of the bold, frank approach of the righteous to a trustworthy Lord.[2] Jesus' loud cries and tears are therefore the very hallmarks, not of fear, but of the appropriate attitude of a son to his heavenly father. His filial obedience was not only expressed in his prayer, but in the sacrifice which accompanied that prayer. 'Although he was a Son, he learned obedience through what he suffered' (v. 8).

This reference to Jesus' obedience through suffering should not simply be interpreted in the light of Heb. 12.5-11. There, drawing upon Prov. 3.11-12, our author employs a traditional Jewish understanding of human suffering as God disciplining His children. He encourages his readers to look positively at their present difficulties as evidence that they are truly sons of God. The same explanation of suffering as God's fatherly, educative discipline ($\pi\alpha\iota\delta\epsilon\iota\alpha$[3]) can be seen in Elihu's response to Job (Job 32.2–37.24; cf. Wis. 11.9-10; 12.22). After the Maccabaean revolt in the second century BCE it was used to give positive significance to the deaths of those who refused to accept the oppressive measures of Antiochus Epiphanes IV (see 2 Macc. 6.12-16; *4 Macc.* 10.10-11). There may be an echo of this martyr tradition in Hebrews' reference to Jesus learning obedience through

---

1. C. Westermann (*The Praise of God in the Psalms* [London: SCM Press, 1965]) has drawn attention to the presence of confidence and praise even in psalms of lament. Whether Jesus' citation of Ps. 22.1 from the cross (Mk 15.34; Mt. 27.46) should be understood as a 'cry of dereliction' or, against the background of the end of the psalm, as an affirmation of faith in his ultimate vindication, is open to debate. As far as the author of Hebrews' use of Ps. 22 is concerned there is no doubt; in 2.12 he uses Ps. 22.22 as an affirmation of praise.

2. Attridge ('Reverence', pp. 90-93) cites Philo, *Rer. Div. Her.* 6-19; *3 Macc.* 1.16; 5.7; 5.25.

3. Cf. Dey, *Intermediary World*, pp. 221-25, who sees in 'perfecting' in Heb. 2.10; 5.8-9; 7.28 an assimilation to ideals of Greek $\pi\alpha\iota\delta\epsilon\iota\alpha$.

suffering. Yet in exhorting his readers to endure hardship the author makes no appeal to the example of Jesus. If 5.7-8 is a reference to the suffering of the cross rather than Gethsemane, this would make sense. We have seen in the paraenetic sections that a martyr's death was not what his readers were facing, and therefore the example of Christ would not be particularly appropriate. For Hebrews it is Jesus' death which is the supreme example and culminating expression of a life which was one of learned filial obedience. It was the act whereby he was made perfect, that is, entered heaven.

For his purposes of presenting a re-interpretation of the Levitical cult, our author focuses almost exclusively on Christ's Passion. He shows scant interest in the life which led up to it. In our exegesis we should therefore respect the limits which he himself has set, neither attempting to read in references to the earthly ministry of Jesus, nor expecting him to answer questions which are outside his particular purview. Hebrews' concentration upon the cross has its limitations, if taken as the sole approach to a Christian understanding of the role of Christ in salvation. Yet it has an important contribution to make—not least as a powerful piece of Passion apologetic. Presenting the cross as the essential means of Jesus' access to God, explored both through its analogy with the high priest's entry into the holy of holies, and also viewed as a sacrificial offering, Hebrews (unlike for example the Synoptic Gospels[1]) has no need to stress the injustice of the crucifixion nor to defend the innocence of the condemned, since Christ's death was an essential prerequisite for his entry into heaven, and his 'sinlessness' the *sine qua non* of his role as both priest and victim. Hebrews, therefore, concentrates upon the effect rather than the cause of the crucifixion.

Furthermore, Hebrews' schema has no need of the language of resurrection[2] as the divine vindication of Jesus' righteousness and the means whereby the disaster of death was turned into a glorious victory.[3] By depicting Christ's death as the expiatory sacrifice offered

1. So the testimony given at Jesus' trial was false (Mt. 26.59-60; Mk 14.56-57), and his innocence recognized by Judas (Mt. 27.4), Pilate (Mk 15.14; Lk. 23.4), Pilate's wife (Mt. 27.19) and one of the thieves crucified alongside him (Lk. 23.39-40).

2. Heb. 13.20 is the only reference to the resurrection of Jesus in the Epistle. 6.2 refers to the resurrection of the dead in general. See also 11.19.

3. Luke especially depicts the resurrection as the act whereby God brings victory

on the Day of Atonement it requires no justification. Its necessity is axiomatic. Equally, within the terms of this analogy, the entry into the holy of holies is not synonymous with the slaughter of the victim. The latter precedes the former. Hence, unlike the Fourth Gospel, the two are not fused in such a way that Jesus' crucifixion becomes his moment of glorification.[1] The sacrifice and the entry into the holy of holies are two separate acts, although, unlike the Lukan tradition of ascension, there is no 43-day gap between them.[2] On the Day of Atonement analogy they took place on the same day—although Hebrews does not pursue that point. Our author, therefore, clearly stands (as we shall see in Chapter 4) within that strand of early Christian tradition which adopts the pattern of cross/exaltation, rather than cross/resurrection. Jesus' death is depicted as the process whereby he moves from his earthly and temporary subordination to the angels to his superior place in heaven where he is now 'crowned with glory and honour' (2.9).

We have seen so far, then, that the language of perfection is integral to our author's presentation of Christ's exaltation in heaven in terms of the provisions made by the Levitical cult for the high priest's approach to God in the holy of holies. The same can be said of the sinlessness of Jesus, which is clearly related to our author's depiction of him as both victim and priest. All sacrificial victims, according to the Levitical regulations, had to be without physical blemishes if they were to be acceptable to God. So, as victim, Christ 'offered himself without blemish (ἄμωμον) to God' (9.14). Coming as this does within a section of the Epistle which argues that Jesus was the *superior* victim (9.11-14), this is more than a claim that he lacked any physical defect. That would have made him merely comparable with them. Our author is interpreting ἄμωμον in terms of the moral superiority of a death willingly accepted in obedience to the will of God (cf. 9.12, 14). As we shall see in the next chapter, it is Jesus' sonship, even more than his high priesthood, which makes him superior to all other mediators. Therefore it is his filial obedience which makes his the superior sacrifice. Once more, therefore, we can see our author starting from a

out of apparent defeat, thereby vindicating the mission of Jesus. See Lk. 24.13-35; Acts 2.24-36; 3.15; 4.10-11; 5.20-31; 13.26-27.

   1. See Jn 3.14; 12.27-33.

   2. Acts 1.1-11.

cultic model, in this case of the sacrificial victim, and yet breaking out of its confines.

Interestingly, in the three other instances outside Hebrews where we meet overt reference to Jesus' sinlessness in the New Testament, the analogy of Jesus with a sacrificial victim is not far off. Thus in 1 Pet. 2.22, 'He committed no sin (ἁμαρτία); no guile (δόλος) was found on his lips', the innocent suffering of the servant whose death is compared to that of a lamb's slaughter (cf. Isa. 53.9) is clearly alluded to. In the same letter the blood of Christ is 'like a lamb without blemish or spot' (ὡς ἀμνοῦ ἀμώμου καὶ ἀσπίλου, 1 Pet. 1.19). It is unlikely that this, too, is an echo of Isaiah.[1] Yet the outcome of that particular scholarly debate is not vital to the point I am making, which is that in the self-same work we have both the sinlessness of Christ and his depiction as a spotless (ἄμωμος; cf. Heb. 9.14) victim. The same connection can be seen in 2 Cor. 5.21, 'For our sake he made him to be sin (ἁμαρτίαν ἐποίησεν) who knew no sin', if Paul is here depicting Christ's death as a sin-offering.[2] Finally, our last reference to Jesus' sinlessness outside Hebrews, 'You know that he appeared to take away sins, and in him there is no sin' (1 Jn 3.5), is also found within a work which applies expiatory sacrificial language to the death of Christ. 'He is the expiation (ἱλασμός) for our sin' (1 Jn 2.2). It seems plausible to suggest, therefore, that what was subsequently to develop into the Christian doctrine of the sinlessness of Christ had its beginnings in the image of Jesus as sacrificial victim.

In Hebrews, of course, the sinlessness of Jesus is not confined to his portrayal as victim; it is also applied to him as superior high priest.

---

1. See M.D. Hooker, *Jesus and the Servant: the Influence of the Servant Concept of Deutero-Isaiah in the N.T.* (London: SPCK, 1959), pp. 124-25. E.G. Selwyn (*The First Epistle of Peter* [London: Macmillan, 1955], pp. 145-46) sees in 1 Pet. 1.19 a reference to the paschal lamb.

2. The interpretation of ὑπὲρ ἡμῶν ἁμαρτίαν ἐποίησεν (2 Cor. 5.21) in terms of Jesus' death depicted as a sin-offering goes back to the early church fathers (Ambrose, Augustine, Cyril of Alexandria). F.F. Bruce (*1 and 2 Corinthians* [NCB; London: Oliphants, 1971], p. 210) continues the tradition. For arguments against this, however, see P.E. Hughes, *Commentary on the Second Epistle to the Corinthians* (NICNT; Grand Rapids: Eerdmans, 1962), pp. 214-15; C.K. Barrett, *The Second Epistle to the Corinthians* (BNTC; London: A. & C. Black, 1973), p. 180. The closest parallel to Heb. 9.14 is Rom. 8.3 where περὶ ἁμαρτίας is more evidently used in the technical sense of a 'sin-offering'. See Käsemann, *Romans*, pp. 214-17.

Our author, moreover, also uses it as a point of comparison between the purity of Christ and that which was required of all priests officiating in the sanctuary, and which separated them off from the profane:

> For it was fitting that we should have such a high priest holy (ὅσιος[1]), blameless (ἄκακος[2]), unstained (ἀμίαντος[3]), separated from sinners, exalted above the heavens. . . ' (7.26).

It is not until the last phrase in the verse, 'exalted above the heavens', that we meet anything which could not have been said of any priest's necessary condition of ritual purity. With these words, however, we move beyond the realm of the Levitical and into that of a Melchizedekian priesthood, the superiority of which has been the main burden of the whole of ch. 7.

In the same vein of contrast our author continues:

> He has no need, like those high priests, to offer sacrifices daily, first for his own sins and then for those of the people; he did this once for all when he offered up himself (7.27).

G.W. Buchanan,[4] followed more recently by R. Williamson,[5] sees in the second half of this verse the implication that Jesus' death was at one and the same time an offering for his own sin as well as for that of the people. Therefore, he was not sinless prior to the crucifixion. As Williamson puts it:

> Jesus achieved sinlessness as his life of growing obedience to the will of God was consummated on the cross in his supreme act of self-abnegation.[6]

Yet surely in 7.27 the contrast is not merely between the 'daily' (καθ' ἡμέραν) offerings of the Levitical system over against the 'once for

---

1. ὅσιος is the LXX translation of *ḥâsîd* (e.g. Ps. 16.10), and is therefore better translated as 'devout' rather than 'holy'.
2. ἄκακος denotes an innocence born of guilelessness. Cf. Rom. 16.18 where it means 'simple-minded'.
3. Cf. 1 Pet. 1.4.
4. Buchanan, *Hebrews*, pp. 129-31.
5. R. Williamson, 'Hebrews 4.15 and the Sinlessness of Jesus', *ExpTim* 8 (1974), pp. 4-8. *Contra* Peterson, *Hebrews and Perfection*, pp. 187-90.
6. Williamson, 'Sinlessness'.

all' (ἐφάπαξ) of Jesus' death, but also between his one offering and their two—a bull for themselves and a goat for the expiation of the sins of people and the pollution of the cult place. The following verse (28) continues this theme of contrast, emphasizing the weakness (ἀσθένεια) of the high priests over against 'a son who has been made perfect for ever' (εἰς τὸν αἰῶνα τετελειωμένον), that is, one who has now an exalted state in heaven. In 7.26-28, therefore, Hebrews' claim that Christ's sinlessness pre-dates his death arises wholly out of the author's concern to present Jesus as a superior high priest. One of his ways of doing this is to see in his one death (as victim) the implication that Jesus needed to make no expiatory offering for himself.

Such a claim for any priest in the Levitical system would have been unprecedented. In order to officiate in the shrine the priests had to be in a state of 'sinlessness', that is, ritual purity. But that state was brought about via expiatory sacrifice and was therefore its result rather than its precondition. The high priest was certainly not thought to be morally infallible. Indeed if that had been the case the expiatory sacrifice which he was obliged to offer on his own behalf before he could offer for the people would have been unnecessary. R.A. Stewart has brought together what evidence there is for notions of 'sinlessness', understood as moral perfection, applied as a characteristic of priesthood, and current in first-century Judaism.[1] He concludes that only the *Testament of Levi* together with some passages in Philo might have some bearing on the issue. *T. Levi* 18.2-15 is a messianic hymn in which God's salvific figure is cast in a priestly mode: 'Then shall the Lord raise up a new priest' (v. 2). For Stewart, this passage is the only evidence we have of a sinless priest in Jewish literature, and even here it is within an eschatological context and is not about the mortal successors of Aaron.[2] More importantly, he admits that *T. Levi* does not state that the priest was to be personally free from

1. R.A. Stewart, 'The Sinless High-Priest', *NTS* 14 (1967–68), pp. 126-35.
2. Stewart, 'Sinless', p. 131. *Pss. Sol.* 17.41, 'And he himself will be pure from sin so that he may rule a great people', provides evidence of a similar messianic hope in the mid first century BCE. The figure here, however, is Davidic rather than Levitical. It is also far from certain in what sense he was to be 'pure from sin'. Cf. the apostle Paul (Phil. 3.6) who can say that in terms of the Law's righteous demands (δικαιοσύνη) his previous mode of life as an observant Pharisee was 'blameless' (ἀμέμπτος).

sin; it merely implies it.[1] I would even question the presence of the implication. Furthermore, we need to bear in mind that the *Testament of the Twelve Patriarchs* is a notoriously difficult work to appeal to for evidence of pre-Christian Judaism. In the form in which we have it, the Greek text comes from the end of the second or beginning of the third century CE, and shows evidence of strong Christian influence at the very least. Scholars are divided as to whether it is a Jewish writing with Christian interpolations, or a Christian work drawing upon Jewish sources.[2]

With Philo, an older contemporary of the apostle Paul, we have no such problems of dating, and (as we have seen in Chapter 1) a number of scholars have looked to him for insight into the thinking of the author of our Epistle. Certainly, along with Josephus (who was himself a member of a priestly family[3]) he shares many of the author of Hebrews' priestly theocratic presuppositions.[4] Yet it is also important to notice the differences between the two, not least in Philo's presentation of the sinlessness of the high priest who enters the holy of holies on the Day of Atonement. The Aaronic figure, as well as his role, is allegorized in such a way as to enable Philo to see in him the *logos*, that principle of the divine which makes contact between God and the world possible. So, in the entry of the high priest into the inner sanctuary may be seen the *logos* which has entered the temple of the cosmos, as well as that other inner sanctum, the human mind (νοῦς).[5] Hence, Philo's exposition of Leviticus 16 quickly leaves behind the earthly high priest—so much so that he can interpret the injunction of Lev. 16.17 that there shall be no one present in the shrine with the high priest (LXX καὶ πᾶς ἄνθρωπος οὐκ ἔσται ἐν τῇ σκηνῇ) to mean that while he is there his humanity is temporarily suspended and he is in a state mid-way between the human and divine.[6] At that moment he is immune from sin,[7] born of incorruptible parentage,

1. Stewart, 'Sinless', p. 129.
2. See M.E. Stone (ed.), *Jewish Writing of the Second Temple Period*, II (CRINT; Assen: Van Gorcum, 1984), pp. 331-44.
3. *Life* 2, 6.
4. See Horbury, 'Aaronic Priesthood', pp. 43-71.
5. See Stewart, 'Sinless', pp. 131-34.
6. Philo, *Rer. Div. Her.* 84; *Somn* 2.189, 231; cf. *Fug.* 108, 'οὐκ ἄνθρωπον ἀλλὰ λόγον θεῖον'.
7. *Spec. Leg.* 1.293.

with God as his Father.[1] This depiction of the high priest has clearly lost all contact with its exegetical point of departure, the earthly figure of Aaron. Philo's identification of Melchizedek with the *logos*[2] is further confirmation of the fact that priesthood merely serves as a peg on which he can hang his *logos* doctrine.

In Hebrews, however, we find something quite different in the way Christ is presented as a sinless high priest. True, he is 'after the order of Melchizedek', but (as we shall see in Chapter 3) this is not linked with a doctrine of the *logos*. More importantly, Christ's sinlessness is no metaphysical abstraction, nor, unlike subsequent Christian apologetics, is it presented as the grounds for claiming his divinity. In our Epistle the superior sinlessness of Jesus, as both victim and priest, lies in his life of filial obedience which culminates in the cross. Thereby it not only mirrors but exceeds the sinlessness expected within the cult.

Furthermore, as we meet it in Hebrews, Jesus' sinlessness, unlike that of Philo's high priest/*logos*, it not that which cuts him off from the rest of humanity:

> For we have not a high priest, who is unable to sympathize with our weaknesses (ἀσθενείαις), but one who in every respect has been tempted (πεπειρασμένον) as we are, yet without sin (χωρὶς ἁμαρτίας) (4.15).

Here the theme of testing (πειράζειν) is picked up from the preceding chapter (cf. 3.8) where it concerned the wilderness generation which had put God to the test and thereby had its own faith tested and found wanting. He now addresses his contemporaries, as those living equally through a time of testing, to look to one who in his role as high priest has similarly been put to the test, and yet not failed. It is significant that Jesus' own endurance should now be described in terms of sinlessness, since at this point our author is to begin his exposition of Jesus in cultic terms. Unlike Philo, our author has not lost sight of the essentially representative character of the priestly role. Any priest must be genuinely part of the humanity which he represents. Thus this very first mention of the sinlessness of Jesus should not be isolated from the section which it introduces (4.14–5.10)—one which stresses not only the compassionate nature of his high priesthood, but also his human solidarity with us. Common

1. *Fug.* 109-110.
2. *Leg. All.* 3.82.

humanity, personal testing and compassion have already been depicted as essential qualifications for priesthood in 2.17-18:

> Therefore he had to be made like his brethren in every respect, so that he might become a merciful and faithful high priest in the service of God, to make expiation for the sins of the people. For because he himself has suffered and been tempted (πειρασθείς) he is able to help those who are tempted (τοῖς πειραζομένοις).

This is, moreover, no contrast between Levitical priesthood and that exercised by Jesus. The two are comparable. Precisely as a point of comparison, our author seems to pick up the pentateuchal themes of priestly solidarity and compassion, which had developed in Jewish tradition from 2 Maccabees onwards,[1] and apply them to Jesus.

So 5.1-4 sets out his three ideal criteria for any high priest: (1) his common humanity, evident from his sharing human weakness (ἀσθένεια; cf. 4.15); (2) his tolerant understanding (μετριοπαθεῖν[2]) of those who commit unwitting sin; and (3) his divine call and appointment. In his application of these qualifications to the high priesthood of Jesus in 5.5-10, our author treats them in inverse order. He therefore starts with the last—Jesus' divine appointment to the office. He appeals to Ps. 2.7 (cf. 1.5) and Ps. 110.4 as evidence of this. In the former psalm God has spoken of him as 'My son' and in the latter as 'A priest forever after the order of Melchizedek'. The theme of Christ's humanity and compassion (begun in 2.17-18) is then picked up, but this time not in terms of his sharing human weakness (ἀσθένεια)—at least not understood as sin. At 4.14 the author has already modified his earlier appeal to Jesus' common exposure to testing or temptation (πειράζειν 2.18) by adding the rider χωρὶς ἁμαρτίας—without sin. (This is going to become one source of his superiority over the Levitical priesthood in 7.27.) Therefore it is to Jesus' suffering that he turns for evidence of his genuine humanity and the source of his effectiveness in his priestly role (see 5.8-10).

So far we have seen how the author of Hebrews compares and contrasts the death of Jesus with both the victim and the role of the high

---

1. See Horbury, 'Aaronic Priesthood', pp. 59-65.

2. μετριοπαθεῖν is used in the Aristotelian philosophical tradition to mean 'to moderate one's feelings', i.e., to avoid excess. In Hebrews, however, it means to moderate one's attitude to others, i.e., to treat them with magnanimity. See P.E. Hughes, *Hebrews*, p. 176.

priest in the Day of Atonement ceremonies. Only by appreciating that at one and the same time he reconstructs and deconstructs the cult can we see the inner logic of his arguments and understand his own theological construction.

He levels two further major criticisms at the Levitical system: (1) its priesthood was not 'after the order of Melchizedek'; and (2) it operated within an earthly rather than a heavenly shrine. I shall deal with these in the following chapters. Meanwhile we must look at how our author views the Sinai covenant, the basis of Mosaic Torah which legislated for the cult.

4. *Mosaic Torah and Sinai Covenant*

Whatever gave rise to the writing of the Epistle to the Hebrews it was not the problems associated with the emergence of a Gentile Christianity within a still predominantly Jewish-Christian church. That situation, as we have already noted (pp. 75-76), lay behind the apostle Paul's attitude to the Mosaic Torah. Our author, by contrast, seems to be facing an entirely different situation—one which required him to focus on those parts of the Law which dealt with the land and the cult place. Rather than discuss Torah as a total salvation system, therefore, he focuses on pentateuchal passages which deal with these specific topics.

Our author is aware, nonetheless, that his abrogation of the Levitical cult inevitably implies an abrogation of the Law of which it is an integral part:

> For if perfection had been attainable through the Levitical priesthood (for under it the people received the law), what further need would there have been for another priest to arise after the order of Melchizedek, rather than one named after the order of Aaron? For where there is a change in the priesthood, there is necessarily a change in the law as well (7.11-12).

In the biblical account, of course, it is the Law which establishes the priesthood and not vice versa. Yet far from this parenthesis demonstrating our author's ignorance of Jewish tradition, as we have already seen (pp. 76-77) it places him firmly within a contemporary strand of it, wherein the priesthood was elevated as the principal expression of theocratic rule. In the particular context which I am suggesting as the *Sitz im Leben* of Hebrews, the author is holding up Christ as the

Melchizedekian priest, divinely intended as the replacement for an order which has recently been displaced.

This is not to say that the Pentateuch ceases to be Scripture for the Christian community. Not least, our author looks to it for the very figure of Melchizedek who is to play such a major role as a type of Christ. Yet, as we shall see, even the Melchizedek of Genesis 14 can only be seen to supersede the Aaronic priesthood which succeeded Abraham in the light of Ps. 110.4. It is therefore the psalm which becomes Hebrews' mandate for abrogating pentateuchal priestly Law. He claims that the law pertaining to Levitical priesthood was demonstrably weak (7.18), since that priesthood failed to gain access to the true holy of holies, that is, heaven. This is what our author means when he says 'the law made nothing perfect' (7.19).

The 'law has but a shadow (σκία) of the good things to come instead of the true form (εἰκών) of these' (10.1). The author of Hebrews has similarly categorized the wilderness tabernacle as mere σκία. Yet neither with reference to the sanctuary (see pp. 52-56) nor Mosaic Torah is this Platonic vocabulary of inferior copy over against the Ideal used in the Epistle in its metaphysical sense of second- and first-order worlds. The reference to 'the good things to come' precludes such an interpretation, alerting us to the presence of a more typically Jewish eschatology of two succeeding ages. Hence, for our author, Mosaic Torah's validity is confined to the age of the past (see 2.2; 3.5). It is no longer operative in the new age inaugurated by Jesus, whose new priesthood has inevitably brought about a change in the Law. It is possible that the author of the Epistle believed that a new Law—that of Christ—now replaces that of Moses. If so this is not actually articulated, since it is in terms of covenant—the very foundation of Law in Israelite thinking—rather than Law *per se* that the argument is pursued. Although one implies the other, our author concentrates upon the new covenant rather than upon the new Law. Not least in Jer. 38(MT 31).31-34 our author finds clear scriptural warrant for the former.

Although in Old Testament tradition there is more than one covenant made between God and his people (e.g. Noah, Gen. 9.1-17; Abraham, Gen. 17.1-14; David, 2 Sam. 7[1]), the 'new covenant' is

---

1. Cf. also covenant renewals under Joshua (Josh. 24); Josiah (2 Kgs 23.1-3); Ezra (Neh. 8–10).

contrasted with that made with Moses on Mount Sinai (Exod. 19). Old
Testament scholars are divided as to the antiquity of Israel's covenant
traditions.[1] In his book, *God and His People: Covenant and Theology
in the Old Testament*, Ernest Nicholson concludes:

> On the whole, however, it is fair to regard 'covenant' as a theological
> theory about God's relationship with Israel which, though first formulated
> in earlier times, came into its own at the hands of the Deuteronomic circles
> in the years leading up to the Exile.[2]

Since Jeremiah is thought to have been associated with Deuteronomic
circles, his promise of a 'new covenant' should therefore be seen as
part of that flowering of covenantal theology mentioned by Nicholson.
In this movement 'covenant' is the central expression of Israel's faith
that it has been chosen as God's people.

Covenant is thereby the basis of the relationship between God and
Israel. The LXX, followed by Hebrews, chooses to translate the
Hebrew *berīt* as διαθήκη, rather than the more usual term for an
agreement, συνθήκη, perhaps because the latter could convey the idea
of a contract between two equal partners. In the case of the bond
between God and Israel that would have been quite erroneous. It
would be equally wrong, however, to infer from this that there is no
contractual element in the idea of covenant.[3] So Ernest Nicholson
reminds us,

> In various formulations in the Old Testament the description of the making
> of a covenant between God and Israel is characterized by two foci: on the
> one hand, Yahweh's appropriation of, and commitment to, Israel; on the
> other, the solemn binding of Israel to the service of Yahweh alone and
> obedience to his commandments. . . . God's covenant with Israel was
> conceived of as bilateral in nature.[4]

It is precisely because Israel had broken her part of the contract that,
according to Jeremiah, the covenant made 'with their fathers when I

---

1. For a discussion of the present state of research with regard to the Sinai
covenant, see E.W. Nicholson, *Exodus and Sinai in History and Tradition* (Oxford:
Clarendon Press, 1973).
2. E.W. Nicholson, *God and His People: Covenant and Theology in the O.T.*
(Oxford: Clarendon Press, 1986), p. vi.
3. Even the secular meaning of διαθήκη, i.e., a will (as in 'last will and
testament'), carries with it a contractual agreement on the part of the testator.
4. Nicholson, *Covenant and Theology*, pp. 210-11.

took them by the hand to bring them out of the land of Egypt' (Jer. 31.32) is now annulled and to be replaced by a new one.

That it is the Mosaic covenant which is also to the forefront of the author of Hebrews' exposition is evident from the way it is interwoven with the themes of priesthood, sanctuary, sacrifice and Law. Here he is clearly following Exodus 19–28 where the self-same institutions are linked. Yet whereas Jeremiah's promise of a new covenant is acknowledged by our author as indicating that God finds fault with his people (8.8), Hebrews insists that the weakness is not merely on their part; it is inherent in the covenant itself:

> For if that first covenant had been faultless, there would have been no occasion for a second (8.7).

So once more our author criticizes Israel's religious institutions as inherently transitory, ordained from their very beginning to be superseded by something better, promised by prophet and psalmist. At best these previous means of access to God were intended to serve as a foretaste or preview of better things to come. Disobedience was earlier given by our author as the reason why the wilderness generation did not attain the promised land. Yet even there, the land of promise quickly becomes re-interpreted as heaven itself, unattainable before the death of Christ. This theme of disobedience, which Jeremiah saw as necessitating a new covenant, is thus not used by the author of Hebrews as a paraenetic warning to his readers.

Rather his citation and exposition of Jer. 38(MT 31).31-34 forms part of a doctrinal section on the theme of the replacement of the old by the new religious order, which begins at 7.1 and continues uninterrupted by paraenesis up to 10.18. Only at 12.18-24 is the Sinai theme overtly used in exhortation. (We shall return to this passage shortly.) Having concluded that his Melchizedekian high priesthood 'makes Jesus the surety (ἔγγυος) of a better covenant' (7.22), our author quickly moves from the superior sanctuary in which he is now installed (8.1-6) back to the theme of a better covenant. This time it is in term of Jesus as its mediator (μεσίτης, 8.6; cf. 9.15; 12.24[1]) rather than its guarantor. It becomes clear in what sense Jesus is spoken of as

---

1. μεσίτης is also used of Jesus in 1 Tim. 2.5. In Gal. 3.19-20 it is applied to angels as mediators of the Law. In 2 Cor. 3.6 Christians are διάκονοι (rather than μεσίται) of the new covenant.

'mediator' at 9.15-22, where the death of Christ is interpreted once more as a sacrifice; not this time as the sin-offering of the Day of Atonement, but as the sacrifice which accompanied the making of the covenant.

But first, in 8.8-12, he cites Jer. 31.31-34, the better promises upon which the new covenant is enacted (8.6). This passage is one of a number which confirm that our author is using a septuagintal[1] rather than a Hebrew text of the Scriptures. Hence, with the LXX he reads, 'And so he paid no heed (ἠμέλησα) to them' (v. 9), rather than the MT, 'Though I was a husband to them'.[2] At the heart of Jeremiah's new covenant lies the same notion of adoption which lay behind the old. 'I will be their God and they shall be my people'.[3] Its new features are: (1) an interiorization and transformation of the people's will, which would lead to radical Torah obedience—'I will put my laws into their minds and write them on their hearts' (v. 10); and (2) universal knowledge of the Law's demands, which will make its teachers and interpreters redundant. In this connection we should note that one of the functions of the priest in Israelite religion was to teach the Law.[4] Concentrating as he does upon the priest's cultic role, the author of Hebrews does not specifically draw out from the Jeremiah prophecy this further evidence of the redundancy of the priestly office. As in fact with the rest of the content of this oracle, it is left undeveloped. Except, that is, for the last promise—'For I will be merciful toward their iniquities, and I will remember their sins no more' (8.12). The second half of this verse is repeated at 10.17 to conclude his argument that the very repetition of sacrifice was a demonstration that it did not mediate a permanent forgiveness of sins (10.1-18). Citing this time a shortened form of Jer. 38(MT 31).33-34,[5]

---

1. Heb. 8.8-12 largely follows LXX Jer. 38.31-34 with a few minor variations, e.g., συντελέσω ἐπί instead of διαθήσομαι (v. 8); ἐποίησα instead of διεθέμην (v. 9).

2. It is possible that the LXX is based on a Hebrew text which read *gā'althî*. The *Vorlage* of the MT, on the other hand, read *bā'althî*.

3. Heb. 8.10. See Exod. 6.7; 29.45; Lev. 26.12; cf. Jer. 7.23.

4. Deut. 33.10; Lev. 10-11; Ezek. 44.23; Hag. 2.11-13.

5. The form in which Jer. 38(MT 31).33-34 is cited in Heb. 10.16-17 is not identical to that in 8.10-12. Apart from the omission of most of Jer. 38.34, the 'house of Israel' becomes 'them' (v. 16); ἐπὶ replaces εἰς; ἐπιγράψω is used twice; ἁμαρτιῶν replaces ἀδικίαις; and ἀνομιῶν replaces ἁμαρτιῶν at v. 17.

he picks up the promise of forgiveness in Jeremiah's prophecy to conclude that, 'Where there is forgiveness of these [i.e. sins], there is no longer any offering for sin'. In other words, since the new covenant has been inaugurated by Jesus, sin has been dealt with and there remains no need for the expiatory sacrificial system to continue. Our author concludes his first citation of Jeremiah with an even more sweeping claim; the very mention of a 'new' covenant implies that the first has been outworn:

> In speaking of a new covenant he treats the first as obsolete (πεπαλαίωκεν). And what is becoming obsolete (παλαιούμενον) and growing old (γηράσκον) is ready to vanish away (ἐγγὺς ἀφανισμοῦ) (8.13).

The first covenant is therefore part of the passing age which is ready to disappear. Here once more we see that, contrary to the opinion of some commentators, the tension between the 'now' and the 'not yet' of linear history has not become lost in spatial, timeless metaphor. Like the promised land which the author holds out to his readers as their imminent inheritance, so the new covenant is part of that future age on whose boundaries they already stand (see 6.5; 12.22) and which they are about to cross at any moment (see 9.10, 28; 10.25, 27).

As we have seen, throughout his Epistle our author has been concerned to present the death and exaltation of Jesus as the replacement for Israel's previous God-given means of access to God. It is wholly within this vein that he depicts Jesus as the sacrificial victim whose death ratifies the new covenant. This is the topic of 9.15-22. It begins by using a secular analogy; the necessity for the death of a testator before a will (διαθήκη) may be proved (vv. 16-17), before moving, via a clever double entendre, to the septuagintal meaning of διαθήκη as covenant, and appealing to the biblical account of the ratification of the Sinai covenant (Exod. 24.4-8) as confirmation that Jesus' death was essential for the inauguration of the new covenant.

Our author has, moreover, introduced into the Exodus account certain features from other biblical rites. Textual variants in v. 19 make it difficult to decide whether our text originally contained a reference to goats or whether it has been added as a result of scribal assimilation to v. 12, where the goat is the Day of Atonement victim.[1]

---

1. See Wilson, *Hebrews*, p. 160.

Be that as it may, we find no mention of water, scarlet wool and hyssop (v. 19) in the covenant ceremony. All play a part in the cleansing of a leper (Lev. 14.4-7), yet it is the ceremony of the red heifer (Num. 19.2-20) which is the more likely source.[1] In this the animal is burned along with hyssop and scarlet 'stuff' with cedar wood, and the resultant ashes, mixed with water, are then used for the purification of sin. It is this latter aspect which appeals to the author of Hebrews. In the covenant ceremony the blood may well have functioned as the means whereby the whole people, and not only the priestly caste,[2] were consecrated 'a kingdom of priests and a holy nation' (Exod. 19.6), and this would explain why half the blood was sprinkled over the people.[3] But it is not thought of as expiatory. Interestingly our author, unlike the sectarians of Qumran,[4] does not address his audience as 'sons of the [new] covenant', nor like the author of 1 Peter (2.9) as 'a royal priesthood, a holy nation'. His use of the covenant theme is predominantly in terms of Jesus as covenant victim, rather than the Christian church as a covenant community. Since the dominant sacrificial model for Hebrews, however, is that taken from the expiatory rites of the Day of Atonement, he introduces this element, probably from the red-heifer ceremony, even into his summary of the inauguration of the Mosaic covenant. He has already introduced the theme of forgiveness in the very first verse of the section (i.e. 9.15), where he speaks of the death of Christ as the means of redemption (ἀπολύτρωσις)[5] from transgressions committed under the first covenant.

In his anxiety to make blood (interpreted as the death of Christ) the all-pervasive medium of expiation (see v. 22), he states that it was

---

1. See Childs, *Exodus*, pp. 509-11.

2. See Exod. 29.30 where blood is sprinkled on Aaron and his sons in their priestly consecration. Cf. Lev. 8.22-40.

3. So Nicholson, *Covenant and Theology*, p. 172.

4. See Vermes, *Qumran in Perspective*, who thinks that the Qumran sectarians' self-understanding, as the righteous remnant now in a new and final covenant with God, is so central that he organizes his summary of their religious ideas around it (pp. 163-70).

5. ἀπολύτρωσις in secular Greek refers to the manumission or redemption of a slave. Paul uses it as an image of salvation. See Rom. 3.24; 8.23; 1 Cor. 1.30; cf. Eph. 1.7. In Hebrews, since it occurs in the context of 'covenant', it may well have resonances of God's manumission of Israel from Egyptian bondage.

used to sprinkle not only the people but also the book of the Law
(v. 19), the tabernacle and all its vessels (v. 21). In the biblical
account of the inauguration of the Mosaic covenant there is no mention of the book being sprinkled, and, of course, since at that stage the
tabernacle was not even constructed, no reference to its consecration.
It is not until Exodus 40 that everything is finally prepared and the
tabernacle is erected. And then the medium of its consecration is oil,
not blood (Exod. 40.9-10). This may be a simple error on the part of
the author of Hebrews. On the other hand, since we find the addition
of 'the blood of bulls and rams' to the oil in Josephus (*Ant.* 3.206), it
may possibly be that he is drawing upon a piece of established
midrashic tradition.

Hebrews is not the only New Testament work which presents Christ
as the covenant victim. Yet elsewhere this is within the context of the
Last Supper seen as a celebration of the Passover.[1] With, 'This cup is
the new covenant in my blood' (1 Cor. 11.25), Paul places upon Jesus'
own lips the interpretation of his death as the offering which inaugurated the new covenant. When we compare this with the Synoptic
Gospels, however, only the longer text of Luke (20.20) refers to the
new covenant. In Mk 14.24 we have simply, 'This is my blood of the
covenant which is poured out for many', to which Mt. 26.28 adds,
'for the remission of sins'. Only in the case of Paul and Hebrews,
therefore, do we have undisputed evidence of the death of Jesus being
interpreted in terms of a *new* covenant theology.

In Hebrews, however, this is not within a eucharistic context, and it
would be misleading to understand it as such. At 9.20 our author cites
Exod. 24.8:

> This is the blood of the covenant which God commanded you (τοῦτο τὸ
> αἷμα τῆς διαθήκης ἧς ἐνετείλατο πρὸς ὑμᾶς ὁ θεός).

Clearly 'the blood of the covenant' is common to Mk 14.24, Mt. 26.28
and Hebrews, yet this is no reason to suppose that here our author has
the Last Supper in mind or indeed that it reflects his own eucharistic
tradition. Neither can significance be read into Hebrews' preference
for τοῦτο instead of the LXX ἰδού (claiming it as an echo of Mk
14.24; Mt. 26.26), since in some LXX manuscripts of Exod. 24.8 we

---

1. For the Last Supper as a Passover meal see Jeremias, *Eucharistic Words*,
pp. 41-88.

find both—ἰδοὺ τοῦτο. More importantly, at this stage in his argument it is the blood of the first covenant victim which is being referred to. His replacement of ὁ θεός for the LXX κύριος makes that abundantly clear. Therefore we may conclude that the author of Hebrews, unlike other New Testament writers, does not associate Jesus, the new covenant victim, with any Last Supper traditions. Ronald Williamson, having examined this passage, together with all others in the Epistle which have been seen by commentators as eucharistic in reference, convincingly concludes that nowhere do we find evidence of such an interest in Hebrews.[1] Whether or not Williamson is equally right that our author's whole theology would militate against a sacramental approach depends largely upon what kind of eucharistic theology is in mind. Any which presented the Lord's Supper as a re-enactment of the sacrifice of Jesus would certainly run counter to his whole presentation. As far as Hebrews' contribution to contemporary Christian eucharistic doctrine is concerned Williamson concludes,

> the Epistle to the Hebrews would seem to invite, if eucharistic faith and practice be retained, a view of the Eucharist which sees it in no sense as a sacrifice, but as at most a moment in the liturgy when the once-for-all sacrifice of Christ is remembered and the End is anticipated, or at least saluted.[2]

But this takes us beyond the scope of this particular study. In the Epistle itself we see that our author has brought together Jeremiah's promise of a new covenant with the sacrifice which accompanied the inauguration of the Mosaic covenant, and has used this as the basis of his model of Jesus as the new covenant victim. In so doing he has incorporated also the expiatory element from the Day of Atonement. Thereby the death of Jesus purges sins committed under the first covenant.

Finally,[3] we meet an appeal made to the new covenant mediated by Jesus in the exhortation with which our author concludes his homily. Using alternately carrot and stick, he urges his readers not to lose confidence in God's promises, but to go forward in faith. To this end in 12.18-24 he reminds them of the differences between the two

---

1. Williamson, 'Eucharist', pp. 300-12.
2. Williamson, 'Eucharist', p. 312 n. 2.
3. One further reference to covenant occurs, i.e., in the doxology at 13.20.

covenants, largely by way of contrasting their respective sites, Sinai and Zion. Although ὄρει is not found in the best manuscripts in v. 18 (and Sinai is not explicitly mentioned) it should probably be taken as implicitly understood.[1] It makes better sense of the list of portents in the rest of the sentence, and clearly vv. 18-21 stand in contrast to Σιὼν ὄρει (Mt Zion) in vv. 22-25. Even without an overt reference to Mt Sinai, we have here a paraphrase of the biblical account of the events which accompanied the making of the Mosaic covenant and the reception of the Torah, combining features of the Sinai tradition from Exod. 19.12-19, 20.18-21 with those found in Deut. 4.11-12, 5.23-27. In the latter Mt Sinai becomes Mt Horeb, but just as the geographical locality of the site had long since ceased to be known with any certainty, so Sinai and Horeb had long since become one within the tradition.[2]

The awesomeness of the events which accompanied the making of the first covenant are singled out and dwelt upon in Hebrews. The biblical account emphasizes the sacred nature of the mountain as the seat of the deity. Precisely because it is holy ground the people are not permitted to venture beyond the boundaries of its foot. To so much as touch its soil is to be liable to punishment by death. Even the prescribed method of execution—stoning—was to ensure that the sanctity of its forbidden territory (upon which the offender was presumably still standing) was not further violated. In Exodus Moses alone (followed by Aaron) is allowed to breach this taboo with its theophanic warning portents of thunder, lightning, cloud and trumpet blast, and to ascend the mountain to meet God.

Standing within the Christian tradition, however, the author of Hebrews is unwilling to concede such a unique place to Moses. Hence he makes Moses as well as the people terrified by the Sinai events: 'Indeed, so terrifying was the sight that Moses said, "I tremble with fear"' (12.21). Since Scripture mentions Moses' fear on two other occasions (in the presence of the burning bush [Exod. 3.6; cf. Acts 7.32], and when he comes before God, having discovered Israel's idolatrous fashioning and worship of the golden calf [Deut. 9.19]), it is possible that a haggadic tradition had already arisen which had introduced the motif of fear into the Sinai theophany as well. Yet given the tendency of Judaism in this period to magnify rather than

---

1. Bruce, *Hebrews*, p. 369.
2. See Schmidt, *Faith*, pp. 41-42.

reduce the figure of Moses,[1] Christian tradition (perhaps in the person of our author himself) would seem the more likely origin for this particular piece of haggadic expansion. As is brought out clearly in vv. 22-24, for the author of Hebrews Jesus alone has set foot upon the supreme sacred territory where God dwells, that is, heaven. Compared with this site, Mt Sinai is merely 'tangible'. Our author utilizes biblical tradition which forbids the people's touch, to claim that Mt Sinai itself was merely that which could be touched, being earthly. Thus, having begun the section with, 'For you have not come to what may be touched' (v. 18) he goes on to claim the superiority of the site of the new covenant, 'Mount Zion', 'the city of the living God, the heavenly Jerusalem' (v. 23), access to which is not barred.

So the thought moves from one holy mountain, Sinai, to another, Zion, the hill and former Jebusite stronghold captured by David (2 Sam. 5.6-9) which was to expand into the city of Jerusalem;[2] the site of the first and second Temples; the repository of the ark (2 Sam. 6.2); and the symbol of the very dwelling place of God.[3] For the author of Hebrews, however, the Jerusalem he speaks of is not to be identified with Israel's earthly capital. It is 'heavenly' (ἐπουρανίος, v. 22) not simply because it appertains to God, but because it is located in heaven. As we have already noted, the idea of a 'heavenly Jerusalem' can be found in Jewish and Christian sources contemporary with the Epistle.[4] As a concept it contains both the idea of the earthly and heavenly Jerusalem as representations of simultaneous, parallel worlds, and the two cities as symbols of two sequential ages.[5] Our author's language of 'approach' (vv. 18, 22) similarly contains a double reference to time and location. He addresses his Christian readers as those standing on the very brink of the boundary of heavenly Jerusalem, understood as both 'soon' and 'there'.

Yet the heavenly Jerusalem, like God's 'rest' and the holy of holies entered by Jesus, is more than simply the counterpart of its earthly

---

1. See, e.g., Philo's two treatises as the *Life of Moses*.
2. Zion and Jerusalem become synonymous in Israel's tradition. See Ps. 122.3-4; 147.12-13; Amos 1.2; Mic. 4.2.
3. See 1 Kgs 14.21; Ps. 78.68-69; cf. Isa. 24.23; Mic. 4.7; Zeph. 3.14-20; Zech. 1.16; Jer. 31.3-4; Joel 3.7.
4. See p. 59 n. 4; Bruce, *Hebrews*, p. 374. For rabbinic evidence see Strack–Billerbeck, III, pp. 573-74.
5. See pp. 58-59.

type, the earthly Jerusalem. The holy city, like all of the rest of Israel's sacred ground, is but a foretaste of the real thing—which is heaven itself. This holy mountain, the heavenly Zion, has been scaled by someone closer to God than Moses; Jesus the Son of God. He has thereby desacralized its holy ground, making access to God open to the people. A new covenant[1] has been inaugurated by a victim whose blood, unlike that of Abel which cried out for vengeance (Gen. 4.10-11), speaks of forgiveness and reconciliation between God and His people (v. 24).

Yet the desacralization of Israel's established meeting ground between God and His people and its relocation in heaven does not imply that our author thereby does away with all ideas of the sacred. If anything, the opposite is true, since holy ground takes on a new ultimacy. Hence his sermon ends (vv. 25-29) with a solemn and fearsome warning of the need to take seriously the awesome responsibility of having access to God:

> See that you do not refuse him who is speaking. For if they did not escape when they refused him who warned them on earth, much less shall we escape if we reject him who warns from heaven. . . Therefore let us be grateful for receiving a kingdom that cannot be shaken, and thus let us offer to God acceptable worship, with reverence and awe; for our God is a consuming fire (12.25, 28, 29).

1. Heb. 12.24 has διαθήκη νέα rather than the more usual διαθήκη καινή. There is no significance in the change of adjective, however, since νέος and καινός can be used synonymously (cf. Eph. 4.24 // Col. 3.10).

Chapter 3

JESUS AS THE DEFINITIVE MEANS OF ACCESS

1. *The Role of Mediator*

That neither the Hebrew nor the Greek Old Testament has a single
term for 'mediator'[1] should not lead us to assume that ancient Judaism
had no such notion. Even the most cursory reading of the Jewish
Scriptures reveals various mediatorial figures who act as go-betweens
in the relationship between God and Israel. Principally this is the
function of angels, of Moses, of the prophets, of the high priest, and
of the Davidic king. We shall see that the author of the Epistle to the
Hebrews draws on all of these established mediatorial categories in his
presentation of Jesus as the definitive mediator between God and His
people.

Interestingly, our author is one of the few in the New Testament[2]
who employ the vocabulary of mediator. He does so mainly in his
depiction of Jesus as the new and better Moses, the mediator
(μεσίτης) of a new (9.15; 12.24) and better (8.6) covenant. In Jewish
tradition Moses was certainly not thought of as a 'mediator' in the
sense in which that term was understood in secular Greek, that is, as
the neutral middle-man, trusted by both sides in a transaction and
therefore acceptable as an umpire or negotiator.[3] True, as covenant-
maker and Law-giver he acts both for Israel and Yahweh; but from
neither perspective is he impartial. This is equally true of the role of
Jesus in Hebrews.

On the other hand, the only occurrence of the verb 'to mediate'

---

1. The verb μεσιτεύω (I mediate, negotiate) is not in the LXX. μεσίτης (mediator)
occurs only once (Job 9.33).
2. In the New Testament μεσιτεύω is only to be found in Heb. 6.17. Apart from
Hebrews, the noun μεσίτης occurs in Gal. 3.19-20; 1 Tim. 2.5.
3. See A. Oepke, 'μεσίτης', *TDNT*, IV (1967), pp. 598-624.

(μεσιτεύειν) in our Epistle does seem to demand a translation which
conveys the neutrality of one who acts as a guarantor:

> So when God desired to show convincingly to the heirs of the promise the
> unchangeable character of his purpose, he interposed (ἐμεσίτευεν) with
> an oath (6.17 RSV).

Here the author is alluding to God's promise to Abraham that he
would be blessed with progeny. Although this promise occurs more
than once in Genesis (cf. Gen. 12.1-4; 17.1-8; 15.21), Heb. 6.13-18
seems to have Gen. 22.16-18 particularly in mind, since this is the one
occasion on which the promise is accompanied by an oath. After
Abraham has demonstrated his obedience, even to the point of being
prepared to sacrifice Isaac, God emphatically (i.e. by swearing an
oath) renewed his promise:

> By myself I have sworn, says the Lord, because you have done this, and
> have not withheld your son, your only son, I will indeed bless
> you . . . (Gen. 22.16, 17a).

Our author appeals to this twofold word of God, that is, the promise,
'guaranteed by an oath' (= NEB translation of ἐμεσίτευεν at 6.17), as
a double surety of God's unshakeable fidelity to the promises made to
Abraham's heirs.[1]

The guarantor of the promise is God Himself. The guarantee is the
oath. Our author is not concerned with the problem of how God can
be called to testify on His own behalf as to the truth of His word.
Philo, on the other hand, was, and discusses how God can swear by
Himself. He concludes:

> God is the strongest guarantor (βεβαιωτής), first for himself and then for
> his works, so that it was reasonable for him to swear by himself in giving
> assurance regarding himself, which was impossible for anyone else.[2]

The author of Hebrews is also aware that, 'Men indeed swear by a
greater than themselves', but continues, 'and in all their disputes an
oath is final for confirmation' (6.16). Rather than speculate about how
God can be said to swear an oath, he is more concerned to focus upon
the definitive character of an oath. It is the last word.

Hence he appeals to the oath to affirm the definitive character of

---

1. For Christians as heirs of the promise to Abraham, see Rom. 4.13, 16.
2. *Leg. All.* 3.207.

Jesus' Melchizedekian high priesthood. It is clearly superior to the Aaronic priesthood since the latter was not inaugurated by God swearing an oath (7.20). Thus Hebrews interprets Ps 109(MT 110).4 as confirmation of the supremacy of Jesus' Melchizedekian high priesthood:

> The Lord has sworn and will not change his mind, 'Thou art a priest forever after the order of Melchizedek'. This makes Jesus the surety (ἔγγυος) of a better covenant (7.21-22).

By appealing to Scripture's silence with regard to an oath on the occasion of the institution of the Aaronic priesthood, he is able to deny (*contra*, for example, Exod. 29.9; 40.14) its eternal validity. By drawing upon mention of an oath in the psalm he is able to claim a finality for Christ's Melchizedekian priesthood, just as, via an appeal to the oath of Genesis 22, he has been able to demonstrate that God has not reneged upon His promises to Abraham, and that they remain for 'the heirs of the promise' (6.17). Mediatorial language, applied to promise and priesthood in chs. 6 and 7, is used, therefore, not so much in the sense of a middle-man between God and His people, but as God's own guarantee of Jesus as His final word.

Yet if we are to appreciate the Epistle's presentation of Jesus as mediator we must look much further than the rare use of μεσίτης, to Judaism's established mediatorial figures with which he is compared and contrasted. But before we can do this we must discuss some of the issues concerning the role of intermediaries in first-century Judaism's theological understanding; not least because either implicitly or explicitly our conclusions about these will inevitably influence the way we read our Epistle.

From the Scriptures themselves it is evident that God is depicted as employing various agents, both human and angelic, who are permitted to cross the sacred/secular divide. The issue is whether there is any evidence that first-century Jewish tradition interpreted these as 'intermediaries', essential for the very possibility of contact between God and His world. Certainly for Platonic philosophy, in all its stages, such contact between a transcendent deity and a material world was a problem. In neo-Platonism, from Plotinus[1] in the third century CE

---

1. See A.H. Armstrong, 'Plotinus', in *The Cambridge History of Later Greek and Early Medieval Philosophy* (ed. A.H. Armstrong; Cambridge: Cambridge University

onwards, a hierarchy of intermediaries between the divine 'One beyond being' and the multiplicity of the world was postulated as a means of bridging the gap. These intermediaries formed the essential rungs of the ladder between the human and the divine. The very One itself was not without its gradations, with being, life and intellect as three hypostases in descending order in the 'godhead'. These philosophical speculations were to influence Christian trinitarian formulations, but were they present even in the period of the New Testament? Although scholars would not claim a full-blown neo-Platonic doctrine of intermediaries for first-century Judaism or Christianity, there is an ever present danger of reading the philosophical problems of one generation and culture back into the theological writings of another. Hence, there are those who see, for example in the writings of Philo of Alexandria, that self-same philosophical concern to reconcile a transcendent God with a material universe which we find in Platonism. On that assumption, Philo's presentation of mediatorial figures such as angels, Moses and the high priest is conditioned by a philosophical necessity, wherein God Himself is unable to act directly in the world. Philo's development of such agents as God's word (λόγος), wisdom (σοφία), spirit (πνεῦμα) and powers (δυνάμεις) are then seen as dictated by the same Platonic necessity, and become the divine hypostases of a lower order, able therefore to communicate with the world.

It is undoubtedly true that in Philo we meet a Judaism which has been influenced by contemporary Hellenistic philosophy. Furthermore, he was evidently sensitive to the philosophical difficulties inherent in attempting to maintain, at one and the same time, both the transcendence and the immanence of God.[1] Platonism asserted the one and Stoicism the other. True to biblical Judaism, Philo maintained both. Where it served his theological purposes he was not averse to drawing upon Hellenistic philosophical traditions, but eclectically and rarely without modification. So, for example, while he is content to adopt a Platonic cosmology of a two-stage creation, with the creation of the world of Ideas followed by the creation of the material universe

Press, 1967), pp. 195-271; A.C. Lloyd, 'The Later Neoplatonists', in *Cambridge History*, pp. 272-325.

1. See Isaacs, *Concept of Spirit*, pp. 27-31; H. Chadwick, 'Philo', in *Cambridge History*, pp. 137-57.

patterned upon it, by making the Ideas the very thoughts of God,[1] he emphasized to a far greater extent than Platonism the correspondence between the Ideal and its material form. Like the pseudo-Aristotelian tract *De Mundo*, Philo believed that God was both above the world and yet a vital, pervading force within it. God cannot be known in Himself. As τὸ ὄν—the Existent—He is incomprehensible and can only be known through His appearance rather than in His reality.[2] By the less enlightened these appearances are mistaken for God Himself,[3] whereas even for these images we are dependent upon God's gracious self-revelation.[4]

Philo sometimes refers to these media of God's self-revelation as though they were lower levels in the being of God. Certainly that is how God's wisdom, word, spirit and powers function in Philo. They are the 'face' God turns to the world. Henry Chadwick has described this as a

> stage on the way towards middle Platonist and Neoplatonist speculations about two or three levels of being in God. *It is, however, no more than a stage . . .* [5] (italics mine).

We meet no more 'Platonized' form of Judaism than that espoused by Philo. Yet even here there is nothing which demands an interpretation of God's agents as Middle or neo-Platonic intermediaries. Long ago G.F. Moore refuted the suggestion that rabbinic Judaism provides any evidence of such,[6] and more recently H.A. Wolfson came to the same conclusion with regard to Philo. His opinion is aptly and succinctly summed up in his sub-title, 'The Fiction of Intermediaries'.[7] So we

1. Philo, *Op. Mund.* 20; *Conf. Ling.* 63; *Cher.* 49; *Spec. Leg.* 1.47-48. See Chadwick, 'Philo', p. 142, who claims that Philo is the earliest witness to this belief. Cf. Seneca, *Ep.* 65.7.

2. Philo, *Mut. Nom.* 27.

3. Philo, *Mut. Nom.* 28; *Somn.* 2.189; *Omn. Prob. Lib.* 43; *Det. Pot. Ins.* 161; *Vit. Mos.* 1.158.

4. Philo, *Leg. All.* 3.78; 1.31-42.

5. Chadwick, 'Philo', p. 142.

6. G.F. Moore, *Judaism in the First Centuries of the Christian Era: The Age of the Tannaim*, I (Cambridge, MA: Harvard University Press, 1927), p. 417; *idem*, 'Intermediaries in Jewish Theology', *HTR* 15 (1962), pp. 41-85. See also Strack–Billerbeck, III, pp. 302-33; J. Abelson, *The Immanence of God in Rabbinical Literature* (London: Macmillan, 1912), pp. 146-73.

7. Wolfson, *Philo*, I, p. 282.

may conclude that these mediatorial agents in Philo no more have an independent, hypostatic existence than do plans in an architect's mind. They are personifications of divine attributes; those aspects of God by which He chooses to reveal Himself.[1]

It is true that, like Platonism, Judaism felt a need to justify the possibility of a relationship between God and the world. Unlike Platonism, however, this was not due to a perceived disjunction between the phenomenal world of sense perception and the Ideal, immaterial world. Sin was what constituted the barrier between the human and the divine, even for a Hellenized Jew such as Philo. The problem for Judaism, unlike later Platonism, was not how a diverse world could emanate from a God who is one, simple and indivisible, but how sin came into a world created by a good God, and, in the face of its presence, how a holy God can have dealings with a sinful world. This will become evident as we look at the mediatorial role assigned to angels, Moses and the high priest in Jewish thinking of the period. Similarly, we shall see that the author of Hebrews' presentation of the mediatorial role of Jesus is dominated by his understanding of the need to overcome the barrier of sin in order to gain approach to God. Hence, neither Jesus nor the mediators whom he supersedes are 'intermediaries' of a Platonic cosmology, but guardians and agents of the sacred, divinely appointed to cross the divine/human divide.

In Jewish tradition God is not obliged to use an intermediary. He can and does on occasion act without an agent. The same can be said of His activity in the future. According to some Jewish hopes He will personally intervene without any mediator.[2] In others it is thought that He will operate via an agent or agents to bring about the final consummation of His purposes. Where a place is made for such figures, they are clearly modelled on those established mediators between God and Israel of the past, enshrined in Scripture. Thus in Israel's eschatological hopes in the postexilic period, we find not one but a number of salvific figures—Mosaic, priestly, Davidic, angelic—espoused by one

1. See Isaacs, *Concept of Spirit*, pp. 52-58, for a refutation of those who would see πνεῦμα as an 'intermediary' in Hellenistic Judaism.

2. On the absence of a messianic figure in 1 and 2 Macc.; Tobit; Wis. Sol.; Ecclus; *Jub.*; *1 En.* 1–36; 91–104; *Ass. Mos.*; *1 Bar.*; and *2 En.*, see D.S. Russell, *The Method and Message of Jewish Apocalyptic* (Philadelphia: Fortress Press, 1964). 'These particular writers apparently see no need for a human agent, for the coming of the kingdom is the work of God himself' (p. 309). Cf. also 1QM 18.1-3.

group or another as the model for God's agent, who would inaugurate His sovereign reign on earth or in heaven. In his presentation of Jesus as the final, definitive agent of God, the author of Hebrews, therefore, compares and contrasts him with Israel's principal mediators who have gone before.

2. *Jesus and Moses*

In the Qumran Covenanters we have a group for whom 'a prophet like Moses' played a part in their eschatological hopes for God's new age. 'There shall come the prophet and the messiahs of Aaron and Israel.'[1] Exactly what is meant by 'messiahs of Aaron and Israel' is disputed, as we shall shortly see. Most scholars, however, are agreed that 'the prophet' in Qumran's eschatological schema was either envisaged by the Covenanters as Moses *redivivus*, or as a prophet in the same mould as Moses, who would come in fulfilment of the prophecy:

> The Lord your God will raise up for you a prophet like me from among you . . . and I will put my words in his mouth, and he shall speak to them all that I command him (Deut. 18.15, 18bc).

This passage was used by the Covenanters as part of their *Testimonia*.[2] It is not clear, however, whether the prophet is to precede the messianic figures[3] or whether he is to be part of a triumvirate consisting of prophet, priest and king. In some Jewish traditions the prophet is identified with Elijah[4] rather than Moses, and functions as the forerunner who announces the impending 'Day of the Lord'.[5] Synoptic tradition assigns this role to John the Baptist.[6]

---

1. 1QS 9.10; Vermes, *Dead Sea Scrolls in English*, p. 87.
2. 4QTest; Vermes, *Dead Sea Scrolls in English*, pp. 247-48. This prophecy is applied to Jesus in Mk 9.7; Jn 6.14; 7.20; Acts 3.22-23; 7.37.
3. So M.A. Knibb, *The Qumran Community* (Cambridge: Cambridge University Press, 1987), p. 139.
4. Mal. 3.1; 4.5.
5. J. Fitzmyer (*The Gospel according to Luke* [I–IX] [AB; New York: Doubleday, 1979], pp. 671-72) maintains that in pre-Christian Judaism, Elijah functions as the precursor of the Day of the Lord rather than the forerunner of the messiah.
6. Mk 6.14-16; Mt 11.7-15. *Contra* Jn 1.21 where the Baptist denies that he is either Elijah or the prophet.

The figure of Moses has clearly influenced the portrayal of Jesus in the Fourth Gospel. Here he is acclaimed by the people as the new Moses. 'This is indeed the prophet who is to come into the world' (Jn 6.14). Albeit as a greater than Moses (see Jn 1.17-18; 6.32-35), Jesus is the fulfilment of the hope of Moses' return.[1] Some scholars have suggested that this was due to the input of Samaritan converts who joined the Johannine community at some point in their history.[2] In its failure to depict Jesus as a second Moses, the Epistle to the Hebrews is quite unlike either Qumran[3] or John's Gospel, however. Although our author discusses certain similarities between Jesus and Moses, he is emphatic in contrasting, not prophet with prophet, but prophet with son:

> In many and various ways God spoke of old to our fathers by the prophets; but in these last days he has spoken to us by a son (1.1-2).

With these opening words he makes it abundantly clear that the model he is using for Jesus is not that of 'a prophet like Moses', but Son of God.

Hence it is as son over against servant that he is superior to Moses in 3.1-6. But first the two are shown to be comparable in fidelity. C. Spicq heads this section of his commentary, 'La fidélité du Christ est supérieure à celle de Moïse'.[4] Yet Hebrews is not claiming for Jesus a superior fidelity, but a superior relationship to God as son:

---

1. See T.F. Glasson, *Moses in the Fourth Gospel* (London: SCM Press, 1963); W.A. Meeks, *The Prophet-King: Moses Traditions and the Johannine Christology* (Leiden: Brill, 1967).

2. See G.W. Buchanan, 'The Samaritan Origin of the Gospel of John', in *Religions in Antiquity. Essays in Memory of E.R. Goodenough* (ed. J. Neusner; Leiden: Brill, 1968), pp. 149-75; C.H.H. Scobie, 'The Origins and Development of Samaritan Christianity', *NTS* 19 (1972–73), pp. 390-414; Cullman, *Johannine Circle*, pp. 43-49, 57; R.E. Brown, *The Community of the Beloved Disciple* (London: Geoffrey Chapman, 1979), pp. 35-40. The figure of Moses seems to be the model for the Samaritan's salvific figure. Significantly Deut. 18.15-18 comes at the end of the Samaritan Pentateuch. A Moses Christology is also later attested among Ebionites (cf. *Clem. Recog.* 1.36-38; 4.5; *Clem. Hom.* 3.47-49; 8.5-7).

3. See Braun, *Qumran*, II, p. 182, who contrasts Hebrews' Christology with Qumran's 'messianic prophet' expectations.

4. Spicq, *Hébreux*, II, p. 63.

He was faithful (πιστός) to him who appointed him, just as (ὡς καὶ)
Moses was faithful in (all[1]) God's·house (ἐν [ὅλῳ] τῷ οἴκῳ αὐτοῦ)
(3.2).

The theme of the faithfulness (πιστός) of Jesus was introduced at 2.17
with reference to his high priesthood. Now it is picked up with regard
to his relationship to Moses, his faithful forerunner. For our author,
Moses' fidelity lies, not least, in that he was 'to testify to the things
that were spoken later' (3.5b). He functions, therefore, as a faithful
witness to what is to be God's final and definitive word—Jesus. This
point is made succinctly, yet clearly with postexilic Judaism's estimate
of the role of Moses in view. Here, among other scriptural mediatorial figures, as God's agent of revelation Moses reigned supreme.
Num. 12.1-8 is one such estimate (cf. Exod. 33.11) which upholds the
uniqueness of Moses' access to God. All other prophets only know
God indirectly via vision or dream (Num. 12.6):

> Not so with my servant Moses; he is entrusted with all my house. With
> him I speak mouth to mouth, clearly, and not in dark speech; and he
> beholds the form of the Lord (Num. 12.7-8).

In Heb. 3.2, 5, Num. 12.7 is cited from the LXX, where, instead of the
MT 'who is entrusted with all my house', the Greek translators have
'who is faithful in all my house' (ἐν ὅλῳ τῷ οἴκῳ μου πιστὸς ἔστιν).
This version enables our author to stress, not that Moses was supreme
among the people of God, but that among the wilderness generation he
alone was faithful—a theme which we have seen plays an important
role in his exhortation to his readers not to emulate the faithlessness of
the past. It also accounts for the reference to Christ's superior glory
(δόξα) since Num. 12.8 (LXX) reads 'and he [i.e. Moses] saw the
glory of the Lord' (καὶ τὴν δόξαν κυρίου εἶδεν).

> Yet Jesus has been counted worthy of as much more glory than Moses as
> the builder of a house has more honour than the house (3.3).

The superiority of a builder to his building was an established commonplace in the ancient world.[2] We do well to remind ourselves of
this before drawing from it unwarranted inferences. The author of

---

1. ὅλῳ is omitted in P13, P46, B, the Coptic versions, Cyril and Ambrose. Its
inclusion may well be a secondary assimilation to v. 5, where it is cited from Num.
12.7 (LXX).
2. See Bruce, *Hebrews*, p. 57 n. 13.

Hebrews is not employing this metaphor in order to deny the existence
of the people of God, His household, prior to the establishment of the
Christian church! As we have already seen, he is far too sensible of
the continuity of faith among men and women of the past and the
present. As the following verse shows, furthermore, his Christology is
always subservient to his theology. Ultimately it is God who is the
creator of the whole universe. 'For every house is built by someone,
but the builder of all things is God' (3.4). In the Epistle's prologue, to
the son has been ascribed the work of God's agent in creation,
'through whom he also created the world' (1.2). In the light of this it
is possible that in 3.3 he means that Christ is the builder of the household of God, although, since he does not say so, here he may have
nothing more in mind than the use of an established *a fortiori* argument for supremacy. If he is referring implicitly to the son as God's
agent in creation, then 'the house' he builds is God's people of faith in
all generations. Hence our author stresses (3.6) that even its present
members only remain so if they keep steadfast, confidently looking to
God's future.

Mary R. D'Angelo has suggested that our author cites not Num.
12.7 but 1 Chron. 17.14 at 3.2.[1] This is Nathan's oracle to David,
confirming the reign of his dynasty in perpetuity:

> But I will confirm (LXX πιστώσω) him in my house and in my kingdom
> forever (1 Chron. 17.14).

S. Aalen had earlier suggested that this passage, as well as Num. 12.7,
lay behind Heb. 3.1-6. Apart from the Septuagint's associative
πιστώσω (I will entrust, confirm), the Targum on 1 Chron. 17.14
has, 'I will maintain him [i.e. the Davidic son] faithful among my
people and in my house forever'.[2] In which case, Jesus, the faithful
Davidic son, is contrasted with Moses, the faithful household servant
(θεράπων). Since, as we shall see, in ch. 1 our author cites other
biblical texts, which by the first century CE had established themselves
as 'messianic', to demonstrate that Jesus is Davidic son, Aalen may
well be right in seeing a reference to David as well as Moses in 3.2.
We must not lose sight, however, of the fact that 3.1-6 is dealing

---

1. D'Angelo, *Moses*, pp. 69, 89.
2. S. Aalen, '"Reign" and "House" in the Kingdom of God in the Gospels',
NTS 8 (1961), pp. 215-40.

principally with Num. 12.1-8, a passage which rebukes even Moses' own family, Aaron and Miriam, for questioning his supremacy. It is evident that the author of Hebrews is aware of the unique role ascribed to Moses in Scripture and tradition, and wishes, equally by an appeal to Scripture, to demonstrate that Christ has superseded him.

Jesus' status as son is the principal argument our author uses to this end. In chs. 1 and 2 he has laid the scriptural foundation for this claim. Now in ch. 3 he draws out the implications of this for the respective positions of Moses and Jesus. In God's household they stand as servant to son; of common household membership and fidelity, but with a different status. Since the role of son is the dominant one in the first three chapters, and not that of a royal priest,[1] it is unlikely, as D'Angelo suggests, that we have here also a reference to 1 Sam. 2.35:

> And I will raise up for myself a faithful priest. . . and I will build him a sure house, and he shall go in and out before my anointed forever.

This oracular promise, that the sons of Eli would be replaced by a faithful priest (LXX ἱερέα πιστόν) officiating in a sure house (LXX οἶκον πιστόν [faithful house]), had already been brought together with the Nathan oracle, she believes, in Jewish interpretative tradition, functioning as twin testimonies to a Davidic son and a messianic priest. Even prior to Christianity, therefore, in some Jewish circles the messianic and the priestly had coalesced in one figure.[2] That our Epistle draws upon a priestly model in its depiction of Christ is evident. That it does so in 3.1-6, however, is not. Although the chapter begins with a call to 'consider Jesus, the apostle (ἀπόστολον) and high priest (ἀρχιερέα) of our confession', it is the respective roles of the two emissaries (ἀπόστολοι), Jesus and Moses, that is pursued, not the theme of Jesus' high priesthood. That is not picked up again until 4.14. In the meantime the topic is the wilderness generation, introduced by a discussion of that generation's leader, Moses.

There are traditions in first-century CE Judaism which extol Moses not only as Law-giver and king, but also as high priest,[3] although it is not as an exemplar of priesthood that we meet him in Hebrews.[4]

---

1. *Contra* D'Angelo, *Moses*, p. 83.
2. D'Angelo, *Moses*, pp. 65-93.
3. See Philo, *Vit. Mos.* 2.66-186; *Praem. Poen.* 52-55; *Gig.* 52-54.
4. *Contra* Dey, *Intermediary World*, pp. 157-63, who maintains that 'high priest' is one of Moses' titles, appropriated for Christ by Hebrews.

Neither does our author present him as king, unlike Philo[1] who
idealizes Moses with colours taken from Plato's portrait of the
philosopher-king, the one who alone is able to grasp reality.[2] For
Philo, as the friend of God,[3] Moses has been granted a unique beatific
vision.[4] Although no one can see God Himself (τὸ ὄν), to Judaism's
founder has been given, albeit indirectly via the operation of God's
'powers' in the world,[5] an unparalleled revelation of God. This is why
Exod. 4.16 and 7.1 can speak of him as god (LXX θεός). Philo denies
that this means that Moses was divine,[6] although some of the language
he uses of his hero on occasion gets close to it. Carl Holladay's discussion of those passages which seem to divinize Moses has convincingly shown that nowhere does Philo make him divine.[7] Holladay
concedes that the Alexandrian rabbi has an 'undeniable tendency to
overstate'[8] in his presentation of Moses. Yet only marginally more so
than Josephus,[9] for whom Moses is 'the noblest Hebrew of them all'.[10]
Unlike Philo, who thought that he was translated to heaven like
Elijah,[11] Josephus was prepared to concede that Moses had an ordinary mortal's death.[12] His birth, however, had more than the ordinary

---

1. For Philo's treatment of Moses see Meeks, *Prophet-King*, pp. 100-63;
Williamson, *Philo*, pp. 449-91; *idem*, 'Philo and New Testament Christology', in
Studia Biblica 1978, III (ed. E.A. Livingstone; Sheffield: JSOT Press, 1980),
pp. 439-45; C. Holladay, *Theios Aner in Hellenistic Judaism: A Critique of the Use
of this Category in N.T. Christology* (Missoula, MT: Scholars Press, 1977),
pp. 104-67.
   2. Philo, *Rer. Div. Her.* 301; *Conf. Ling.* 1.
   3. Philo, *Vit. Mos.* 1.148-63.
   4. Philo, *Poster. C.* 388; *Mut. Nom.* 2; *Quaest. in Exod.* 2.29.
   5. Philo, *Spec. Leg.* 1.40-42.
   6. Philo, *Vit. Mos.* 1.155. Cf. also Philo's firm insistence on the impossibility of
any human being God (*Vit. Mos.* 1.283; 2.194; etc.). Hence he castigates emperor
worship (*Leg. Gai.* 114, 118, 154), and ridicules the notion of demigods (*Vit. Cont.*
6).
   7. Holladay, *Theios Aner*, pp. 104-67.
   8. Holladay, *Theios Aner*, p. 96.
   9. Holladay, *Theios Aner*, pp. 47-73.
   10. Josephus, *Ant.* 2.229.
   11. Philo, *Vit. Mos.* 2.288-91; *Quaest. in Exod.* 2.29.
   12. Josephus, *Ant.* 4.326. Cf. Jn 3.13 which denies that anyone (other than
Christ) has ascended to heaven.

about it. It was not only predicted by priests;[1] it was miraculously free from labour pains.[2] Like Philo, Josephus's Moses is cast in the Stoic-Cynic mould of the ideal philosopher-king, the very quintessence of stoic virtue (ἀρετή), such virtue now being redefined as religious piety (εὐσεβής),[3] and thereby 'baptized' into Judaism.

In presenting Moses as the acme of all human virtue and the unique recipient of divine revelation, Philo and Josephus are principally concerned to extol the supremacy of Judaism over all other religions and philosophies. Here they stand in an established tradition of Jewish apologetics, as we can see from fragments of the works of their predecessors preserved by Alexander Polyhistor and quoted by Eusebius.[4] According to these apologists for Judaism, Moses was the fount of all learning and culture, who invented writing[5] and instructed the Egyptian priests in hieroglyphics.[6] He was a prince in Egypt,[7] who was called Hermes by the Egyptians.[8] Aristobulus would have him father of all culture—Greek as well as Egyptian.[9]

A few haggadic elements are present in the author of Hebrews' presentation of Moses in 11.23-27. Following the LXX (Exod. 2.2), both parents, rather than his mother only, take the initiative in concealing the newborn (v. 23). In singling out for mention the child's beauty (ἀστεῖον; cf. Exod. 2.2; Acts 7.20) even from birth, as does Philo,[10] our author too may well be intending 'to infer that there was something about the appearance of the child which indicates that he was no ordinary child, but was destined under God to accomplish great things for his people',[11] as F.F. Bruce suggests. In the biblical account

---

1. Josephus, *Ant.* 2.205.
2. Josephus, *Ant.* 2.288.
3. See Holladay, *Theios Aner*, pp. 89-99.
4. See H.W. Attridge, 'Historiography', in *Jewish Writings of the Second Temple Period* (CRINT, 2.2; ed. M.E. Stone; Assen: Van Gorcum, 1984), pp. 160-75.
5. Eupolemus (*Praep. Ev.* 9.26).
6. Artapanus (*Praep. Ev.* 9.27; cf. Clement, *Strom.* 1.23, 154).
7. Ezekiel the Tragedian, 'The Exodus' (*Praep. Ev.* 9.29; cf. Clement, *Strom.* 1.23, 155).
8. Artapanus (*Praep. Ev.* 9.27).
9. Aristobulus (*Praep. Ev.* 7.12; 13.12).
10. Philo, *Vit. Mos.* 1.9 emphasizes that Moses was more than usually beautiful (ἀστειοτερὰν) at birth.
11. Bruce, *Hebrews*, p. 317.

(Exod. 2.5-10) Moses was raised as the son of Pharaoh's daughter, whereas in Hebrews (11.24) he repudiates the title. There is no mention, however, of the tradition we find in Josephus, according to which, when Moses was a child and a diadem was placed upon his head, he tore it off, threw it on the ground and trampled it under-foot.[1] On the other hand, neither does our author mention overtly the reason why Moses was obliged to leave Egypt, that is, because he killed an Egyptian overseer (Exod. 2.11-12). 'He left (κατέλιπεν[2])' Egypt no more afraid of the anger of the king (11.27) than his parents had been intimidated by the royal edict (11.23). Yet it is not Moses' fearlessness which is dwelt upon. Unlike Josephus, who depicts him as the courageous military commander leading his people to freedom,[3] the author of Hebrews makes faith[4] not courage the motivation for his departure from Egypt (11.24). Far from a fearless Moses, we have already encountered (pp. 124-25) him as equally terrified by the Sinai events as the rest of the people (12.21).[5]

It is therefore as a man of faith rather than courage that Moses is presented in Hebrews. This is evident from the fact that Moses is one (11.23-28) of a whole gallery of heroes of the past whose lives have been prompted by faith not fear, and who are paraded before us in ch. 11.[6] They have not themselves received the promised rewards of God. Nonetheless they have seen and greeted their future inheritance, albeit at a distance (11.13, 39). Similarly, Moses 'looked to the reward' (11.26; cf. 10.35; 11.6) which was not to be in his lifetime, but which lay in the future.

Like the others in the list, Moses is here used as an example of the endurance which our author wishes to instil in his readers. Hence he

1. Josephus, *Ant.* 2.232-34.
2. Like the LXX (Exod. 2.15 ἀνεχώρησεν = withdrew), Hebrews also weakens the MT 'fled'. Cf. also Philo, *Leg. All.* 3.12-14, for whom Moses' departure from Egypt is more in the nature of a strategic withdrawal rather than an enforced flight.
3. Holladay, *Theios Aner*, pp. 47-73.
4. It is also faith which prompts him to keep the Passover (Heb. 11.28; cf. Exod. 12.3-12).
5. This is in contrast to Josephus, *Ant.* 2.267-69, who makes Moses unafraid even in the presence of the burning bush.
6. From their presence in both Jewish and Christian sources (cf. Ecclus 40–50; Wis. Sol. 10; 1 Macc. 2; *4 Macc.* 16.20-28; Acts 7; *1 Clem.* 4–6, 7, 10–12, 31, 45, 55) it would seem that such lists were well-established in paraenesis.

stresses the patriarch's willing preference to 'share ill-treatment with the people of God rather than enjoy the fleeting pleasures of sin' (11.25):

> He considered abuse suffered for the Christ (τὸν ὀνειδισμὸν τοῦ Χριστοῦ) greater wealth than the treasures of Egypt, for he looked to the reward (11.26, RSV).

There are a number of problems about this verse. (1) From the immediately preceding reference to Moses' suffering in v. 25, logically he continues to be the subject, and therefore is the one who suffers 'reproach' (ὀνειδισμός). Yet τὸν ὀνειδισμὸν τοῦ Χριστοῦ in terms of the Greek language more naturally refers to the reproach which Christ endures, rather than that undertaken for his sake by Moses. (2) To whom does ὁ Χριστός—the anointed one—refer? The NEB translation, 'the stigma that rests on God's Anointed', captures something of the ambiguity of the phrase. In its present context it could well refer to Moses as one who was privileged to be identified with the hardships suffered by his fellow Israelites (see v. 25). In Old Testament tradition 'the anointed', in either the plural (cf. 1 Chron. 16.22; Ps. 105.15) or singular, can designate the collective people of God. So the psalmist can say

> The Lord is the strength of his people; he is the saving refuge of his anointed (Ps. 28.8; cf. Hab. 3.13).

Like 'servant',[1] 'anointed' can therefore have a corporate as well as an individual reference. This is evident in Ps. 89.50-51 (LXX 88.51-52):

> Remember, O Lord, how thy servant is scorned (LXX τοῦ ὀνειδισμοῦ
>   τῶν δούλων σου);
> how I bear in my bosom the insults (LXX ὠνείδισαν) of the peoples,
> with which thy enemies taunt (LXX ὠνείδισαν) O Lord,
> with which they mock the footsteps of thy anointed
> (LXX with which they have reproached the recompense of thine
>   anointed—οὗ ὠνείδισαν ἀντάλλαγμα[2] τοῦ χριστοῦ σου).

The author of Hebrews seems to be echoing this passage with its reference to the Lord's 'anointed' (Χριστός) who endures insult

---

1. Cf. Isa. 41.8; 43.10; 44.2, 21; 49.3.
2. ἀντάλλαγμα usually means that which is given or received in exchange. Here it should probably be translated 'recompense', 'gain' or 'reward'.

(ὀνειδισμός). Perhaps also he has Ps. 69.7a, 9 (LXX 68.8a, 10) in mind:

> For it is for thy sake that I have borne reproach (ὀνειδισμόν). . .
> For the zeal of thy house has consumed me,
> and the insults of those who have insulted thee (ὀνειδισμοὶ τῶν
>   ὀνειδιζόντων σε) have fallen on me.

The apostle Paul alludes to this passage in Rom. 15.3, and makes Jesus the one who endures insult. This should not, of course, dictate how we understand its use in Hebrews. Our author's other two uses of ὀνειδισμός do not decide its meaning in this verse, either. In 10.33 it is his Christian readers who have been subject to the insults (ὀνειδισμοί) of outsiders,[1] whereas in 13.13 it is the abuse which Jesus endured which is held out as the exemplar for Christians to follow. (3) If τὸν ὀνειδισμὸν τοῦ Χριστοῦ is taken as a reference to the disgrace suffered by Jesus in his Passion (as in 13.13), in what sense can Moses' actions be motivated by events which were to come in the future?

The answer to this last question can be seen if we read the verse in the light of the whole of ch. 11. Here Israel's heroes of old are depicted as men and women, driven by their faith in an as yet unseen future—a future which culminates in Christ. Moses, as one of their number, is sustained in his obedience and perseverance by that vision also, 'for he endured as seeing him who is invisible' (11.27b). Here our author has far more than the vision granted to Moses in the burning bush (Exod. 3.2-6) in mind.[2] As the unique mediator chosen by God to be the recipient of the Torah (see Exod. 33–34), Moses is able to meet God 'face to face' (Exod. 33.11).[3] Unlike John's Gospel, which denies this vision of God to any other than the son (Jn 1.18), Hebrews accepts Moses as a 'visionary'. As in the Fourth Gospel, he is subordinate to Jesus. Yet our author arrives at this conclusion by a different route. He makes the self-same point not by denying vision to

---

1. In 1 Tim. 3.7 anyone who aspires to the office of overseer (ἐπίσκοπός) in the church must ensure that his life does not evoke the reproach (ὀνειδισμός) of the non-Christian.

2. See Bruce, *Hebrews*, p. 323, who, rather than confining it to one occasion, interprets this as a reference to Moses' life-long vision of God.

3. Cf. Philo, *Mut. Nom.* 7, where Moses' entering the darkness (Exod. 20.21) is interpreted as his entering the realm of the invisible (ἄορατος).

Moses, but by making Christ the subject of that vision. Which is not to suggest that the one who is invisible in 11.27b is Jesus. Clearly God is intended (cf. 11.6b). Yet in 11.26 the future Christ seems to be included in the content of Moses' vision of unseen realities. The insult suffered by the Lord's 'anointed' is, as P.E. Hughes puts it,

> not simply the reproach accepted by identifying himself with the people of God but, more precisely, the reproach of the coming Messiah with whom he was united by faith.[1]

It refers, therefore, not only to the suffering of Moses, the Lord's anointed. It also implies his obedience to and solidarity with the reproach to be endured by the future Christ, foreknowledge of which has been granted to Moses through divine vision or inspiration. Christ's future Passion, therefore, constitutes part of God's revelation of the as yet 'invisible', that is, his plan of salvation operative in the future. By making Jesus' experience the motivating force and model for Moses' actions, the latter thereby conforms to the former and not vice versa. Thus the author of Hebrews is enabled to make Judaism's supreme mediatorial figure both the forerunner of Christ, and subordinate to him who is the content of Mosaic revelation.

And this surely is what our author is trying to achieve—to make Scripture subject to Jesus by making Jesus the subject of Scripture. He is not trying to promulgate a doctrine of Christ's pre-existence; he is trying to lay claim to Christology as the overriding hermeneutical principle by which Scripture is to be understood. In this sense Christ can be seen as walking the streets of the people of God's previous history. It is doubtful, however, whether we can infer from this that our author believed that it was a pre-existent Christ who appeared to Moses.[2] In this connection, we need to exercise caution in reading the Christology of Hebrews as though it is identical to that of Paul or the author of the Fourth Gospel. J.D.G. Dunn's *Christology in the Making*[3] has questioned the tendency to read a doctrine of pre-existence into a number of New Testament works. He concludes that it is

---

1. P.E. Hughes, *Hebrews*, pp. 496-97.

2. *Contra* A.T. Hanson, 'Christ and the O.T. according to Hebrews', *Studia Evangelica* 2 (1964), pp. 394-97; *idem*, *Living Utterances*, p. 107; D'Angelo, *Moses*, pp. 155-86.

3. J.D.G. Dunn, *Christology in the Making: An Inquiry into the Origins of the Doctrine of the Incarnation* (London: SCM Press, 1980).

not to be found in Paul's writings,[1] and maintains that only the Fourth Gospel has a Christology of an incarnation of a pre-existent being.[2] Whether we agree with all his conclusions or not, Dunn's work should certainly make us cautious about seeing pre-existence as extensive in the New Testament. There are certainly dangers in trying to build a case for a belief in Christ's pre-existence in Hebrews upon supposed Pauline parallels. In our Epistle, for example, we find no christological utilization of earlier Jewish exegetical traditions, wherein both the rock (cf. 1 Cor. 10.4) from which Moses struck water and the manna (cf. Jn 6.25-71) became identified with God's wisdom.[3] Rather we meet the claim that Moses was granted foresight of God's plan. Therefore to see Christ in the Scriptures is not to read something new into them. As part of the 'better things to come' he had always been integral to God's plan, even at the time of Moses. Indeed, Moses himself has been privy to God's future intention. The Torah of which he was God's mediator is and always was, therefore, intended as a witness to Christ.

Thus we can see that our author's estimate of the figure of Moses is all of a piece with his view of Scripture. It is inherently christological, and has been from its very inception. Therefore both Moses and Scripture function as servants in God's household, whose task is to serve the son.

3. *Jesus, the High Priest and Melchizedek*

The most obvious mediatorial figure in Judaism in the period of the Second Temple was the high priest. As we have already seen (pp. 88-

---

1. Dunn, *Christology*, pp. 127-28, 194-96.
2. Dunn, *Christology*, pp. 249-50.
3. Philo (*Det. Pot. Ins.* 115; *Leg. All.* 2.86) identifies the rock with divine wisdom. See H. Conzelmann, *1 Corinthians* (Hermeneia; Philadelphia: Fortress Press, 1975), p. 167, who suggests that here both Paul and Philo are drawing upon common haggadic tradition. Since Philo allegorically equates rock, water and manna (*Det. Pot. Ins.* 118), we may infer that he is also aware of Jewish tradition, wherein the manna was identified with God's wisdom/word (cf. *Leg. All.* 3.169-77)/law (cf. Ecclus 24; *Congr.* 170, 173-74). For a discussion of the respective treatments of the manna by Philo and the Fourth Gospel see P. Borgen, *Bread from Heaven: An Exegetical Study of the Concept of Manna in the Gospel of John and the Writings of Philo* (NovTSup; Leiden: Brill, 1965).

115), the Aaronic priesthood as a whole functioned as divinely appointed guardians of the sacred. The priest's specific role of offering all or part of the victim[1] sacrificed by the worshipper was intended to sanctify the offerer through the offering, thereby admitting the secular into the orbit of the sacred. In the case of expiatory sacrifices the barrier of sin was removed and access to God facilitated. *Par excellence*, this can be seen in the role played by the high priest in the Day of Atonement ceremonies. On that day only, he alone (albeit as representative of all the people of Israel) went behind the dividing curtain and entered that most sacred space—the holy of holies, the innermost sanctum of the shrine.

So far we have discussed how Hebrews 8–10 draws a parallel between the death and session of Jesus and the actions of the high priest on the Day of Atonement. The basic point of comparison between the two is the offering of a purificatory sacrifice as the *sine qua non* of entry into the presence of God. For our author it is the death of Jesus which constitutes the necessary sacrifice, by virtue of which he has been enabled to enter that ultimate sphere of the sacred—heaven.

The Epistle to the Hebrews itself has accustomed us to a priestly model for the work of Christ; so much so that we can fail to appreciate how innovative it is when compared to the rest of the New Testament. There Judaism's priesthood is more often than not depicted as antithetical to Jesus and his followers.[2] What, then, led our author to draw upon the role of the high priest in the Jewish cult and make it the cornerstone of his soteriology?

Some scholars see this merely as the extension of a process which we can see at work in other part of the New Testament, wherein cultic

---

1. The individual worshipper normally killed his own victim (Lev. 5.3; 2.8, 13; 4.24, 29, 33) except on public occasions, when the animal was slaughtered by one of the lower ranks of the priesthood on the people's behalf (2 Chron. 30.17; Ezek. 44.1). The priest's specific function was to pour the blood of the sacrifice around the altar, and there present any other part of the victim prescribed for that specific category of sacrifice. In the case of the holocaust (*'ōlāh*) that was the animal in its entirety, whereas in the communion offering (*zebaḥ šĕlāmîm*) the carcase was shared between God, the priest and the worshipper. See de Vaux, *Ancient Israel*, pp. 415-21.

2. See Lk. 10.31-32; Mt. 26.3; Jn 11.49; Mt. 26.65; Mk 14.63; Lk. 22.71; Jn 18.13-14, 19-24, 28; Acts 4.6. Acts 6.7, however, claims that the early church gained converts from the ranks of the Jewish priesthood.

imagery is applied to the person and work of Jesus. So, from Jesus as
sacrificial victim it is but a short step to Jesus the high priest who
offers the sacrifice. Certainly, as we have seen, Hebrews depicts the
death of Jesus as an expiatory offering. Yet why of all New Testament
authors is he the only one to go further and present Jesus, not only as
sacrificial victim, but also as high priest?

The question remains unanswered if we look to New Testament
traditions which utilize other cultic vocabulary, such as 'temple' or
'shrine', as the source of our author's priestly model. In Mk 14.58 the
false testimony of Jesus' accusers at his trial is:

> We heard him say I will destroy this temple that is made with hands and in
> three days I will build another not made with hands (cf. Mk 15.29).

In the Fourth Gospel, however, the words, 'Destroy this temple and in
three days I will raise it up' (Jn 2.19), are placed on the lips of Jesus
himself, in response to the Jews' demand for a sign to justify his
actions in 'cleansing' the Temple. John clearly denies that any reference to the Jerusalem Temple was intended by Jesus (Jn 2.20). Rather,
'He spoke of the temple of his body' (Jn 2.21). By understanding
'temple' as a metaphor for Jesus' body the saying is transformed from
an accusation into a confident prediction of his death and resurrection.
Yet this can hardly be the source of Hebrews' priestly model for
Jesus. Not least, the word employed in both John and Mark for
temple/shrine is ναός, whereas our author uses σκηνή or ἅγια.
Whether or not the temple image was originally used of Jesus and
subsequently transferred to the church, or vice versa,[1] the Christian
community soon saw itself as the new Temple, and it is this tradition,
rather than Jesus as the new Temple, which we find predominantly in
the New Testament.[2]

For the author of Hebrews, the cult place has not been replaced by
the church, but superseded altogether, and re-located in heaven.
Therefore, to apply the image of the Temple, even a new Temple, to
the church would undermine his analogy between the work of Jesus
and the role of the high priest on the Day of Atonement. A central
part of that argument is that Christ is superior to the Aaronic high

---

1. See p. 64 nn. 1, 2.
2. See 1 Cor. 3.16 (cf. 6.19); 2 Cor. 6.16; Eph 2.20-22; 1 Pet. 2.4-5; Rev. 11.1-
3 (?).

priesthood, not least in that the shrine he has entered is not located on earth but is heaven itself. The people of God have not yet entered heaven. Jesus alone has done that. It seems highly unlikely, therefore, that the author of Hebrews has developed his priestly model for Jesus from the language of 'temple', applied in other Christian traditions either to Christ or (more often) to the church.

The intercessory role assigned to Jesus in both Pauline and Johannine tradition has been suggested as another possible source of Hebrews' depiction of Jesus as high priest. In Rom. 8.34 session and intercession are linked. 'Christ Jesus. . . who is at the right hand of God, who indeed intercedes for us.' C. Spicq looks to John rather than Paul for the origin of our author's priestly model of Jesus.[1] He categorizes the prayer of Jesus for his disciples in John 17 as 'high priestly', since to plead the people's cause before God was part of the function of the high priest on the Day of Atonement. The latter contention is certainly true, as can be seen, for example, in the description of Aaron's vestments. Engraved upon each onyx stone attached to the shoulder-pieces of the high priest's ephod are the names of six of the twelve tribes of Israel (Exod. 28.5-14; 39.6-7). Each of the twelve stones on the breastplate also contains the name of one of the tribes (Exod. 39.8-21). These are described as 'stones of remembrance for the sons of Israel' (Exod. 28.11), which Aaron shall bring before the Lord. There is no doubt that the author of Hebrews draws upon this priestly model for the intercessory function he ascribes to the ascended Christ. So, like the high priest, he now appears in the presence of God on our behalf (9.24). His enduring priestly work[2] is not

---

1. C. Spicq, 'L'origine johannique de la conception du Christ-prêtre dans l'épître aux Hébreux', in *Aux sources de la tradition chrétienne. Melanges offerts à M.M. Goguel* (Neuchâtel: Delachaux & Niestlé, 1950), pp. 258-69; *idem, Hébreux*, I, pp. 109-38.

2. At 7.24 Jesus' priesthood is described as ἀπαράβατος. *Contra* Phillips, TEV, Héring, Spicq, Montefiore and Moffatt, it is unlikely that this is to be understood in the passive sense of 'without successor', since there is no evidence of such usage in contemporary Greek. Rather it should be taken in its active sense of 'permanent' or 'unchangeable' (so RSV, NEB, Knox, Windisch, Bruce, Wilson *et al.*). P. Ellingworth ('The Unshakeable Priesthood: Hebrews 7.24', *JSNT* 23 [1985], pp. 125-26) suggests that it is a synonym for 'unshakeable (ἀσάλευτος; see 12.27). P.E. Hughes (*Hebrews*) points out that most early Greek fathers understood

that of offering the sacrifice (that is the prerequisite of his entry into the heavenly shrine), but of interceding on behalf of the people of God:

> Consequently he is able for all time to save those who draw near to God through him, since he always lives to make intercession for them (7.25).

It would be reading too much into John 17, however, to see this self-same high priestly model at work there. It is one thing to claim an intercessory function for the high priest in Judaism. It is quite another to confine this to the priesthood. Advocacy before God on behalf of the people can also be exercised by the patriarchs,[1] by the king[2] or by angels.[3] We cannot, therefore, assume that whenever Jesus is depicted as interceding he is being clothed, as it were, in the high priest's ephod.[4]

In the case of 1 John there is more to be said for a cultic background to Jesus' intercessory function, since his role as advocate (παράκλητος) is overtly linked with expiation (ἱλασμός):

> if anyone does sin, we have an advocate with the Father, Jesus Christ the righteous; and he is the expiation for our sins, and not ours only but also for the sins of the world (1 Jn 2.1-2).

Yet this does not allow us to interpret John's Gospel as portraying Jesus in priestly terms. In the Gospel παράκλητος is a designation of the Holy Spirit's activity,[5] which is to defend and guide the disciples in

---

ἀπαράβατος here to mean 'intransmissable', however, and therefore suggests that it may convey both active and passive meanings. 'In our view, the appropriateness of the term is enhanced by its ambivalence: the priesthood of Christ does not pass to another, precisely because it is a perpetual priesthood' (*Hebrews*, p. 269 n. 34).

1. E.g. Abraham (Gen. 18.22-33); Moses (Exod. 32.30-34). The prophets are also depicted as intercessors. See Amos 7.2; Jer. 14.11; 18.20; Ezek. 9.8; 11.13.

2. E.g. Solomon (2 Chron. 6.12-21); Hezekiah (2 Kgs 20.2-11).

3. Job 5.1; 33.19-25; Zech. 1.12. The intercessory function of Israel's heroes on her behalf comes to the fore in postexilic, apocalyptic works, which also stress the role of angels (especially Michael) in this respect. See S. Mowinckel, 'Die Vorstellung des Spätjudentums vom Heiligen Geist als Fürsprecher und der johanneische Paraklet', *ZNW* 32 (1933), pp. 97-100; J. Behm, 'παράκλητος', *TDNT*, V, pp. 810-11.

4. *Contra* Spicq, 'L'origine johannique', p. 263, who takes the reference to Jesus' seamless robe (Jn 19.23) to be a conscious echo of the high priest's vestment.

5. Jn 14.16, 26; 15.26; 16.7.

the world, rather than plead their cause before God in heaven.[1]

The suggestion that Hebrews' high priestly presentation of Jesus is but a variant of the suffering servant 'concept' of Deutero-Isaiah,[2] or that it represents a sublimation and re-interpretation of the servant,[3] is equally unconvincing as an explanation of its origin. Apart from Morna D. Hooker's contention that no such servant figure had been isolated within Israel's interpretative tradition of the Isaianic corpus, and that we find scant evidence of the utilization of any such suffering servant 'concept' in the New Testament,[4] our author nowhere calls Jesus παῖς or δοῦλος. Some[5] see an allusion to Isa. 53.12 (LXX), 'he bore the sins of many (καὶ αὐτὸς ἁμαρτίας πολλῶν ἀνήνεγκε)'[6] in Heb. 9.28:

> So Christ, having been offered once to bear the sins of many (ἅπαξ προσενεχθεὶς εἰς τὸ πολλῶν ἀνενεγκεῖν ἁμαρτίας) will appear a second time, not to deal with sin but to save those who are eagerly waiting for him.

The most Hooker is prepared to concede is that Isaiah 53 may have been a source from which Hebrews derived the idea of Christ as a victim for sin.[7] Therefore, if Hebrews is dependent upon the Isaianic tradition, it is not for a supposed 'servant Christology', but as a model for Christ as victim.

Which leads us back once more to the all-important point; that whereas in other New Testament writings we can find Jesus depicted in cultic terms, as sacrificial victim, or (more rarely) new Temple, nowhere outside the Epistle to the Hebrews is that cultic imagery extended in terms of Christ as priest. Even his intercessory activity is only identified as an overtly priestly act in our Epistle.

---

1. Jn 14.26; 15.26; 16.13. See M.E. Isaacs, 'The Prophetic Spirit in the Fourth Gospel', *HeyJ* 24 (1983), pp. 391-407.
2. O. Cullmann (*The Christology of the New Testament* [London: SCM Press, 2nd edn, 1963], p. 91) also closely relates Jesus' high priesthood in Hebrews with the suffering servant.
3. J.R. Schaefer, 'The Relationship between Priestly and Servant Messianism in the Epistle to the Hebrews', *CBQ* 30 (1968), pp. 359-85.
4. Hooker, *Servant, passim*.
5. E.g., Wilson, *Hebrews*, p. 169, 'an echo'; Bruce, *Hebrews*, p. 223, 'a plain echo'; P.E. Hughes, *Hebrews*, p. 388, 'a plain allusion'.
6. Cf. 1 Pet. 2.24.
7. Hooker, *Servant*, pp. 123-24.

The most obvious source of the author of Hebrews' priestly model for Jesus is the one he cites himself; Psalm 110. We have already noted[1] that the first verse:

> The Lord says to my Lord:
> 'Sit at my right hand,
> till I make your enemies your footstool,

is appealed to by a number of New Testament writers, including our own (1.3, 13; 8.1; 10.12-13; 12.2). In first-century Jewish and Christian tradition this psalm was interpreted as referring to the messiah. Hence, in Mk 12.35-37, the fact that it has a messianic referent is common ground between Jesus and the scribes.[2] Yet in the theological exposition of Hebrews, this psalm is used, not only as scriptural affirmation of Christ's session in heaven, but as warrant for viewing his entry into heaven as analogous to the entry of the high priest into the holy of holies on the Day of Atonement. Hence, unlike other New Testament writers, our author moves beyond v. 1 to v. 4:

> The Lord has sworn
>   and will not change his mind,
> 'You are a priest forever
>   after the order of Melchizedek,[3]

and links the two. Hebrews is the only Christian work before Justin Martyr (2nd century CE) to mention Melchizedek, let alone to interpret the work of Christ in Melchizedekian terms. So in Hebrews, not only the presentation of Jesus as a priest, but his depiction as 'a priest after the order of Melchizedek' is quite without precedent in early Christian tradition. The most likely source of this innovation is Psalm 110, with its reference to a non-Aaronic priest, which our author sees as evidence of a superior high priesthood now vested in Jesus.

This is the main theme of 4.14–7.28, which begins with an affirmation of Jesus as high priest in heaven, and quickly moves to lay claim to the office by virtue of his divine appointment:

---

1. See p. 90 n. 4.
2. See D.M. Hay, *Glory at the Right Hand: Psalm 110 in Early Christianity* (SBLMS, 18; Nashville: Abingdon Press, 1973), p. 30. For evidence of its acceptance as messianic in rabbinic tradition see Strack–Billerbeck, IV, pp. 452-65.
3. Ps. 109(MT 110).4 is quoted in Heb. 5.6; 6.20; 7.17 and alluded to in Heb. 4.14; 5.10; 7.3, 11, 21, 24; 8.1.

So Christ did not exalt himself to be made a high priest, but was appointed[1] by him who said to[2] him. . . 'Thou art a priest forever after the order of Melchizedek' (5.5a, 6b).

It is God who has designated Jesus as high priest (5.10), and his ascension, therefore, may be seen as entry into the holy of holies, where he has gone as our forerunner (6.19-20). Which brings our author to his major exposition of Jesus as Melchizedekian priest (7.1-28).

Melchizedek is mentioned only twice in the Old Testament in Psalm 110 and Gen. 14.17-20. Having introduced this non-Aaronic model of priesthood via the psalm, in ch. 7 (vv. 1-3) our author introduces the pentateuchal narrative of the meeting between Abraham and Melchizedek, the Canaanite priest-king. That he omits in his paraphrase of Genesis 14 any mention of Melchizedek providing bread and wine is probably indicative of his general lack of interest in the eucharist. Philo, on the other hand, when dealing with this passage, contrasts Melchizedek's provision of bread and wine with the refusal of the Ammonites and Moabites to supply so much as bread and water to the Israelites in the wilderness. He then proceeds to make them symbols of the divine *logos* or reason, with which God feeds the soul.[3] Both Hebrews and Philo, however, advance the same etymologies for the king's name and city, that is, king of righteousness (zedek = *sedeq*, righteousness),[4] and king of peace (salem = *shâlōm*, peace).[5] In some Jewish traditions Salem becomes identified with Jerusalem,[6] although this is not indicated in our Epistle. Since etymologies in the ancient world were more often than not allegorizations, we can only rely upon those them for evidence of secondary interpretation. It has been suggested that Melchizedek's name may originally have contained a

---

1. In the Greek text there is no verb at this point. It may be inferred, however, from the preceding sentence which speaks of Christ 'being called' (καλούμενος) by God.

2. πρὸς αὐτόν should perhaps be translated 'concerning him' rather than 'to him'. Cf. 1.7, 8.

3. Philo, *Leg. All.* 3.82.

4. *Leg. All.* 3.82.

5. *Leg. All.* 3.79. See also Josephus, *Ant.* 1.10.

6. Cf. Ps. 76.2 where Salem seems to indicate Zion. 1QGen 22.14-15 also identifies Salem with Jerusalem. Josephus (*Ant.* 1.10) makes Melchizedek the founder of the Canaanite city of Jerusalem.

reference to a Canaanite deity, Zedek.[1] In which case it would have meant, 'Zedek's king', which would lend support to the hypothesis that he was originally a Canaanite priest-king.

For the author of Hebrews, the important factor is that he was a priest of non-Levitical descent. That he received tithes from Abraham and blessed him demonstrates not only his superiority to the patriarch, but to those of the descendants of Levi who are to come after him (7.4-9):

> One might even say that Levi himself, who receives tithes, paid tithes through Abraham, for he was still in the loins of his ancestor when Melchizedek met him (7.10).

It is as if our author were anticipating the possible objection that Melchizedek's priesthood had been superseded by the later Levitical order. Hence he claims that, although as yet unborn, Levi was seminally present in the person of his great-grandfather, Abraham, and as such was included in the acceptance of the supremacy of Melchizedek. Hence the Melchizedekian priesthood antedates and has precedence over that which was to begin with Aaron. Although Hebrews assigns to the priests rather than the Levites the task of receiving tithes directly from the people (*contra* Num. 3.5; 18.25; Neh. 10.38), by the first century CE this seems to have been the practice.[2] Clearly by 'descendants of Levi' our author is referring to priests rather than their cultic subordinates, the Levites.[3] The latter are nowhere mentioned in the Epistle, where the only distinction made is between priest and high priest. Our author's interest in Levi is as patriarch of the Aaronic priesthood, in which role he comes to the fore from the second century BCE onwards.[4]

Genesis 14 therefore demonstrates that the type of priesthood which finds its antitype in Jesus has existed since the time of *the* patriarch,[5] Abraham. Furthermore, its silence as to Melchizedek's origins enables our author to infer that:

---

1. In Josh. 10.1 the name of the King of Jerusalem is Adonizedek = 'the Lord is Zedek'. See Horton, *Melchizedek*, p. 44.
2. See Horbury, 'Aaronic Priesthood', p. 50.
3. For the role of the Levites see Exod. 28–30; 40.12-16; Lev. 8.
4. See Ecclus 45.6; *Jub.* 31.16-17; 32.1-5.
5. Note the emphatic position of ὁ πατριάρχης at the end of the sentence (7.4).

He is without father (ἀπάτωρ) or mother (ἀμήτωρ) or genealogy (ἀγενεαλόγητος), and has neither beginning of days nor end of life (7.3ab).

Yet he is not thereby claiming an eternity for the figure of Melchizedek so much as for the type of priesthood which he represents. The rest of v. 3 makes this abundantly clear: 'but resembling the Son of God he continues a priest forever'. Although his initial appeal to Genesis might lead us to suppose otherwise, it is Jesus rather than Melchizedek who is our author's starting point and pattern. Here once more we see that Christ is the exegetical norm by which Scripture is tested and understood. Hence our author does not pursue the mystery of Melchizedek's origins, other than to stress that they are non-Levitical.[1] Rather he concentrates on the permanency of this priesthood, and its on-going inviolable character. This he gets from the 'forever' (εἰς τὸν αἰῶνα) of Ps. 109(MT 110).4. Compared with the Levitical priesthood, which is impermanent by virtue of the inevitable death of its members (cf. 7.8, ἀποθνήσκοντες ἄνθρωποι), that exercised by Jesus continues, since 'his is an indestructible life' (7.16):

The former priests were many in number, because they were prevented by death from continuing in office; but he holds his priesthood permanently,[2] because he continues for ever (εἰς τὸν αἰῶνα). Consequently he is able for all time (εἰς τὸ παντελές) to save those who draw near to God through him, since he always (πάντοτε) lives to make intercession for them (7.23-25).

Thus the resurrection and ascension of Christ are understood as the 'for ever' of the psalm, and constitute the grounds for claiming a supremacy for his ministry over that exercised by the Jewish priesthood.

1. Philo, *Leg. All.* 3.79-82, on the other hand, interprets Melchizedek's lack of antecedents and the self-taught (αὐτομαθῆ or αὐτοδίδακτος), instinctive character of his priesthood allegorically. They represent the *logos* which, likened to intoxication, divinely inspires the soul by displacing mere sense perception. In some later Christian circles it was inferred from his lack of genealogy that Melchizedek was not really a man, but an angel, or a theophany of the holy spirit, or the *logos*. Among some Gnostic groups he became the pattern of Christ rather than vice versa. Epiphanius, Hippolytus and Jerome attempted to refute such notions. See P.E. Hughes, *Hebrews*, pp. 239-45.
2. See p. 147 n. 2.

Just as in the following chapter Hebrews asserts the inefficacy of the Mosaic covenant, and claims that mention of a new covenant in Jeremiah is evidence that God did not intend the first to be eternally binding (8.7-13), so with the priesthood:

> Now if perfection had been attained through the Levitical priesthood (for under it the people received the law), what further need would there have been for another priest to arise after the order of Melchizedek, rather than one named after the order of Aaron? (7.11)

Furthermore, we meet the self-same appeal to God's oath. Not this time as a double surety of the promise made to Abraham (as in 6.13-18), but as confirmation that Jesus' Melchizedekian priesthood is God's final word. Thus, although previously regarded as permanent (cf. Exod. 29.9), the Aaronic priesthood, since it was not confirmed by an oath (Heb. 7.21a), is now abrogated and replaced by a Melchizedekian one, of whom the psalmist has written:

> The Lord has sworn and will not
> > change his mind,
> 'Thou art a priest forever' (LXX Ps. 109.4 = Heb. 7.21c).

Modern biblical scholarship may well be unsure as to whether or not Gen. 14.17-20, as a literary composition, predated Psalm 110.[1] Our exegete, however, working within the presuppositions of his time, accepts the Mosaic authorship of the Pentateuch and a Davidic date for all the Psalms. This particular psalm does indeed seem to be an oracular blessing addressed, possibly by some unnamed prophet, to the Davidic king. He is extolled as seated at the right hand of God, that is, as granted a position of highest eminence,[2] and empowered to rule with divine authority. Furthermore, he is promised victory over all his enemies, whom he will utterly destroy. Yet how can the Davidic king be addressed as a priest? In this connection it is as well to remind ourselves that, long before the institution of the Hasmonaean high

---

1. See Horton, *Melchizedek*, p. 33.

2. To be seated at the right hand was to be in the position of highest esteem (see 1 Kgs 2.19; Ecclus 12.2). Hence the righteous martyrs will have thrones at God's right hand (*Apoc. Elij.* 37.3-4); the righteous will have their thrones near God (*4 Macc.* 17.5; *1 En.* 108.12). Cf. Wisdom, who sits beside God's throne (Wis. 9.4; 18.15). The Qumran Covenanters expected the messiah, the branch of David, to occupy a 'throne of glory' in the last days. See Hay, *Glory at the Right Hand*, p. 55.

priesthood in the second century BCE, Israel's kings exercised priestly functions. Thus, clad in the priestly ephod (2 Sam. 6.14), David offered sacrifices (2 Sam. 6.13, 17), and blessed the people (2 Sam. 6.18). He also interceded for the people (2 Sam. 24.17). Similarly, Solomon was privileged to stand before the Ark of the Covenant, and to offer sacrifices on behalf of the nation (2 Kgs 3.15; cf. 9.25). In Jeremiah's vision of a restored Israel (Jer. 30.21) the prince will once more be enabled thus to approach God. This is not to suggest that Davidic monarchs were themselves priests, let alone claimed to combine in themselves the office of high priest and king as did the Maccabees from the time of John Hyrcanus.[1] The Hasmonaeans, of course, could lay no claim to Davidic descent, coming as they did from the tribe of Levi rather than Judah. There were those who questioned their credentials as rightful heirs to the high priesthood, but that was because they disputed their Zadokite lineage, not their Levitical descent.[2] They did not claim the title 'king' by virtue of a supposed descent from David. That would have entailed membership of the tribe of Judah, and, as Hebrews (7.14b) puts it, 'in connection with that tribe Moses said nothing about priests'! Conversely, if the author of our Epistle is to utilize a priestly model for Jesus, he cannot use a Jewish one, 'For it is evident that our Lord was descended from Judah' (7.14a).

In other words, although he wishes to draw parallels between the death and ascension of Christ and the work of the high priest, accepting as he does the early church's belief that Jesus was Davidic messiah,[3] he is obliged to find another scriptural model of priesthood.

---

1. Jonathan Maccabaeus had been granted first the high priesthood and then the title 'military governor' (στρατηγός) in 151/150 BCE by Alexander Balas, pretender to the Seleucid throne (1 Macc. 10.15-21; Josephus, *Ant.* 13.43-46; 1 Macc. 10.51-66; *Ant.* 13.80-85). This was not confirmed by the people, however, until the reign of Simon in 140 BCE, when he was declared high priest, military ruler (στρατηγός) and ethnarch (ἐθνάρχης) in perpetuity (1 Macc. 14.42). Simon's successor, John Hyrcanus (135/34–104 BCE), became the first to inherit this dual religious and civil role. According to Josephus (*Ant.* 13.301), Aristobulus I (104/103 BCE) was the first Hasmonaean to use the title 'king'. See E. Schürer, *The History of the Jewish People in the Age of Jesus Christ*, I (rev. G. Vermes, F. Millar and M. Black; Edinburgh: T. & T. Clark, 1973), pp. 178-81.

2. See Schürer, *History*, I, pp. 211-15.

3. Acts 2.34-36; 5.31; 10.42-43; Rom. 1.2-4; etc.

This he does in Genesis 14 and Psalm 110 in the person of Melchizedek. More importantly, in this figure he finds one who is non-Levitical and yet combined in himself the office of priest and king. Given that this psalm had already been accepted in both Jewish and Christian circles as a prophecy of the coming messiah, it is all the more useful, since it enables Hebrews at one and the same time to maintain that Jesus is the fulfilment of this promise of Davidic kingship, and to depict his work in priestly terms.

Does this mean that pre-Christian Judaism looked forward to a priestly messiah? This is a complex issue, made more so by the various ways scholars use the terms 'messiah' or 'messianic'. In this connection it needs to be remembered that in the Old Testament, anointing is the means whereby something or someone is set apart as belonging to God, and thereby placed in the category of the taboo or the sacred. Thus we read that, not only Aaron and his sons (Exod. 28.41; 29.7; 30.30; Lev. 4.1-5, 16; 6.19-22; 7.35-36; 8.12; 17.32; Num. 3.2-3; 35.25), but the very furniture in the tabernacle was anointed (Exod. 29.36-37; 30.26; 40.9-15; Lev. 8.10-12). In 1 Kgs 19.16 Elijah is told to anoint Elisha (cf. Ps. 105.15), although it is not clear whether, in the case of prophets, anointing is used as a metaphor for consecration (cf. Isa. 45.1) rather than indicating a literal action. The most frequent references to anointing, however, are in connection with kings (e.g. Judg. 9.7-8, 14-15; 1 Sam. 16.12-13; 26.9-11, 16; 2 Sam. 22.51; 1 Kgs 19.15-16).

Zechariah (3.1–4.14; 6.11-14) presents us with a duumvirate of those anointed, in the persons of Joshua the high priest, and Zerubbabel, the royal Davidic representative. Yet after Israel's return from Babylonian captivity, there was in fact no restoration of the Davidic monarchy. Now the only 'anointed one' (*māshîaḥ*) is the high priest, who governed a theocratic state as Yahweh's representative. It is only with the acceptance of the non-Davidic Hasmonaean dynasty, in the late second century BCE, that we find once more Israel governed by a monarch. What is more, this is the only time in its entire history in which the offices of king and high priest were united in the same person, and that was only made possible by the sacrifice of Davidic descent. With the rise of Herod the Great and Rome's conferral of the title 'king' upon him,[1] in the late first century BCE the two offices

1. Herod the Great was nominated King of Judaea by the Roman Senate in 40 BCE (Josephus, *Ant.* 14.381-93; *War* 1.282-85), although it took him some years to

separated once more. It is likely that the *Book of Jubilees*, in which the tribe of Levi outranks that of Judah (*Jub.* 31.12-20) came from circles which initially supported the Hasmonaean high priesthood.[1] *The Testament of the Twelve Patriarchs* also gives pre-eminence to a Levitical figure over a Davidic one.[2] More often, however, it combines both features in one person.[3] The dating of this work, however, is problematic. Many scholars believe that in its present Greek version it is Christian in origin.[4] At the very least it has been heavily interpolated by second-century Christian editors.[5] It is therefore safe to assume that its 'priestly messianism' has been influenced by Christianity, and cannot therefore afford us evidence of pre-Christian Jewish eschatological expectations.

What we can say with more confidence is that in postexilic Judaism the priestly office came to the fore. Thus, in Ezekiel's vision of the restored Temple (Ezek. 40–48), the king is given a very limited role (Ezek. 34.23-24; 37.22-25). Moses' blessing of Levi (Deut. 33.8-11) now becomes a covenant made by God with Levi (Mal. 2.4-8), analogous to that made with David (Jer. 33.14-20).[6] Like the Davidic covenant (cf. 2 Sam. 7.12-16), this is to be permanent:

> For thus says the Lord: David shall never lack a man to sit on the throne of the house of Israel, and the Levitical priests shall never lack a man in

gain control of the country. As an Idumaean, he was neither of pure Jewish descent nor of sacerdotal lineage, and therefore ineligible to hold the high priestly office.

1. See G.W.E. Nickelsburg, *Jewish Literature between the Bible and the Mishnah* (London: SCM Press, 1981), pp. 73-80.

2. See *T. Jud.* 21.29; 24.1-3 where the priest has pre-eminence over the king.

3. It is difficult to get a clear picture from *Test. XII Patr.* as we have it. Thus, although in *T. Levi* 18.18 Judah will establish a new priesthood, in *T. Dan* 5, *T. Gad* 8 and *T. Jos.* 19, Judah and Levi seem to coalesce into one person.

4. So, e.g., M. de Jonge, *The Testament of the Twelve Patriarchs: A Study of their Text, Composition and Origin* (Assen: Van Gorcum, 1953), pp. 118, 121-25, 130-31, who assigns it to the 2nd century CE. Its Christian authors may have utilized an earlier Jewish Testament.

5. So, e.g., R.H. Charles (ed.), *The Apocrypha and Pseudepigrapha of the O.T. in English*, II (Oxford: Clarendon Press, 1913), p. 291.

6. Jer. 33.14-26 is probably a postexilic interpolation. See J. Bright, *Jeremiah* (AB; New York: Doubleday, 1965), p. 298, *et al.* E.W. Nicholson (*Jeremiah 26–52* [Cambridge Bible Commentary; Cambridge: Cambridge University Press, 1975], pp. 87-89) suggests an exilic date.

my presence to offer burnt offerings, to burn cereal offerings, and to make sacrifices for ever (Jer. 33.17-18).[1]

Even prior to the Hasmonaean establishment, therefore, we can see that, among some groups, the high priest had already been endowed with royal features.

This is not to say that with the advent of the Hasmonaeans there did not also arise opposition to their incumbency. The Qumran Covenanters, for example, seem to have had their origins in just such disaffection, which led them to withdraw from the Temple and its services altogether.[2] Their complaint, however, seems to have been not with the Hasmonaean claim to kingship, but to the dubiousness of their Zadokite descent. On these grounds they regarded their ministry as a defilement of the sanctuary.[3] It was not only the Covenanters who objected to the Hasmonaeans. In the first century CE the Pharisaic party also criticized the way their Sadducean, high priestly rivals performed some of the cultic rituals.[4] This seems to lie behind the story we find in Josephus of the crowd, on the occasion of the feast of *Sukkot*, pelting the high priest with fruit as he processed to the Temple.[5]

Given their origins in a protest against the validity of the Hasmonaean incumbency of the high priestly office, it is not surprising that the distinction between the laity and the priesthood was not only maintained but intensified by the Covenanters. The priests among their number, the true 'sons of Zadok',[6] were supreme in the government of the community in all matters, whether secular or sacred:

> The sons of Aaron shall command in matters of justice and property, and every rule concerning the men of the community shall be determined according to their word (1QS 9.7).[7]

1. Cf. Num. 25.11-13; Ecclus 45.6-21.
2. See pp. 39-41.
3. See 1QpHab 12.7-8; 10.10; CD 12.2.
4. For the ritual and juristic issues which divided the Pharisees from the Sadducees, see L. Finkelstein, *The Pharisees: The Sociological Background of their Faith*, II (Philadelphia: Jewish Publication Society of America, 3rd edn, 1963), pp. 637-753.
5. Josephus, *Ant.* 13.372-73. This incident also appears in rabbinic writings; cf. *m. Suk.* 3.16; *t. Suk.* 3.16; *b. Suk.* 48b.
6. 1QS 5.6.
7. Vermes, *Dead Sea Scrolls in English*, p. 87.

Hence it is equally unsurprising that their eschatological hopes should be expressed in priestly terms.

Scholars are divided, however, as to whether or not the true Zadokite priest to whom they looked forward was envisaged as the messiah. The Qumranic material is neither uniform nor unambiguous on the issue. In the *War Scroll*, for example, there is no messianic agent; God is to intervene himself (1QM 18.1-3). In the *Damascus Document*, on the other hand, the messiah will be a Davidic king, 'the Branch of David', 'the messiah of Israel', 'the Prince of the congregation' (cf. also 1QSb 5.21, 25, 28), although, like the first David he is also to exercise certain priestly functions.[1] In one passage in the *Community Rule*, the matter is further complicated by the mention of two messiahs. 'There shall come a prophet and the messiahs of Aaron and Israel' (1QS 9.9b-11). The 'prophet', as either contemporaneous with,[2] or forerunner of[3] the messiah, we have already discussed when we considered the influence of the figure of Moses[4] upon Jewish eschatological thinking (pp. 133-44). Also, in Samuel's anointing of David (1 Sam. 16.13) we can find biblical precedent for the prophet as the one who is deputed by God to consecrate His chosen king. Not infrequently in the Old Testament prophets are depicted as king-makers and breakers.[5] Is Qumran's eschatological prophet to anoint two figures,[6] one priest and the other king, on the Joshua–Zerubbabel model, or is one figure intended, combining both royal and priestly

1. CD 19.16; 12.23; 14.19.

2. So N.A. Dahl, 'Eschatology and History in the Light of the Qumranic Texts', in *The Crucified Messiah* (Minneapolis, MN: Augsburg, 1974), p. 134.

3. Since so little is said about him, it is difficult to be certain about the precise role of the prophet in Qumran's expectations. If Mal. 4.5, which prophesies the return of Elijah as herald of the day of the Lord, has contributed at all to the Covenanters' thinking, then he could well have been thought to function as a precursor.

4. Deut. 18.18-20. Cf. 1 Macc. 4.46; 14.41 which sees Hasmonaean rule as lasting only until such time as a 'trustworthy prophet' should arise.

5. See 1 Sam. 9.1–10.1; 16; 1 Kgs 14.1-6; 15.29; 16.1-7, 12; etc.

6. See K.G. Kuhn, 'The Two Messiahs of Aaron and Israel', in *The Scrolls and the New Testament* (ed. K. Stendahl; London: SCM Press, 1957), pp. 54-64; J. Liver, 'The Doctrine of the Two Messiahs in Sectarian Literature in the Time of the Second Commonwealth', *HTR* 52 (1959), pp. 149-85; R.E. Brown, 'The Messianism of Qumran', *CBQ* 19 (1959), pp. 53-82; Knibb, *Qumran Community*, pp. 139-40; Schürer, *History*, II, pp. 550-54.

functions?[1] From the rest of the Qumran material, where we meet
'messiah' only in the singular, the latter might seem more likely.
Some scholars, however, cite 4QTestimonia as evidence to support the
two messiahs hypothesis. In this collection of messianic proof-texts, a
prophecy concerning the royal messiah (Num. 24.15-17) is followed
by a citation of Deut. 33.8-11, the blessing of the Levites (4QTest 14-
20). Is this an implicit reference to the 'messiah of Aaron' of the
Community Rule?[2]

We need to bear in mind in any discussion of the Covenanters that
the evidence from Qumran and its surroundings is disparate, and this
partly due to its fragmentary and incomplete state, and partly because
it represents writings accumulated over the two centuries of the sect's
existence. It is unlikely that their thinking would have remained
unchanged throughout that entire period. J. Starcky has accordingly
attempted to correlate what palaeography can tell us about the date of
the various Qumran writings with the different eschatological ideas
we find in them. On the basis of this he suggests that the Covenanters'
messianism went through four successive stages. (1) In the
Maccabaean period no messiah was anticipated. (2) In the Hasmonaean
period a belief in two messiahs, one priestly and one royal, emerged.
(3) Throughout the period of the Roman general Pompey's virtual
control of Judaean affairs (60–30 BCE), the Covenanters looked to one
messiah, a Davidic king, who would exercise some priestly functions.
(4) With the Herodian rise to power, they once more set their hopes
on a duumvirate, 'the messiahs of Aaron and Israel'.[3]

Any developmental model has its drawbacks—not least the problem
of accurately dating the material. Yet this approach has the virtue of
recognizing the complexity of the evidence as we have it. Perhaps the
reason those of us who come from the Christian tradition, where Jesus
is claimed as *the* messiah, find it so difficult to understand the diversity of first-century Judaism's messianic expectations, is because we
have assumed that there was only *one*; an anointed Davidic king.
Whereas biblical and extrabiblical sources alike bear witness to a

---

1. So A.J.B. Higgins, 'The Priestly Messiah', *NTS* 13 (1966–67), pp. 211-39.
2. So Vermes, *Dead Sea Scrolls in English*, p. 247; Knibb, *Qumran Community*,
p. 139.
3. J. Starcky, 'Les quatres étages du Messianism à Qumrân', *RB* 70 (1963),
pp. 481-505.

whole plethora of beliefs in Jewish 'messianism', some of which have
no messiah at all! For the rest, Davidic king and Levitical priest,
singly or in combination, can be looked to as God's messiah(s),
entrusted with the inauguration of the new age. If in 11QMelch[1] the
'messenger' is none other than the eschatological prophet who is to
announce the coming of the reign of Melchizedek, then he is also
designated 'messiah'.[2] At the very least, a prophetic figure is to function as the one who anoints, even if we dismiss a reading of the text
which would have him anointed also. What is clear from the Qumran
material is that this particular sect drew upon all three: prophet, priest
and king, and used these figures of past tradition as salvific models for
their future hope.

When we compare this with the author of Hebrews' depiction of
Jesus, we find some very important differences. Early Christian tradition drew heavily upon the Davidic strand within contemporary
Jewish messianism, and we must not lose sight of its contribution to
our own author's Christology. Like Qumran he assigns priestly functions to a Davidic messiah. Unlike Qumran, however, he claims that
this self-same royal messiah belongs to a priestly order. Without
resorting to a messianic duumvirate, this would be impossible if that
priesthood were Levitical. According to the laws of descent, it was
impossible to belong to two tribes; in this case that of Judah and Levi
(see 7.14). Furthermore, he does not wish to portray Jesus as the ideal
high priest of the existing system (like Qumran's hoped-for 'messiah
of Aaron'), but as one exercising a wholly different and superior type
of priesthood.

This is how Melchizedek functions in Hebrews; as the type of non-
Levitical priest, who both preceded Levi and, at the same time, was
recognized by him while he was still 'in the loins of Abraham', that is,
was as yet unborn. Furthermore, as Psalm 110 attests, in Scripture it
is the only order of priesthood ascribed to a Davidic king. With the
coming of the messiah in the person of Jesus, his Melchizedekian
priesthood has now brought the interregnum of the Aaronic order to
an end. Having established this Melchizedekian model for Jesus in

1. See Vermes, *Dead Sea Scrolls in English*, p. 267.
2. See Horton, *Melchizedek*, pp. 78-79, following de Jonge and van der Woude,
'11Q Melchizedek', pp. 306-308; *contra* Fitzmyer, 'Further Light', p. 40, who
identifies the messenger as Melchizedek.

ch. 7, our author proceeds in the following chapters to demonstrate how, in his death and ascension, Jesus has definitively carried out the work of the high priest. As Otto Michel has put it, 'Good Friday and ascension become Christianity's great Day of Atonement'.[1] Above all, Hebrews claims, Jesus has achieved what was in the main aim of the cult and the purpose of the high priest's role within it; he has come into the very presence of God. This previous high priests had failed to do.

From all this we can see that the preoccupations of the Epistle to the Hebrews are very different from those we find at Qumran. The Covenanters looked to a restored high priesthood of the true Zadokite line, not the installation of a wholly different priestly order. Furthermore, although they draw upon the figure of Melchizedek, it is not in order to exploit his specifically priestly work. According to a scroll, 13 fragments of which have been found in Cave 11 (= 11Q Melch),[2] Melchizedek played a part in Qumran's eschatological beliefs, although they make no mention of Psalm 110, either here or in the *Genesis Apocryphon*, in which the Gen. 14.18-20 story is retold in Aramaic,[3] without any particular eschatological interpretation being given to the text. In 11QMelch, however, he is to preside over the proceedings on the great day of judgment, which would take place at the end of the tenth Jubilee year. Then 'all the sons of light' will be

---

1. Michel, *Hebräer*, p. 212.
2. See Vermes, *Dead Sea Scrolls in English*, pp. 266-68. It should be borne in mind that the scroll is so fragmentary and badly preserved that almost every line has had to be reconstructed. Scholars are divided in their reconstructions and vary as to how extensively they are prepared to fill in the lacunae. Cf. Horton, *Melchizedek*, pp. 67-72, who is more judicious than some in this regard.
3. In the *Genesis Apocryphon*, Gen. 14.18-20 is largely followed with a few, minor additions (see 1QGen 20.14-16 = Vermes, *Dead Sea Scrolls in English*, p. 223). One of these is to add that the 'food and drink' (*contra* Genesis 'bread and wine') was given by Melchizedek 'to all the men who were with him'. This clearly resolves any ambiguity in the Hebrew text as to who gave the tithe. Nowhere here is any eschatological interpretation given to Melchizedek's actions. Further, as in the biblical account, it is Abraham, not Melchizedek, who has the centre stage. Cf. *Abr.* 235, which is bereft of Philo's usual allegorization and, like 1QGen, largely follows the biblical account. Philo's retelling contains some elements of haggadic midrash, such as Melchizedek's rejoicing at Abraham's victory as if it were his own, his acknowledgment that the victory should be ascribed to God, and the stress upon the friendship between Melchizedek and the patriarch.

atoned for. Yet Melchizedek's primary task on that day is to act as judge rather than priest; specifically he is to exercise judgment on God's behalf, condemning the demonic 'lot' of Belial.

As a judge, he functions like God himself, as the Covenanters point out in identifying him with the *'Elōhîm* of Ps. 81.1 and *'Ēl* of Ps. 7.7-8. This, of course, is not to claim that he is God. He is, however, portrayed as a heavenly being, accompanied in his task by other angelic beings, 'sons of heaven'. Some scholars have suggested that he is thereby identified with the archangel Michael.[1] They point to the *War Scroll* (17.5-9),[2] where Michael is present and active in the final battle between the forces of good and evil. Yet here he is to play the role of the one who comes to the assistance of the 'sons of light', rather than to act as judge. Thus the function of Melchizedek in 11QMelch seems to go beyond that of Michael in the *War Scroll*,[3] and the two cannot simply be equated. That only occurs in later tradition,[4] in mediaeval rabbinic texts. While in the Qumran writings in some respects Michael and Melchizedek have parallel functions, they are never explicitly identified as one person.[5]

The role of Jesus in Hebrews, however, is not that of judge. His return to earth is 'not to deal with sin, but to save those who are eagerly waiting for him' (9.28). Throughout, his earthly ministry is depicted in priestly rather than juridical terms. Furthermore, there is no suggestion that the author of our Epistle was aware of any tradition that made Melchizedek an archangel, or that he believed that he

---

1. E.g. Vermes, *Dead Sea Scrolls in English*, p. 266 and *idem*, *Qumran in Perspective*, p. 184.

2. Vermes, *Dead Sea Scrolls in English*, pp. 145-46.

3. See Horton, *Melchizedek*, pp. 81-82.

4. Subsequently Melchizedek was to capture the imagination of both Jewish and Christian writers. To those mentioned by Horton (*Melchizedek*, pp. 87-151) should be added the Melchizedek tractate from Codex IX of the Nag Hammadi library. See B.A. Pearson, *Nag Hammadi Codices IX and X* (Leiden: Brill, 1981), pp. 19-85. Pearson concludes (pp. 23, 31, 34) that this Christian Gnostic work has been influenced by Hebrews. Unlike our Epistle, however, it identifies Melchizedek with Christ rather than depicting them as type and antitype. Like 11QMelch from Qumran, in this codex Melchizedek is an eschatological holy warrior who destroys the hostile, demonic forces.

5. De Jonge and van der Woude ('11Q Melchizedek', p. 305) draw parallels between Michael and Melchizedek, but do not go so far as to claim that the two are one.

appeared to Abraham as such.[1] Had this been the case it is inconceivable that he would have chosen to use Melchizedek as the type for Jesus' high priesthood, since he is adamant that Jesus is superior to all angels. In 7.3 he clearly subordinates Melchizedek to the son of God, who is in fact the 'type' of the Canaanite king's own priesthood. Yet he does not argue the case, as we would expect had he been aware of angelic speculations about Melchizedek similar to those found at Qumran. Indeed, F. Horton suggests that it is as a direct consequence of our author's failure to amplify the superiority of Christ's priesthood over that of Melchizedek that later Christian heresies arose which subordinated Jesus to Melchizedek.[2] Be that as it may, Hebrews, far from distancing the two, describes the priesthood of Christ as 'after the order of Melchizedek', and here pursues a typology of correspondence rather than one of contrast.

Thus we can see that, while the work of Christ is an enactment of the Levitical high priest's role on the Day of Atonement, he himself is of a wholly different priestly order. In this lies his superiority.

4. *Jesus and Angels*

The topic of Christ's supremacy over angels, which is dealt with in 1.4–2.18, is not raised vis-à-vis his relationship to Melchizedek, but arises out of the affirmation with which Hebrews opens, 'he sat down at the right hand of the Majesty on high' (1.3; cf. Ps. 110.1). But this, he insists, does not mean that Jesus is merely one of the angelic throng. He is exalted above the angels. To make this point our author cites seven biblical texts. It is impossible to be sure whether this was an already existent catena,[3] or one of his own making. In 4QTestimonia we now have evidence of the early existence of such a collection of messianic proof-texts. Yet most of the texts in Hebrews' selection do not appear in the rest of the New Testament, and, as our author employs them, are so geared to his particular argument that it is probable that he brought them together himself. Hugh Montefiore,

---

1. *Contra* de Jonge and van der Woude, '11Q Melchizedek', p. 321.
2. Horton, *Melchizedek*, p. 164.
3. So Montefiore, *Hebrews*, pp. 43-44, who follows Synge, *Hebrews*, p. 3, in suggesting that this collection of texts was originally intended to demonstrate from Scripture Christ's divinity, his incarnation, baptism, resurrection and ascension. Hebrews used it for another purpose—to prove that the son is superior to the angels.

on the contrary, thinks that, 'The selection of the seven *testimonia* seems ill-adapted to his purpose, since only one of them in the LXX contains the actual word angels'.[1] Yet this accusation does not sufficiently take into account that the author of Hebrews uses these texts not only to demonstrate Christ's supremacy over angels, but to confirm his status as son. It is on this basis that he proceeds to demonstrate Jesus' superiority to angels, Moses and the Levitical priesthood.

Thus the most important step in our author's argument is the first: to establish Jesus' incomparable status as son. In Jewish tradition 'son' is a designation that can be used either of Israel as a whole or of the wise and righteous among its number.[2] As we have already noted,[3] moreover, it can also be used of angels, although in the LXX this is rare.[4] More importantly, like other ancient Near Eastern nations, Israel hailed its Davidic kings as sons of God.[5] The first scriptural passage cited (Heb. 1.5a) is from Ps. 2.7:

> Thou art my son,
> today I have begotten thee.

In origin this psalm was probably associated with the enthronement of a Davidic monarch. It came to be applied to David's messianic successor. Hence it is cited in the *Psalms of Solomon* (17.26), a mid-first-century BCE work, which looks forward to the downfall of the Hasmonaeans and the restoration of a Davidic king who would fulfil the hopes expressed in Isa. 11.1-5.[6] It is also to be found among the Qumran writings (1QSa 11). In Synoptic tradition this psalm's address

1. Montefiore, *Hebrews*, p. 44.
2. See M. Hengel, *The Son of God: The Origin of Christology and the History of Jewish-Hellenistic Religion* (London: SCM Press, 1976), pp. 21-22, 42-45.
3. See p. 49 n. 2.
4. See p. 49 n. 1.
5. See H. Frankfort, *Kingship and the Gods: A Study of Ancient Near Eastern Religion as Interaction of Society and Nature* (Chicago: Chicago University Press, 1948), pp. 36-38, 159-63, 299-304, S. Mowinckel, *He that Cometh* (Oxford: Basil Blackwell, 1956), pp. 23-56 and *idem.*, *The Psalms in Israel's Worship*, I (Oxford: Basil Blackwell, 1967), pp. 50-60. For Ps. 2 as the enthronement of a Davidic king as God's viceregent see Mowinckel, *Psalms*, I, pp. 61-64; A.A. Anderson, *Psalms*, I (NCB; London: Oliphants, 1972), pp. 63-70.
6. See Nickelsburg, *Jewish Literature*, pp. 203-12; G.L. Davenport, 'The "Anointed of the Lord" in the Psalms of Solomon 17', in *Ideal Figures in Ancient Judaism* (ed. G.W.E. Nickelsburg and J.J. Collins; Chico, CA: Scholars Press, 1980), pp. 67-92.

of the Davidic king as 'son' seems to be behind the words at both Jesus' baptism (Mt. 3.17; Mk 1.11; Lk. 3.22 [Western text]) and transfiguration (Mt. 17.5; Mk 9.7; Lk. 9.35; cf. 2 Pet. 1.17). Ps. 2.7 is also quoted in Acts 13.33 where it is applied to Christ's resurrection (cf. Rom. 1.4).

2 Sam. 7.14 is used as twin testimony[1] to Jesus' divine sonship:

> I will be to him a father, and he shall be to me a son (Heb. 1.5b).

In its Old Testament context this is Nathan's prophecy to David that he would be the founder of an everlasting dynasty:

> And your house and your kingdom shall be made forever before me; and your throne shall be established forever (2 Sam. 7.16).

As David's successor and God's Temple-builder, this oracle was to find its fulfilment in Solomon (cf. 1 Chron. 29.23). With the demise of the Davidic dynasty however, this prophecy was to take on an eschatological significance. Thus we find it, along with Psalm 2, in 4QFlorilegia[2]—a collection of biblical texts used by the Qumran Covenanters to announce the imminence of the Davidic messiah, prior to whose coming to cleanse and restore the Temple in Jerusalem they are to see themselves as functioning as that Temple's replacement.[3] In 2 Cor. 6.18 we also find an allusion to 2 Sam. 7.14, and, like Qumran, also in a context where the image of 'temple' is applied to the people of God, only here understood as the Christian church:

> And I shall be a father to you and you shall be my sons and daughters, says the Lord.[4]

Although not averse to describing Christians as 'sons' (cf. 2.10), the author of Hebrews does not claim this text as an ascription of the community, however. He prefers to keep it to prove the unique sonship of Jesus.

---

1. See καὶ πάλιν which links the citation of Isa. 2.7 in Heb. 1.5a with 2 Sam. 7.14 in 1.5b.
2. See Vermes, *Dead Sea Scrolls in English*, pp. 245-56.
3. See B. Gärtner, *The Temple and the Community in Qumran and the New Testament* (Cambridge: Cambridge University Press, 1965).
4. Paul's extension of 'sons' to include 'daughters' finds its parallel in such Old Testament passages as Isa. 43.6 and Joel 2.28 (cf. Acts 2.17).

From these two opening citations it is evident that our author's principal model for Jesus' sonship is the Davidic king, as taken up in current Jewish eschatological expectations. George Buchanan, however, will have none of this. He maintains that there is neither direct nor indirect evidence that Hebrews believed Jesus was of Davidic descent. Rather:

> He portrayed a messiah who was a priest-king, which David and his successors certainly were not; but some Hasmonaeans were, and the priest-king described in Hebrews resembles that type of messianic expectation much more closely than any messiahs from the families of David and Aaron.[1]

Yet we have seen, it is precisely because he accepts Jesus as Davidic messiah, 'descended from Judah' (7.14), that he is obliged to establish a non-Levitical model for his priestly office. Had the Hasmonaeans provided our author with his 'type' then we would have expected a positive refutation of Davidic kingship rather than the adoption of a Melchizedekian priesthood.[2] Yet, prior to the establishment of Jesus' priestly credentials (which begins at 4.14), Hebrews sets out his primary status—that of Davidic son. Thus Ps. 2.7 is picked up once more at 5.5 to show that Melchizedekian priesthood, like Jesus' royal sonship which has already been established via this psalm, is equally dependent upon divine appointment. Only after his sonship has first been demonstrated does Hebrews move on to an extended discussion of his priesthood. Buchanan is therefore misleading when he claims that our author presents us with a priest-king; rather in Hebrews we meet Jesus as a king-priest.

As royal son, his supremacy over the angels is therefore axiomatic. Hebrews goes on to demonstrate this by citing Deut. 32.43 (Heb. 1.6b), 'Let all God's angels worship him'—a phrase which is only

---

1. Buchanan, *Hebrews*, p. 15.

2. It is most unlikely that the messiah's Davidic descent is denied in Mt. 22.41-46; Mk 12.35-37a; Lk. 20.41-44. Rather, what is emphasized is that the messiah is both David's son *and* Lord. See J. Jeremias, *Jesus' Promise to the Nations* (SBT, 24; London: SCM Press, 1958), p. 58; Cullman, *Christology*, pp. 130-33; J.A. Fitzmyer, 'The Son of David Tradition and Mt. 22.41-46 and Parallels', in *Essays on the Semitic Background of the New Testament* (London: Geoffrey Chapman, 1971), pp. 113-26. Although the Hasmonaeans probably used Ps. 110 to defend their position (see Hay, *Glory at the Right Hand*, pp. 24-25), there is no evidence that they claimed Melchizedekian rather than Levitical priestly descent.

found in the LXX, and then only in one manuscript which has come
down to us. The others read 'sons' (υἱοί). The discovery of fragments
of a Hebrew version of Deuteronomy at Qumran has lent support to
the suggestion that a Hebrew *Vorlage* may lay behind what was previously regarded as a septuagintal interpolation at Deut. 32.43. Thus in
4QDeut we have, 'and prostrate yourselves before him, all gods'.[1] It
would seem that our author's version of Deuteronomy read 'angels'
rather than 'sons' or 'gods', however, and this fits his purpose
admirably. He is thereby able to prove the superiority of Jesus over
the angelic inhabitants of heaven. It is their appointed task to minister
to him rather than vice versa (a point he is to repeat at 1.14). Of
course, in the original song of Moses this phrase referred to God, as
the recipient of heaven's worship. In Hebrews its application is now
shifted to Jesus the son, seated at the right hand of God in heaven.

To make his point even more strongly, the author of Hebrews
claims that Jesus is not only son; he is the oldest or firstborn
(πρωτότοκος,[2] Heb. 1.6a). In the Old Testament we find Israel so
designated (Exod. 42.44; Jer. 31.9). More importantly it is used of
David (Ps. 88[MT 89].29).[3] In the *Life of Adam and Eve* (13–14) we
find a Jewish tradition in which the angels were summoned to worship
Adam at his birth. This they did, with the sole exception of Satan, who
refused.[4] We cannot infer from this, however, that the author of
Hebrews was aware of this story and drew upon it to depict Jesus as a
second Adam. In spite of the fact that the Epistle to the Hebrews has
been handed down to us as by Paul, it would be erroneous to read the
apostle's presentation of Christ as the last Adam[5] into our text.

---

1. See P.W. Skehan, 'A Fragment of the "Song of Moses" (Deut. 32) from
Qumran', *BASOR* 136 (1954), pp. 12-15.

2. Only here in the New Testament is ὁ πρωτότοκος used as an absolute title for
Christ. Elsewhere (Rom. 8.29; Col. 1.15; Rev. 1.5) he is the firstborn of a new
creation.

3. Philo (*Conf. Ling.* 146) describes the *logos* as God's first born, but uses the
synonym τρωτόγονος.

4. See Davies, *Paul*, p. 42. (Cf. Job 38.7 where angels are joyful spectators at
creation.) *The Life of Adam and Eve* is a Jewish work, midrashic in character and
probably to be dated near the end of the first century CE. See M.D. Johnson, in *The
Old Testament Pseudepigrapha*, II (ed. J.H. Charlesworth; London: Darton,
Longman & Todd, 1985), pp. 249-95.

5. Rom. 5.12-21; 1 Cor. 15.20-23, 45-49. See C.K. Barrett, *From First Adam to
Last: A Study in Pauline Theology* (London: A. & C. Black, 1962). Increasingly,

The next step in our author's argument (1.7-12) is to contrast the changeable nature of angels with the eternal sovereignty of the son. To this end he cites the LXX version of Ps. 104.4:

> who makes his angels winds and his servants flames of fire (Heb. 1.7).

Unlike the Masoretic text (see p. 49), this enables him to claim that angels are so unstable that God can reduce them to the elemental forces of wind and fire. We meet a similar interpretation in *4 Ezra* 8.21:

> before whom (heaven's) hosts stand trembling and at thy word change to wind and fire.

It is not difficult to see that the following two proof-texts, taken from the Psalms, also continue the theme of the contrast between the son and the angels, although at this point our author's somewhat condensed style has created problems for subsequent interpreters. First, although the first two citations in his catena (Ps. 2.7; 2 Sam. 7.14) are clearly understood to be a direct address by God to the son, the same cannot be said of those which follow in 1.8-12, where he lays claims to the son's eternal rule. Here it is more likely that the πρὸς δὲ τὸν υἱόν (v. 8) with which he introduces Psalms 45 and 102 means 'concerning the son' rather than 'to the son'.[1] πρός has already been employed in this way in v. 7 where the translation 'concerning the angels' makes the most sense.

Ps. 44(MT 45).6-7 is one which poses difficulties both in its Old Testament context and in the one in which we find it cited in Hebrews (1.8-9). As its opening, 'I address my verses to the king', indicates, it was originally composed as an encomium for Israel's monarch,[2] probably on the occasion of a royal wedding. Yet both in Hebrew, and in the Greek version which we find followed here, v. 6, ὁ θρόνος σου ὁ θεὸς εἰς τὸν αἰῶνα τοῦ αἰῶνος is amenable to more than one translation. So, for example, the RSV renders Ps. 45.6, 'Thy divine throne endures for ever and ever', relegating the alternative, 'Thy throne, O God is for ever and ever', to the margin. Old Testament

---

scholars are understanding Phil. 2.6-11 as a depiction of Christ as superior to Adam. See Dunn, *Christology*, pp. 113-28.

1. See Buchanan, *Hebrews*, p. 19.
2. Probably a Davidic king. See Bruce, *Hebrews*, p. 19.

scholars are divided as to how far the royal ideologists of Jerusalem
were prepared to go in praise of the king. Were they prepared to
assimilate to their foreign neighbours to the extent of designating an
Israelite king 'God'?[1] Although subsequent Christian theology was to
claim the title 'God' for Christ is that how Heb. 1.8 is to be understood? If ὁ θεός is a vocative then that indeed is so. Thus, in contrast
to their translators' preference in Ps. 45.6, when we meet it cited in
Heb. 1.8 the RSV reads, 'Thy throne, O God, is for ever and ever'. If
on the other hand, ὁ θεός is to be understood either as the subject,
'God is your throne',[2] or predicate, 'Your throne is a throne of
God/divine',[3] then Jesus is not here called God. On the whole, current
scholarship is inclined to the opinion that both the psalmist and his
Christian interpreter were prepared to designate the Lord's anointed
(v. 9 ἔχρισεν) as θεός.[4] If this is true it would strengthen the argument that Hebrews depicts Jesus as royal messiah, which is how our
author seems to understand the Greek version of the Psalm. The reign
of the messiah is characterized by righteousness and justice (1.9) and
therefore, the occupant of the throne of that kingdom,[5] since he
exercises rule on God's behalf, may be designated 'God'. His is an
anointing which surpasses that of any of his 'comrades' (1.9).

1. So J.R. Porter, 'Psalm XLV 7', *JTS* 12 (1961), pp. 51-53, who also points
out that in all the ancient versions of the psalm it is interpreted as the king being
addressed as 'God'. *Contra* A.R. Johnson, *Sacral Kingship in Ancient Israel*
(Cardiff: Cardiff University Press, 2nd edn, 1967), p. 30 n. 1, who denies a vocative reading and suggests instead, 'Thy throne is an everlasting throne like that of
God'.
2. So Wycliffe, Tyndale, Moffatt, Westcott, Jewett, *et al.*
3. So Buchanan, *Hebrews*, p. 20.
4. See N. Turner, *Grammatical Insights into the N.T.* (Edinburgh: T. & T. Clark,
1965), p. 15; Spicq, *Hébreux*, II, p. 19; Bruce, *Hebrews*, p. 19; Montefiore,
Hebrews, p. 47; Wilson, *Hebrews*, pp. 41-42; *et al.* R.E. Brown ('Does the N.T.
Call Jesus God?', *TS* 26 [1965], pp. 545-73) includes Heb. 1.8-9 (along with Jn
1.1; 20.28) in the affirmative. He suggests that this arose out of the liturgical life of
the church.
5. At 1.8b the reading 'his (αὐτοῦ) kingdom' is strongly attested (p. 46 א, B).
This would support understanding ὁ θεός as the subject or predicate nominative.
'Thy (σου) kingdom', however, follows the LXX, is supported by a wide variety of
good manuscripts, and allows ὁ θεός to be taken as vocative. Therefore it is
accepted by the 3rd edition of the United Bible Societies' Greek New Testament. See
B.M. Metzger, *A Textual Commentary on the Greek New Testament* (London and
New York: United Bible Society, 1971), pp. 662-63.

The sixth text, Ps. 101(MT 102).25-27, provides further evidence of the eternity of the son's rule, which unlike the created order (and presumably the angels, who are part of the created order), is permanent and stable. In its Hebrew form the supplicant is the speaker throughout, whereas in the LXX, from v. 22 onwards we have God's answer, promising that the time will be short before He will restore the fortunes of His servants. In which case it is possible that, following the LXX, our author understands the speaker to be God, either directly addressing the son,[1] or more likely talking about him (see vv. 7 and 8). Thus 'Lord' (κύριος),[2] a title used in Old Testament tradition for God, is transferred to Jesus. 'Jesus is Lord' seems to have been one of the earliest confessions in the church, as we can see from other New Testament works.[3] Our author clearly uses it as an accepted title for Jesus (see 2.3; 7.14). In 1.10-12 it is used to uphold the unchangeableness of his messianic rule:

> Thou, Lord, didst found the earth in the beginning, and the heavens are the work of thy hands; they will perish, but thou remainest; they will all grow old like a garment, and they will be changed. But thou art the same, and thy years will never end.

In the next chapter I shall be discussing the son's role in creation. Here, however, this is not our author's preoccupation. His emphasis, rather, is upon the eternity of Jesus' messianic rule. To a group shaken by events which brought home to them the impermanence of all earthly institutions, even religious ones, this would have been a powerful and timely reminder of the meaning of Christ's ascension. Hebrews concludes its scriptural 'proofs' of the son's supremacy over the heavenly hosts with a citation from Ps. 109(MT 110).1:

> Sit at my right hand,
> till I make thy enemies
> a stool for thy feet (Heb. 1.13).

I shall discuss this psalm in more detail shortly. Here suffice it to say that just as our author began the section with, 'For to what angel did God ever say' (1.5), so here he introduces this quotation with, 'But to

---

1. So Bruce, *Hebrews*, p. 23.
2. 'Lord' is not in the Hebrew although it is in the LXX. At Heb. 1.10a it is omitted by א*, although restored by אca.
3. See Cullmann, *Christology*, pp. 195-237.

what angel has he ever said?' It is this psalm, alluded to in the prologue (1.3), which has led him to discuss the relationship of Jesus to
angels in the first place. Like Jesus, they may occupy heaven, but they
do not have the same exalted status as the son, seated at the right hand
of God. His very posture signifies his pre-eminence.

At this point our author turns to remind his readers of the need for
obedience (2.1-4). If the Law (λόγος, v. 2) mediated through the
angels[1] was binding, how much more is the message of salvation,
proclaimed by the Lord, that is, Jesus, and attested by those who heard
him. Deut. 33.2 (LXX), which speaks of the angels' presence at God's
right hand[2] when Moses was given the Law, may well be in mind
here, although, as we have seen, elsewhere Hebrews focuses upon
Moses as the principal Law-giver.

The author soon returns, however, to his main theme—the
sovereignty of the son:

> For it was not to angels that God subjected the world to come (τῆς
> οἰκουμένην τὴν μέλλουσαν), of which we are speaking (2.5).

It was God's original intention at creation, not that angels but that man
(Adam) should exercise sovereignty over the whole created order on
His behalf (cf. Gen. 1.26-30), as is attested by the psalmist:

> What is man that thou art mindful of him,
> or the son of man, that thou carest for him?
> Thou didst make him for a little while (βραχύ τι) lower than the angels,
> thou hast crowned him with glory and honour,[3]
> and put everything (πάντα) in subjection under
>   his feet (Heb. 2.6-8 = Ps. 8.4-6 [MT vv. 5-7]).

The Masoretic text reads, 'Yet thou hast made him less than God'
(*'Elohim*), that is, it marvels at God's willingness to exalt humanity to
a status only just lower than His own. The septuagintal version
followed by the author of our Epistle, however, makes man's status
'lower than the angels'[4] rather than 'less than God'. Since βραχύς can

---

1. See p. 19 n. 7.
2. See Deut. 33.2 (LXX): ἐκ δεξιῶν αὐτοῦ ἄγγελοι μετ' αὐτοῦ.
3. Some manuscripts (including A C D* P ψ) add 'and didst set him over the
works of thy hands'. This is probably an assimilation to the LXX where the phrase
completes the couplet.
4. This is how it is understood in the Targum.

indicate either stature or duration it could mean 'lower than' in the LXX of the psalm also.

For our author's purpose it is important that it be understood as 'for a little while', since he wishes to interpret the death of Jesus as that brief interlude during which his condition was not one of exaltation but of humiliation:

> But we see Jesus, who for a little while (βραχύ τι) was made lower than the angels, crowned with glory and honour because of the suffering of death, so that[1] by the grace of God (χάριτι θεοῦ[2]) he might taste death for everyone (2.9).

As we have seen, the theme of Jesus' death as the means whereby he enters the presence of God and is enthroned in heaven, is one which plays a vital role in the analogy between the work of Christ and that of the high priest. Like the rest of the Old Testament passages cited in this section (1.4–2.18), therefore, Psalm 8 serves a wider purpose than merely to establish Jesus' sovereignty over the angels. Here it forms part of the scriptural foundation upon which our author is to build his presentation of Christ as superior to all other divinely appointed means of access to God. By virtue of Jesus' entry into heaven and enthronement as son, God's intention for the whole of humanity, that it should exercise sovereignty over the whole of creation (including the angels), has now been fulfilled.

---

1. ὅπως is best understood, not as introducing a purpose clause in 2.9b, but as epexegetical of the preceding phrase. Christ's death is thereby the means by which he tastes death for everyone.

2. The variant reading 'apart from God' (χωρὶς θεοῦ), although not so well attested by manuscript evidence, was accepted by some of the early fathers, and has found favour with some modern commentators. Origen and Theodoret understood 'apart from God' to mean 'God being no exception', and Ambrose and Theodore of Mopsuestia as, 'apart from his divine nature'. Those twentieth-century commentators (e.g. B. Weiss, A. van Harnack and H. Montefiore) who accept this reading understand it as a reference to Jesus' sense of separation on the cross from God (cf. Mk 15.34). See also J.K. Elliott, 'When Jesus was apart from God: An Examination of Heb. 2.9', *ExpTim* 83 (1972), pp. 339-41. The alternative reading, 'by the grace of God' (χάριτι θεοῦ), however, is to be preferred, not only because of its superior attestation, but because χωρὶς θεοῦ would be an extraordinary way for any Greek author to express any of the meanings expressed above. It may well have arisen as a result of an assimilation to 1 Cor. 15.27, where Psalms 8 and 110 are similarly brought together. For a fuller discussion see P.E. Hughes, *Hebrews*, pp. 94-97.

Yet for the present that fulfilment is only to be seen in Jesus; for the rest it remains in the future—part of 'the world to come' (2.5).[1] Writing as he does to a group who have known what it was to suffer for their faith (see 10.33; 12.4), our author is well aware that the world has yet to accept the sovereign reign of God. 'For now (νῦν), we do not yet (οὔπω) see everything in subjection to him' (2.8c). It is not clear whether by 'him' our author is still, like the psalmist, referring to humanity in general, or whether he has already particularized 'him' in Jesus. In either event, the following verse clearly applies the psalm to Jesus, where ascension and exaltation are seen as the fulfilment of God's intention for the whole of humankind.[2] Christ's entry into heaven becomes the surety, not only that *the* son but that 'many sons' will be brought to glory (2.10).

Thus, although Hebrews stresses the unique supremacy of Jesus, he does not do so at the expense of his solidarity with the rest of humanity. Hence he draws upon a psalm which extols the elevation of humankind as a whole, and sees that intention fulfilled in him. 'Son of man' has presented New Testament scholars with a number of problems. In the Gospels it is placed on the lips of Jesus himself, although it is not always clear whether he is referring to himself or some future figure. Did he use the phrase at all, and if so, did he always use it in the same sense? Was 'Son of Man' a messianic title in pre-Christian Judaism, or was it the early church, in giving it that significance, who made it such? The Epistle to the Hebrews does not help us resolve these issues, since it points to Psalm 8, rather than Jesus tradition, as the author's source for the phrase, 'son of man'. In keeping with the psalm, in Hebrews it is used, not in a titular sense, but as a synonym for 'man'. For our author 'son', not 'son of man', is Jesus' God-given unique name.

The latter provides Hebrews with the note of solidarity with which to end the section (2.10-18). On the basis of Jesus' common humanity, our author is able to proceed with his presentation of Christ's priestly role, in which he acts as part of what he represents. This is in accord with what we know of first-century CE Jewish interpretation, where

---

1. Heb. 6.5 'the age to come'; 13.4 'the city to come'. For the variety of designations for the future age in rabbinic literature see Moore, *Judaism*, II, p. 378.

2. See the combination of Psalms 8 and 110 in 1 Cor. 15.25-27 and Eph. 1.20-22, where they are employed to make the same point.

Psalm 8 is not regarded as messianic.[1] Thus, although Hebrews applies this psalm to Jesus,[2] unlike those texts in ch. 1 which were already accepted as messianic, it is not used to stress Jesus' unique identity as son, but to emphasize his solidarity with his followers. 'For he who sanctifies and those who are sanctified have all one origin (ἐξ ἑνὸς πάντες)' (2.11). It seems more in keeping not only with what has gone immediately before but also with the direction to which our author's thought now turns, to understand God, rather than Jesus, as the subject.[3] In which case the emphasis here is not upon Jesus the sanctifier, but on his inclusion among those who are sanctified, and their common unity in God. The following three biblical citations confirm Jesus' solidarity with his followers:

> I will proclaim thy name to my brethren, in the midst of the congregation I will praise thee (Heb. 2.12 = Ps. 22.22);
>
> I will put my trust in him (Heb. 2.13a = Isa. 8.17);
>
> Here am I, and the children God has given me (Heb. 2.13b = Isa. 8.18).

The first two confirm that Jesus is one with the assembled (cf. ἐκκλησία, v. 12) people of God in praising and trusting Him, and the third shows that he too is counted among God's children.

The chapter ends with a powerful affirmation of the true humanity of Jesus—a humanity which alone was ordained to rule on God's behalf:

> For surely it is not with angels that he is concerned but with the descendents of Abraham[4] (2.16).

---

1. *Contra* J.F. Moloney, 'The Re-Interpretation of Ps VIII and the Son of Man Debate', *NTS* 27 (1981), pp. 656-71, who cites the non-Qumranic Targums. An early date for these, however, is highly questionable. See J.A. Fitzmyer, *A Wandering Aramean: Collected Aramaic Essays* (Missoula, MT: Scholars Press, 1979), pp. 17-18, 71-74; S.S. Kaufmann, 'On Methodology in the Study of the Targums and their Chronology', *JSNT* 23 (1985), pp. 117-21.

2. See also Mt. 21.16; 1 Cor. 15.27; Eph. 1.22.

3. See Moffatt, *Hebrews*, p. 31; Wilson, *Hebrews*, pp. 54-55.

4. 'Sons of Abraham' was Israel's own self-designation. Christians, however, also adapted it to designate the church. See Rom. 9.8; Gal. 3.29.

Angelic hosts may 'people' heaven[1] and minister in the heavenly sanctuary,[2] but to be seated at God's right hand (Ps. 110.1) and to share divine sovereignty (Ps. 8) is not their intended destiny.

There is nothing in 1.4–2.18, therefore, which suggests that it was intended as a refutation of the notion that Christ was an angelic rather than a human being. We find such in Tertullian,[3] yet in contrast, our author's treatment is decidedly non-polemical in tone. He is not combatting a docetic Christology. If he were, it would be most unlikely that he would draw upon the figure of Melchizedek for the type of Jesus' priesthood. He would hardly have done so had he been aware of any tradition, like that at Qumran, which paralleled the functions of Melchizedek and the archangel Michael. Had he been at once utilizing and correcting such a tradition for the benefit of an audience composed of former Qumran Covenanters, as some have suggested,[4] it would surely have been vital to establish that neither Jesus nor Melchizedek were angels. In fact he does not treat of the matter with regard to Melchizedek. Furthermore, in his discussion of the supremacy of Jesus over the angels, our author is neither polemical nor corrective. Had his intention been so, we would have expected the subject to be taken up in one of his paraenetic sections. Where it is (2.1-4), it is in terms of the superiority of Jesus, as God's last word, to that granted in the Mosaic Torah. His preoccupations are those of an exegete engaged with a text, not an inquisitor rooting out 'heresy'!

Thus the author of Hebrews does not introduce the topic of angels to refute the suggestion that Jesus was one. Nor is he depicting the ascension of Christ as his victory over hostile aeons who would impede his ascent to heaven, for the benefit of a readership whose background was Gnostic.[5] On the contrary, there is nothing demonic about the angels we meet in Hebrews. Indeed they were mediators of the Law. The author of our Epistle discusses angels because they naturally arise from his use of Psalms 110 and 8, neither of which is cited to introduce the subject of angels. In the former, however, the son is

1. For the presence of angels among the heavenly council see 1 Kgs 22.19-23; Job 1.6-12; Isa. 6.6-7; etc.

2. For angels ministering in heaven see *Jub.* 30.18; *1 En.* 71; Philo, *Virt.* 74; etc.

3. Tertullian, *De Carne Christi* 6.

4. E.g. Kosmala, *Hebräer*; Yadin, 'Dead Sea Scrolls'; *idem*, 'Melchizedek'; Spicq, *Hébreux*; Longenecker, *Biblical Exegesis*.

5. *Contra* V. Narborough, T.W. Manson, E. Käsemann, R. Jewett *et al.*

located in heaven, where he is enthroned with God. The latter extols
Jesus' session as the fulfilment of mankind's destiny to have
sovereignty over the created order. His discussion of angels arises out
of this, and they become the first in the series of mediators whose
ministry he recognizes, but who are nonetheless superseded by Christ.

A tradition arose in postexilic Judaism according to which each
nation had been assigned a guardian angel. We can see this reflected in
the LXX of Deut. 32.8 which reads, 'He set the bands of the nations
according to the number of the angels of God', rather than the MT,
'according to the number of the sons of Israel'.[1] This may well also lie
behind our author's assertion that God has not subjected 'the world to
come' to angels but to man. While the present world may be under the
guardianship of angels, in the future world God's sovereignty will be
entrusted to humankind. Certainly, in late Judaism, especially in
apocalyptic writings,[2] angels came to play an increasingly important
role vis-à-vis the world, acting as God's messengers,[3] or interceding
before God on behalf of the righteous.[4] The author of Hebrews,
however, is more concerned with the angels' presence in heaven than
with their activity on earth. Apart from a brief mention of their
presence when the Law was given, their mediatorial role is not to the
fore. In his concentration upon their heavenly abode the author of
Hebrews may have been influenced by that strand of Jewish mysticism
which aspired to ascend to the heavenly chariot-throne (*Merkavah*).[5]
The Qumran Covenanters in worship also felt themselves in fellowship with the angelic hosts.[6] Principally, however, what determines
our author's interest in angels is that they are located where Jesus is
now—in heaven. Their occupation of the same sacred space does not
mean, however, that they have equal status with him. As son he far
outranks them (1.4).

---

1. Cf. also *1 En.* 10.5; Dan. 10.13; *Jub.* 15.31-32.
2. See Moore, *Judaism*, I, pp. 401-13; Russell, *Jewish Apocalyptic*, pp. 253-
362.
3. See *1 En.* 103.2; *2 Bar.* 81.4.
4. *1 En.* 15.2. Cf. Rev. 5.8 where angels offer prayers on behalf of the people.
5. See p. 61.
6. 1QH 3.21-23; 4.24-25; etc.

5. *Jesus, the Son*

Thus we can see that for the author of Hebrews, Jesus' primary status is not that of Melchizedekian high priest but son of God. Furthermore, in his understanding of son he is largely indebted to a royal, Davidic messianism. Hence he draws upon scriptural passages which have already been interpreted in these terms in Jewish and Christian circles, and makes them the basis of his subsequent claims for the supremacy of Jesus. Only having established Jesus' sonship does our author proceed to demonstrate, by virtue of that status, that he is the definitive means of access to God. In many ways Jesus' work may be compared with that of his biblical predecessors, namely Moses and the high priest, but in each case it is his sonship which is used to highlight the contrast between his status and theirs. Like them his task is to cross the boundary which divides the human from the divine, the sacred from the profane. Yet whereas their achievement is flawed and partial, Jesus has definitively crossed over into the realm of the sacred in entering heaven, the superior Mount Sinai and the true holy of holies. Even there, as son he is superior to heaven's angelic occupants, and destined to reign over the whole created universe on earth and in heaven.

Chapter 4

SESSION, SOVEREIGNTY AND SACRED SPACE

1. *Psalm 110.1 and the Exaltation of the Son*

Psalm 110 is, undoubtedly, the single most important biblical text used in Hebrews. Bringing together as it does the themes of sonship, sovereignty, priesthood and enthronement, it permeates the whole of our author's exposition from beginning to end. We have already seen how v. 4 of the psalm, which predicates Melchizedekian priesthood of the Davidic son, has played a vital role in Hebrews' presentation of the death and ascension of Jesus, the divine son. Now we must consider our author's use of the first verse:

> The Lord said to my Lord,
> 'Sit on my right hand
> till I make thy enemies
> a stool for thy feet.'[1]

This is one of the most widely used texts in the whole of the New Testament.[2] As David Hay's study, *Glory at the Right Hand*, has clearly demonstrated, however, not all early Christian writers use it for the same purpose.[3] Thus in Acts 2.33-36 it occurs in an apologetic context and is used to prove that by virtue of his resurrection and heavenly exaltation Jesus is indeed the messiah.[4] Elsewhere, however,

---

1. Hebrews follows the LXX with slight modifications. When paraphrasing Ps. 110.1 (1.3; 8.1; 10.12; 12.2) the author has ἐν δεξιᾷ. In direct quotation (1.13), however, he retains the LXX ἐκ δεξιῶν.

2. See p. 90 n. 4.

3. Hay, *Glory on the Right Hand*, esp. pp. 45-47.

4. B. Lindars (*New Testament Apologetic: The Doctrinal Significance of the Old Testament Quotations* [London: SCM Press, 1961], pp. 45-51) maintains that in the earliest Christian tradition Ps. 110.1 was seen as a literal depiction of the resurrection.

it is not principally employed in the service of apologetic.[1] In Mk
12.35-37 and parallels the context seems to be an intra-Christian
debate about the appropriateness or otherwise of using the title 'Son of
David' for Jesus. Here the opening phrase, 'The Lord said to my
Lord', plays an essential part in the argument. The author of Hebrews,
on the other hand, nowhere cites this phrase, not least because he uses
the psalm for very different purposes. As we have seen in the previous chapter, although he is content to draw upon a messianism modelled upon Davidic royal ideology, for the author of Hebrews it is
'son' which is the name Jesus attains (1.4) and which gives him his
unique status.[2] Where that sonship is further explicated it is as 'son of
God' (4.14; 7.13) rather than 'son of David'.

Our author's use of Ps. 110.1 does, however, accord with that
which we find in the majority of other New Testament writings which
focus on the theme of session and see therein an affirmation of
Christ's post-resurrection state of heavenly exaltation. Understood
thus, it may have become incorporated into credal and/or hymnic
material early in the life of the church. Many scholars have suggested
a catechetical or liturgical setting as the most likely explanation for its
wide dissemination in the tradition.[3] The author of Hebrews clearly
uses Ps. 110.1 as an established text, already known and accepted by
his readers as an affirmation of Jesus' exalted state. Unlike v. 4 of the
psalm, which he seems to be introducing into the Christian tradition[4]
in order to explore the person and work of Jesus in priestly terms,
v. 1 needs no careful introduction or exposition. So well is it known
to his readers that of the five times he refers to it, only once (1.13) is
it by direct citation rather than allusion.

Strikingly, the first of such allusions is in the prologue:

> When he had made purification for sins, he sat down at the right hand of
> the Majesty on high (1.3).

---

1. See Hay, *Glory on the Right Hand*, p. 47.
2. The anarthrous use of υἱός at 1.2, 5; 3.6; 5.8, far from suggesting that Jesus is
merely one son among many, points to his unique status, and places him in a category wholly different from that of the prophets, the angels and Moses.
3. See Hay, *Glory on the Right Hand*, pp. 39-43.
4. Thus he prefaces his exposition of Ps. 110.4 by stating that it is hard to explain
(5.11). What he has to say is solid food for the mature (5.14; cf. 6.1). This suggests
that the author of Hebrews is conscious that he is introducing a new insight.
Certainly, nowhere else in the New Testament do we find v. 4 of the psalm cited.

This royal psalm originally extolled Israel's king[1] as Yahweh's vice-regent on earth. His session at God's right hand was symbolic not only of his incomparable status but also of the source of his authority and power. This was a rule exercised on behalf of God, upon whom his sovereignty was wholly dependent. By the first century CE in some Jewish circles Psalm 110 seems to have been given a messianic interpretation.[2] For New Testament writers it found its fulfilment in Jesus' present heavenly existence. In some traditions his session is associated with a future last judgment.[3] Mainstream Christian interpretation, however, sees Christ's enthronement as taking place after his resurrection/ascension. So too for our author. Christ's enthronement does not lie in the future; it has already taken place.

This affirmation forms an important starting point for what is to follow, which is largely an explication of the means whereby Jesus achieved his exalted status. In this process we have seen how our author goes on to make heaven not simply a throne room but also a cult place; *the* cult place, to be more precise; the superior holy of holies (see 9.11-12). On this analogy, heaven, like its earthly counterpart, requires the offering of a purificatory sacrifice before the high priest can gain entry. Hence the prologue introduces the theme of Jesus' death *before* his session:

> When he had made purification for sins, he sat down at the right hand of the Majesty on high (1.3).

The cross, interpreted in sacrificial terms, was not merely prior in time to Christ's heavenly exaltation; cultically it was the essential prerequisite of his entry into heaven's sacred territory.

This is made evident in 8.1-2, a passage which both summarizes what has gone before and emphasizes our author's main point:

> Now the point (κεφάλαιον)[4] in what we are saying is this: we have such a high priest, one who is seated at the right hand of the throne of the Majesty in heaven, a minister in the sanctuary and the true tent which is set up not by man but by the Lord.

1. The majority of scholars place Ps. 110 in the time of a Davidic rather than a Hasmonaean king. See Hay, *Glory on the Right Hand*, pp. 19-20.
2. For a summary of the evidence see Hay, *Glory on the Right Hand*, pp. 27-30.
3. See Mk 14.62 and parallels; *Apoc. Pet.* 6.
4. κεφάλαιον can mean both 'summary' and 'main point'.

Thus, to previous Christian tradition which has used this psalm to depict Jesus as the exalted royal son, our author has added his own interpretation of the earthly ministry of Jesus portrayed in priestly terms. In Hebrews, therefore, it is both as king and high priest that Jesus is exalted to the right hand of God.

Although it is the session theme in Ps. 110.1 which most appeals to the author of the Epistle to the Hebrews, he does not entirely neglect the psalm's promise of God's final subjugation of the king's enemies. This theme is most fully developed in vv. 5 and 6 of the psalm, which were not utilized in early Christian tradition. It is present, however, in the concluding phrase of the opening verse, 'Till I make thy enemies a stool for thy feet', and as such is included in its full citation at 1.13. As we have seen, however, here Ps. 110.1 serves to establish the incomparable status of the son above even the angelic occupants of heaven, rather than to look forward to the defeat of his enemies in the future. The latter theme is touched on at 10.12-13:

> But when Christ had offered for all time (εἰς τὸ διηνεκές)[1] a single sacrifice for sin, he sat down at the right hand of God, then to wait (τὸ λοιπὸν ἐκδεχόμενος) until his enemies should be made a stool for his feet.

Thus, like entry into the promised land and the attainment of God's rest, the ultimate subjugation of Christ's enemies lies in the future.

Exactly who these enemies are is not expressed. In Pauline tradition they are identified as supernatural forces of evil,[2] especially epitomized by death itself, the last enemy to be overcome.[3] The apostle also

1. εἰς τὸ διηνεκές is one of our author's favourite expressions. At 7.3 it is used of the perpetual character of Jesus' Melchizedekian high priesthood; at 10.1 it refers to the continual round of sacrifices required by the Levitical system; at 10.14 it is the perfection attained 'in perpetuity' for the believer by Jesus' single sacrifice. At 10.12, however, its meaning is not clear since the syntax of the sentence is ambiguous. The RSV takes εἰς τὸ διηνεκές with the preceding clause, in which case it refers to the once-for-all nature of Christ's sacrifice. If it is taken with the succeeding phrase, however, then it is Jesus' enthronement which is 'in perpetuity'. See Attridge, *Hebrews*, pp. 279-80.

2. 1 Cor. 2.6; 2 Thess. 2.8, etc. The theme of the coming messiah's victory over demonic forces is common in Jewish apocalyptic writings. Cf. *1 En.* 10.13; *4 Ezra* 13.8; etc. From Qumran see also 1QH 6.29; 1QM 1.11, 13, 15, 17.

3. 1 Cor. 15.24-28, 55. Cf. 2 Tim. 1.10; Rev. 20.14; 21.4. In Heb. 2.14-15 Jesus' resurrection is seen as his victory over 'him who has the power of death, that

uses Ps. 110.1c ('For he must reign until he has put all [πάντας][1] his enemies under his feet' [1 Cor. 15.25]) which, in conjunction with Ps. 8.7 ('For God has put all things [πάντα] in subjection under him' [1 Cor. 15.27]), he uses as dual confirmation of the future subjugation of all things to Christ. When that is achieved he himself will be subjected to God. We have seen that Hebrews (2.8) also uses Ps. 8.7. Yet, unlike Paul, our author draws upon it as an affirmation of Jesus' *present* supremacy over the hosts of heaven and not with reference to a future subjugation. Here Hebrews is closer to Eph. 1.20-23 which similarly combines Psalms 110 and 8 to extol the reign of Christ in the present[2] over all angelic powers. In 1 Corinthians 15, however, it is not clear whether, for Paul, Christ's dominion begins at the resurrection or his parousia. In terms of the subjugation of enemies it is clearly the latter. What is evident is that for both Paul and Hebrews, Ps. 110.1 is concerned with Jesus' 'post-existence' rather than his pre-existence, since it depicts his enthronement which took place after his death and resurrection. For the author of Hebrews, that sovereignty is exercised in heaven rather than on earth, where, 'As it is we do not yet see everything in subjection to him' (2.8b).

Yet even in heaven Christ's session is more a symbol of his unique status rather than his active reign. Thus in the final allusion to Ps. 110.1 (12.2) the move from the aorist to the perfect tense, κεκάθικεν, suggests that being seated is the posture of one whose work has been completed. Ceslau Spicq has compared it to 'the rest of an athlete after effort'.[3] And indeed the main thrust of our author's argument is that Jesus' work of removing the barrier between the sacred and the profane has been achieved through his death. He now enjoys an unparalleled proximity to God as a result of his finished work.

Why then should there be any need for intercession—the one

---

is the devil'. Above all the believer is liberated from the bondage of the fear of death. That fear of death rather than death itself is seen to be the main enemy is more typical of Graeco-Roman rather than Jewish thought. See Attridge, *Hebrews*, p. 93.

1. The insertion of πάντας at this point seems to be due to an assimilation to Ps. 8.7 in v. 27. It enables Paul to make the point that everything and everyone (with the exception of God Himself) will be finally subject to Christ.

2. See also 1 Pet. 3.22 where Ps. 110.1 is also used to confirm Christ's present lordship over angelic powers.

3. Spicq, *Hébreux*, II, p. 388.

heavenly activity explicitly mentioned (7.25b; cf. 9.24)? David Hay finds this 'something of a "foreign body" in the epistle's theology',[1] and suggests that our author has probably taken it over from earlier Christian tradition[2] without resolving the tension it creates for his own soteriological schema. This would be true were it not for the fact that in Hebrews' conceptual framework, heaven is not only an existent territory in which the exalted Jesus now resides, it is also the future goal and destiny of the believer, held out as the only true cult place worth journeying to. There is, therefore, undoubtedly a gap between both 'here' and 'there', and 'now' and 'then', which Jesus alone has crossed. Furthermore this divide is not bridged by any Pauline notion of 'incorporation' into Christ's death and resurrection,[3] nor any Johannine idea of the mutual indwelling of disciple and Lord.[4] The exalted Christ of Hebrews has not taken anyone into the presence of God with him, other than in the generally accepted sense that the high priest enters the inner sanctum as the people's representative. Yet for our author this is not enough, and hence he criticizes the Levitical model precisely because the high priest enters alone and does not bring others into God's presence. Jesus' ministry, on the other hand, has as its end more than the representative nature of his priesthood. Its aim is that heaven should be accessible to all the people of God. In the interim period between Jesus' entry and theirs he intercedes for those who are as yet *en route*. Thus, in his depiction of the exalted Jesus interceding for his followers, the cultic and the eschatological intersect.

Nonetheless, Christ in session is a somewhat distant figure, separated from those who have as yet to enter heaven to join him. In our Epistle we find no portrayal of the Holy Spirit as the presence of the

---

1. Hay, *Glory on the Right Hand*, pp. 132, 149-51.

2. Cf. Rom. 8.24. It is possible, however, that here Paul has principally in view Christ's intercessory function on the future day of judgment rather than in the present. See M. Black, *Romans* (NCB; London: Oliphants, 1973), p. 126.

3. E.g. Rom. 6.3-4. E.P. Sanders (*Paul and Palestinian Judaism*, pp. 453-72, 502-508, 549) uses the term 'participation' rather than 'incorporation'. M.D. Hooker prefers 'interchange'. See *idem*, 'Interchange in Christ', *JTS* 21 (1971), pp. 349-61; 'Interchange and Atonement', *BJRL* 60 (1978), pp. 462-81; 'Interchange in Christ and Ethics', *JSNT* 25 (1985), pp. 3-17.

4. See Jn 6.56; 14.20; 15.5.

risen Lord[1] which might bridge the gap. Jesus' intercessory activity goes some way to modify the distance between earth and heaven, as does our author's emphasis upon the human Jesus, who himself endured suffering prior to his exaltation (2.17-18; 4.14-15; cf. 13.13). In this knowledge he exhorts them not to give up on their journey to join him:

> Let us then with confidence draw near to the throne of grace, that we may receive mercy and find grace to help in time of need (4.16).

Even so, it is not principally to the earthly Jesus that the readers are urged to look for encouragement, but to Christ in session—the one who has reached the goal for which they are striving. The picture of Jesus 'seated at the right hand of God' (12.2), therefore, also forms part of the exhortation to perseverance[2] with which the Epistle ends. The addressees are to look not only to God's future for inspiration but to the present glory of Jesus, and to aspire to similar glory (cf. 2.10).[3] What saves Hebrews' exalted Christ from being a wholly distant figure is the author's conviction of his imminent return to earth. Heaven is not discouragingly 'far' because it is 'soon'.

In summary, Ps. 110.1 is used by the author of Hebrews to stress Jesus' unique proximity to God—at His right hand. He has achieved this by virtue of his death, which was the means whereby he entered heaven, there to be enthroned as son of God, and to exercise sovereignty over heaven's hosts. This much our author takes from common Christian tradition, where the psalm has been used as part of a cross/exaltation pattern. This fits in well with his purposes since it enables him to focus on the theme of sacred space, which dominates his exposition of the person and work of Jesus. Hebrews, however,

---

1. In Hebrews the Spirit chiefly functions as the inspirational source of the Scriptures (3.7; 9.8; 10.15). At 2.4, the gifts of the Holy Spirit, together with signs, wonders and miracles, testify to the truth of Jesus' message. At 6.4-5, being a 'partaker of the Holy Spirit' is one of a number of metaphors used to describe conversion (see p. 31 n. 1). Nowhere in Hebrews is the Spirit personalized, nor is it Jesus' replacement or *alter ego*.

2. Col. 3.1 also uses this session psalm as an exhortation, but as symbolic of a type of living, entered into at baptism, which is heavenly rather than earthly. Cf. Eph. 2.6.

3. In Rev. 3.21 'the conquerors', i.e., the martyrs, already share Christ's throne in heaven.

moves beyond the traditional imagery of the psalm where heaven is a
royal court to introduce its depiction as a cult place—*the* shrine *par
excellence*. This enables our author to explore the death and ascension
of Jesus in terms of the actions of the Aaronic high priest on the Day
of Atonement. Like the high priest, he alone has entered the inner
sanctum, although in the case of Jesus this is the superior holy of
holies which is heaven itself. Unlike the high priest, moreover, he is
not forever to be the one who alone is permitted to enter the most
sacred presence of God; in the imminent future he is to return to
gather the elect who will then accompany him into that sanctuary
(9.27-28; cf. 2.10). In the meantime they have reached its borders and
are on the very brink of entry into the promised land.

Thus, to the commonly accepted Christian confession that Jesus is
exalted in heaven (Ps. 110.1), the author of Hebrews has added his
own unique presentation of Jesus' death and ascension in priestly
terms (Ps. 110.4). The result is an innovative soteriology, forged, on
the one hand from inherited Christian traditions and, on the other,
from the contemporary situation of his audience.

2. *The Prologue, its Wisdom Motifs and the Question of the Son's Pre-Existence*

Many commentators have drawn our attention to the rhetorical skill
with which the prologue has been composed. In the Greek text these
opening four verses of Hebrews are one long elaborate sentence,
whose constituent parts are balanced with care and precision.[1] The
rhetorical character not only of the Epistle's opening but of the whole
work is generally recognized by scholars. What is not so clear, however, is exactly what kind of rhetoric our author employs. According
to the accepted rules of the time rhetoric differed according to its
setting and audience.[2] Thus the rhetoric of the political arena was
'deliberative'; its aim was to persuade the hearers both to come to a
right decision and to act upon it. Clearly the paraenetic sections of
Hebrews could be classified as 'deliberative', in that here the author
employs the art of persuasion to move his readers, not only to right

---

1. See Attridge, *Hebrews*, p. 36.
2. See G. Kennedy, *The Art of Rhetoric in the Roman World: 300 B.C.–A.D.
300* (Princeton: Princeton University Press, 1972), esp. pp. 7-23.

beliefs, but to the actions which should follow from them.[1] In the market place or amphitheatre, however, 'demonstrative' (epideictic) rhetoric was employed. Its aim was the reinforcement of what the audience already knew or believed. We can see rhetoric of the 'demonstrative' type[2] in Hebrews at those points where the author seeks to reinforce those Christian traditions which he has in common with his readers. Both kinds of rhetoric, therefore, are at work in the Epistle.

The principal tone of the prologue is demonstrative, that is, it both appeals to and seeks to reinforce the common confession of the exalted status of the son, now seated at the right hand of God. This note is struck in v. 2, even before the allusion to Ps. 110.1 in v. 4, where Jesus is proclaimed as God's definitive spokesman who has entered into his inheritance. From v. 3c, 'when he had made purification for sins, he sat down at the right hand of the Majesty on high', it is clear that he 'whom he appointed heir of all things' (v. 2b, ἔθηκεν κληρονόμον)[3] has been granted nothing less than sovereignty over the entire created order. The rest of the chapter (1.4-14) goes on to demonstrate Jesus' superiority to angels who are included among the πάντα (everything).

To begin with, however, our author asserts Jesus' supremacy over the prophets who preceded him as God's spokesmen:

In many (πολυμερῶς) and various (πολυτρόπως) ways God spoke of old by the prophets; but in these last days he has spoken to us by a son (1.1-2a).

Here the RSV rightly translates the adverbs πολυμερῶς and πολυτρόπως (literally 'of many parts' and 'in many ways'), not as

1. S. Stowers (*Letter Writing in Greco-Roman Antiquity* [Philadelphia: Fortress Press, 1986], pp. 93-95, 107-108) points out that in the ancient world paraenetic letters were usually 'deliberative'. B. Lindars ('Rhetorical Structure', pp. 382-406) would classify the whole of Hebrews as 'deliberative' rhetoric whose aim was to deter the readers from returning to the worship of the synagogue.

2. Attridge (*Hebrews*, p. 14) classifies the whole of Hebrews' rhetoric as 'epideictic'. This, however, is to ignore its 'deliberative' features.

3. This echoes Ps. 2.8, 'As for me I will make the nations your heritage (LXX κληρονομία) and the ends of the earth your possession'. This oracle, in which the Davidic king was proclaimed son of God (Ps. 2.7), is used at Heb. 1.5b as part of the catena of scriptural passages demonstrating the supremacy of Jesus the son.

pejorative terms but as indicating the plurality and diversity of revelation in the past, over against the definitive word spoken through
Jesus. The contrast, therefore, is not so much between the fragmentary or piecemeal character of the inspiration granted to Israel's
prophets, as its multiplicity, which has now been superseded by the
singular, definitive word spoken through the son 'in these last days'.
At the very outset of the Epistle, therefore, we find a Christocentric
approach to revelation which pervades the rest of the work and con-
trols the way its author uses Scripture. Moreover, the inspiration of
the past is not thereby denied but affirmed, since the word spoken
through the son is the fulfilment of that diverse divine address spoken
through the prophets. Thus the prologue contains the twin themes of
continuity with the past and the superiority of new revelation in Christ
which we have seen to be integral to the whole of Hebrews.

In true epideictic style, Hebrews begins with an appeal to what was
already known and accepted by his audience. Thus he describes Jesus
in language previously applied by Judaism to 'wisdom'. It would seem
that such a christological appropriation of the Wisdom tradition was
something with which they were already familiar. Certainly the
author of Hebrews is not unique among New Testament writers in
applying such terminology to Jesus,[1] and there is nothing to suggest
from the way he introduces it in the prologue that it would be new to
his readers:

> through whom also he created the world (δι' οὗ καὶ ἐποίησεν τοὺς
> αἰῶνας). He reflects the glory of God (ὃς ὢν ἀπαύγασμα τῆς δόξης)
> and bears the very stamp of his nature (καὶ χαρακτὴρ τῆς ὑποστά-
> σεως αὐτοῦ) upholding (φέρων)[2] the universe (τὰ πάντα) by the word
> of his power (τῷ ῥήματι τῆς δυνάμεως αὐτοῦ) (1.2c-3b).

Many scholars believe that here our author is beginning his homily by
citing an existing hymn or credal confession with which his audience
were already familiar. They note the presence of certain stylistic

---

1. See Mt. 11.27-30 (cf. Ecclus 51.23-27); Jn 1.1-18; 1 Cor. 1.24, 30; 8.6; Col.
1.15-20.
2. The first hand in B reads φανερῶν (manifesting)—almost certainly a scribal
error. The superfluous letters were deleted by a corrector, only to be reinstated by a
thirteenth-century scribe who added the rebuke, 'Most ignorant and wicked man,
leave the original alone; do not change it!' See Bruce, *Hebrews*, p. 1.

features,[1] namely the use of participial phrases introduced by a relative, together with vocabulary not found elsewhere in the Epistle (such as ἀπαύγασμα and χαρακτήρ) or used in a sense atypical of the rest of the work (such as φέρων)[2] which could be an indication of an outside source or sources. Where such material can be paralleled in other New Testament writing and where literary dependence can be ruled out, then it is reasonable to assume that it is either a citation or an allusion to a common, established tradition, either written or oral. Given its content a liturgical or confessional setting has been suggested for this particular material.

On this criteria most scholars would accept v. 3,[3] which begins with the relative ὅς and continues with the participles φέρων and ποιησάμενος before concluding with an allusion to Ps. 110.1, as a fragment of an existing hymn or credal confession. Some want to extend it beyond v. 3[4] and suggest that it begins at v. 2c, 'through whom he also created the world', and continues to the end of v. 4 to include the reference to the more excellent name which the son has obtained. The justification for this, however, is not so much the style of the passage as its content, which can then be more closely paralleled with other supposed New Testament 'hymns'.[5] The more extensive the

1. See E. Stauffer, *New Testament Theology* (London: SCM Press, 1965), pp. 338-39.
2. Only here in Hebrews is φέρων used in the sense of 'governing'. See R.H. Fuller, *The Foundation of the New Testament Christology* (London: Lutterworth, 1965), pp. 220-21.
3. Fuller, *Foundation*, pp. 220-21; G. Bornkamm, 'Das Bekenntnis im Hebräerbrief', in *Studien zu Antike und Christentum* (Munich: Kaiser, 2nd edn, 1963), pp. 197-99; E. Grässer, 'Hebraer 1, 1-4: Ein exegetischer Versuch', in *Text und Situation: Gesammelte Aufsatz zum Neuen Testament* (Gütersloh: Mohn, 1973), pp. 182-230; J.T. Sanders, *The New Testament Christological Hymns: Their Historical Religious Background* (Cambridge: Cambridge University Press, 1971), pp. 19-20; *et al.*
4. See R. Deichgräber, *Gotteshymnus und Christushymnus in der frühen Christenheit: Untersuchungen zu Form, Sprache und Stil der frühchristlichen Hymnen* (Göttingen: Vandenhoeck & Ruprecht, 1967), pp. 137-45, who suggests that vv. 2 and 4 may also have been drawn from hymnic sources, albeit from different ones from those used in v. 3.
5. J.T. Sanders *(Christological Hymns)* classified Phil. 2.6-11; Col. 1.15-20; Eph. 2.14-16; 1 Tim. 3.16; 1 Pet. 3.18-22 and Heb. 1.3 as 'Christological hymns'. He includes Jn 1.1-18 in this category, although he admits that it is more in the genre

citation the more easily it would fit the pattern of pre-existence, incarnation, death and exaltation which some claim to find in other christological 'hymns' of the New Testament.[1]

The feature which more obviously links the prologue of Hebrews to other such hymnic passages is its christological appropriation of Jewish Wisdom motifs.[2] The divine Wisdom, both in its Hebrew (*ḥokmah*)[3] and Greek (σοφία)[4] guise, comes to the fore in postexilic writings. Now to its traditional revelatory function is added a creative one; Wisdom becomes God's agent in creation. In these traditions two tendencies can be seen: (1) the personification of the divine Wisdom, and (2) the desire to locate Wisdom in the 'beyond' of human history—understood protologically rather than eschatologically. Thus

of religious poetry rather than hymnody.

1. Fuller (*Foundation*, pp. 220-21) detects such a mythological pattern in Heb. 1.1-3; Phil. 2.6-11; Col. 1.15-20 and 1 Tim. 3.16. J.T. Sanders (*Christological Hymns*) believes that a common redeemer myth lies behind all New Testament christological 'hymns'. He is obliged to admit (see pp. 24-25), however, that not every feature is present in each 'hymn'. For Sanders, New Testament 'hymns' reflect a stage in the development of what is to become the myth of the redeemer in second-century Gnosticism (pp. 135-39). However, there are problems with two of the three 'hymns' often claimed to display a pattern common to that found in Heb. 1.1-3. (a) Phil. 2.6-11 (cited by Käsemann, *Wandering People*, pp. 101-15) probably contains no reference to the incarnation. For Paul, Jesus' 'self-emptying' is not his renunciation of a pre-existent glory in order to come into the world, but his death, seen as the supreme act of obedience which overturned the effects of the disobedience of the first Adam. See M.D. Hooker, 'Philippians 2.6-11', in *Jesus und Paulus. Festschrift für W.G. Kümmel zur 70 Geburtstag* (ed. E.E. Ellis and E. Grässer; Göttingen: Vandenhoeck & Ruprecht, 1975), pp. 151-64; Dunn, *Christology*, pp. 113-28; *et al.* Unlike Hebrews, moreover, the name to which Jesus was exalted is not that of 'Son' but 'Lord' (Phil. 2.9, 11). (b) 1 Tim. 3.16 has no reference to the death of Jesus. (c) Col. 1.15-20 (esp. vv. 15-17) is closest to Hebrews. Jesus is the 'firstborn' (πρωτότοκος cf. Heb. 1.6) of all creation. He also has a cosmic function, both in the initial act of creation and in continuing to sustain the universe. See Dunn, *Christology*, p. 206.

2. See Dunn, *Christology*, pp. 163-212 for a discussion of the 'wisdom of God' in Jewish tradition and the New Testament's use of it.

3. See Job 28.23-28; Prov. 1-9 (esp. 8); Ecclus 24.3-24. Ecclus was originally written in Hebrew, although it is mainly preserved in its Greek, Latin and Syriac versions. The Greek translation was made by Ben Sira's grandson in 132 BCE. See M. Gilbert, 'The Wisdom of Ben Sira', in *Jewish Writings of the Second Temple Period* (CRINT, 2.2; ed. M.E. Stone; Assen: Van Gorcum, 1984), pp. 290-301.

4. See esp. Wis. 7 and the writings of Philo of Alexandria.

for Ecclus 24.3-24, Wisdom in her revelatory role is equated with the Torah which did not simply come into being with Moses but went back to creation itself. Similarly in other Jewish sources we find a creative role assigned to Wisdom, in and by whom God brought the world into being.

It remains a matter of conjecture as to how far these writings have been influenced by beliefs about the goddess Wisdom—one of the deities of both Egyptian and Mesopotamian religion. Some scholars have seen the figure of Isis behind Prov. 8.22-31 and Ecclesiasticus 24, while others have detected the influence of Ishtar-Astarte on Prov. 1.20-33; 8.1-33; 9.1-6.[1] Be that as it may, even Bernhard Lang,[2] who numbers Wisdom among Israel's pre-exilic polytheistic pantheon, concedes that by the time we meet her in biblical texts she has become 'absorbed' into the one God of Judaism. Whether or not Wisdom as a female goddess played a role in Israel's early history, therefore, in the tradition in which she has become a part she is not thought of as an independent being. In pre-Christian Judaism it is highly improbable that wisdom was hypostatized. On this issue James Dunn correctly concludes:

> it is very unlikely that pre-Christian Judaism ever understood wisdom as a divine being in any sense independent of Yahweh. . . wisdom never becomes more than a personification. . . a way of speaking about God himself, of expressing God's involvement with his world and his people without compromising his transcendence.[3]

---

1. For the influence of Isis see W.L. Knox, 'The Divine Wisdom', *JTS* 58 (1937), pp. 230-237; Hengel, *Judaism and Hellenism*, I, pp. 157-60; B.L. Mack, *Logos und Sophia: Untersuchungen zur Weisheitstheologie in hellenistischen Judentum* (Göttingen: Vandenhoeck & Ruprecht, 1973), pp. 38-42. For Wisdom and Ishtar-Astarte see R.N. Whybray, *Wisdom in Proverbs* (SBT, 45; London: SCM Press, 1965), pp. 87-92.

2. B. Lang, *Wisdom and the Book of Proverbs: An Israelite Goddess Redefined* (New York: Pilgrim Press, 1986). For a survey of scholarly opinion on the figure of personified Wisdom in Proverbs see C.V. Camp, *Wisdom and the Feminine in the Book of Proverbs* (Sheffield: JSOT Press, 1985), pp. 19-68. Camp herself claims that in Proverbs, Wisdom functions as a metaphor whose various meanings depend upon the values associated with women in Israelite society. In the postexilic era, with the move of Israel's centre from the court to the family, Wisdom filled the role of a mediating, legitimizing figure previously played by the king.

3. Dunn, *Christology*, p. 176. See also Isaacs, *Concept of Spirit*, pp. 52-58.

Language which speaks of God's wisdom as his revelatory and creative power is not intended thereby to suggest the pre-existence of a divine being apart from God, but to affirm that His salvific plan and active involvement with His creation has been from the very beginning.

This conclusion does not of itself preclude the possibility that New Testament writers thought of Jesus as a pre-existent being who became incarnate. It does, however, radically undermine the assumption that the application of Wisdom language to Jesus automatically carries with it this implication for a first-century audience. It also leaves open the question of the mode of Christ's pre-existence. All this needs to be borne in mind as we look at the prologue of our Epistle.

Here, although the word σοφία is not used, language previously applied to Wisdom in Jewish tradition is transferred to Jesus, the son. Thus he it is through whom God created the 'universe'.[1] The Greek text here (1.2c) has οἱ αἰῶνες. Is this to be understood spatially or temporally? Does it refer to the creation of the material universe or the creation of time? Its principal meaning in Greek is temporal, although both in the singular (αἰών) and the plural (αἰῶνες) it can be used of space.[2] Both usages can be found in Hebrews. Thus in 6.5 'the age [singular] to come' is the author's designation of the eschatological future, whose power may be experienced in the present.[3] The same word (in the plural) occurs at 11.3:

> By faith we understand that the world (τοὺς αἰῶνας) was created by the word of God (ῥήματι θεοῦ) so that what is seen was made out of things which do not appear.

Here αἰῶνες clearly refers to the visible material universe which, according to Genesis, came into being at the divine command. Unlike the prologue, however, here our author does not seem to be drawing overtly upon Jewish Wisdom traditions. There is precedent for assigning Wisdom's various functions (including that of agent in creation) to God's 'word' (λόγος) in, for example, Philo of Alexandria, who can happily use σοφία and λόγος as synonyms.[4] In Heb. 11.3, however,

---

1. Cf. Prov. 3.19; 8.27-31.
2. E.g. Exod. 15.18 (LXX); Wis. 13.9; 14.6; etc.
3. It also seems to have a predominantly temporal meaning at 9.26.
4. E.g. *Leg. All* 1.65. Cf. Wis. 9.1. Thus for Philo the archetype of divine light can be σοφία (*Abr.* 40) or λόγος (*Somn.* 1.75), the manna can be either the wisdom

we find ῥῆμα not λόγος.[1] Furthermore, unlike the figure of Wisdom in Jewish sources, here there is no hint of personification. Certainly there is nothing to suggest that God's 'word' (ῥῆμα) is identified with the son. It would be misleading, therefore, to read 1.2c in the light of 11.3. Given the particular combination of spatial and temporal language which is a distinctive feature of the Epistle to the Hebrews, there is much to be said for understanding οἱ αἰῶνες in its prologue as containing a reference to both time and space.[2] Scholars have tended to read the whole of Hebrews exclusively in terms of one or the other, as Middle Platonic metaphysics or Jewish eschatology,[3] whereas, as we have seen throughout this study, the Epistle defies such simplistic either/or categorizations. From its very opening time and space jostle together, and to the son is ascribed pre-eminence in both.

In giving the son a role in creation our author is more obviously indebted to Wisdom traditions as they developed in Greek-speaking Judaism rather than those found in an earlier Palestinian work such as the book of Proverbs. There (Prov. 8.22-31) the description of Wisdom's presence at creation is to emphasize her antiquity rather than her creativity:[4]

> The Lord created (*qānānī*) me at the beginning of his work,
>> the first of his acts of old.
> Ages ago I was set up,
>> at the first, before the beginning of the earth (8.22-23).

In Prov. 3.19 we are told that God in his wisdom created the universe. At 8.22-31 this is expanded. Wisdom is now personified, and her temporal priority to the created universe brought to the fore. In this section, however, the Hebrew of the opening and closing verses poses certain problems for the translator. In v. 22a *qānānī* can be translated as (1) created, (2) begotten, or (3) acquired. Among Old Testament scholars each has its supporters.[5] This verb was to become an

---

(*Mut. Num.* 258-60) or words (λόγοι) of God (*Congr.* 173-74).

1. Occasionally (*Fug.* 137; *Sacr.* 8) Philo can use ῥῆμα as a synonym for λόγος, but this is rare.
2. See Buchanan, *Hebrews*, p. 6.
3. See pp. 56-61.
4. See Whybray, *Wisdom*, p. 103.
5. See W. McKane, *Proverbs: A New Approach* (Philadelphia: Westminster Press, 1970), pp. 352-53.

interpretative crux in the church's later christological debate, especially in the Arian controversy in the fourth century. By that time
Christian tradition had identified Jesus with the Wisdom of the text of
Proverbs. There is no clear evidence, however, that such an
identification took place prior to the second century.[1] Its significance
for our discussion lies in its connection with the issue of how *'āmōn* in
v. 30a is to be understood. This term is not attested elsewhere. The
RSV translation reads:

> then I was beside him, like a master workman (*'āmōn*);
> and I was daily his delight,
> rejoicing before him always,
> rejoicing in his inhabited world
> and delighting in the sons of men (Prov. 8.30-31).

There are, however, both syntactical and etymological problems
with the opening phrase.[2] As far as the syntax of the Hebrew is concerned, *'āmōn* could refer either to Wisdom or God. If it is the latter
then it should probably be translated 'I was at the side of the master
builder', that is, God. Most commentators, on the other hand, take it
as a reference to Wisdom. Even so we are still left with the problem
of how to translate *'āmōn*. Bernhard Lang suggests four possibilities:
(1) master builder/architect, (2) confidant, (3) counsellor or (4)
infant.[3] If the first is accepted then we find a creative role for
Wisdom, not only in Hellenistic Judaism, but in Palestinian tradition
also. Nonetheless it is still true to say that it is more pronounced in the
former. If, on the other hand, taking the fourth suggested meaning,
Wisdom is here depicted as the darling daughter of Yahweh, delight-
ing in the creation which He has made,[4] then Lang is correct in his
conclusion that 'she has no active part in creating the world. She is
just a spectator.'[5] To translate *'āmōn* as 'infant' or 'child' would lend
weight to the possibility that *qānānī* in v. 22 means 'begotten'. In
which case, as we meet her in Proverbs, Wisdom is the daughter of
God and is creation's first witness rather than its artificer.

In Hellenistic Jewish writings, however, a more active role is
assigned to Wisdom. Here she is also present before creation:

1. Justin, *Dial.* 61.
2. See Lang, *Wisdom*, pp. 65-66, 164 n. 20; McKane, *Proverbs*, pp. 356-58.
3. Lang, *Wisdom*, p. 65.
4. Whybray, *Wisdom*, p. 102; McKane, *Proverbs*, p. 357.
5. Lang, *Wisdom*, p. 66.

with thee is wisdom, who knows thy works and was present when thou
didst make the world (Wis. 9.9ab).[1]

The Wisdom of Solomon goes beyond Proverbs, however. Now
Wisdom is not merely a witness; she is 'an associate of his works'
(8.46) and 'fashioner' (τεχνῖτις; cf. 7.22) of what exists (8.6b). Philo
also speaks of Wisdom as the daughter of God who is at the same time
'the first-born mother of all things' (*Quaest. in Gen.* 4.97). His
preferred designation for God's creative power, however, is word
(λόγος) rather than wisdom. By virtue of its existence before
creation, the λόγος is God's firstborn (πρωτόγονος)[2] or elder
(πρεσβύτατος)[3] child, through whose agency He created the world.[4]

Philo's doctrine of the *logos* is complex.[5] Perhaps we should not
call it *a* doctrine, since he does not use the term uniformly. It is certainly misleading to present his writings on the subject in an over-
schematized fashion.[6] On the other hand, neither are Philo's works
simply a hotchpotch of ill-thought-out Hellenistic commonplaces.[7]
There is coherence in the role he gives the *logos*. Not least, in speaking of God's wisdom in terms of λόγος rather than σοφία, he is able
to draw upon the accepted tenets of Stoicism at those points where, in
his judgment, they coincide with Judaism. For the Stoics the λόγος
ἐνδιάθετος was the principle of divine reason which permeates the
cosmos and comes to its expression (λόγος προφορικός) there.[8] The
divine reason (λόγος) is thus at work in the world, where it may be

1. Cf. Ecclus 1.4; Aristobulus fragment 5 (in Eusebius, *Praep. Ev.* 7.14.1).
2. *Conf. Ling.* 146-47.
3. *Conf. Ling.* 146-47; *Rer. Div. Her.* 205-206. Heb. 1.6 uses the synonym
πρωτότοκος (cf. Col. 1.15).
4. *Spec. Leg.* 1.81; *Deus Imm.* 55-58; *Migr. Abr.* 6; *Cher.* 35.
5. For a good introduction to Philo's *logos* see R. Williamson, *Jews in the
Hellenistic World: Philo* (Cambridge Commentaries on Writings of the Jewish and
Christian World 200 BC to AD 200, 1.2; Cambridge: Cambridge University Press,
1989), pp. 103-43.
6. This is the major drawback of H.A. Wolfson's *Philo: Foundation of Religious
Philosophy in Judaism, Christianity and Islam* (2 vols.; Cambridge, MA: Harvard
University Press, 1947).
7. *Contra* A.J. Festugière, *La révelation d'Hermès Trismégiste.* II. *Dieu cosmique*
(Paris: Gabalda, 1949).
8. See Philo, *Migr. Abr.* 70-85; *Abr.* 83.

apprehended by itself, that is, that self-same reason with which humanity has been endowed. Philo, however, wants to emphasize not only the immanence of the *logos* but also its transcendent origin and nature. To this end he appeals to Platonism, with its distinction between the heavenly, immaterial world of Ideas and their earthly, material copies. By making the Ideas the very thoughts of God[1] he is able to unite the divine transcendence of Platonism with the immanentism of the Stoa, with the *logos* as the middle term. The *logos* of Hellenistic philosophy is thereby made to approximate to Jewish Wisdom, through whom God created the universe. It becomes the idea or ground plan which God had in mind for creation even before creation. Once articulated, it becomes the model for that creation.

Philo's *logos*, moreover, has a cosmic function which goes beyond protology. The Wisdom of Solomon can speak of God's spirit/wisdom as that which 'orders all things' (Wis. 8.1). Similarly, for Philo the role of the *logos* does not cease with the original act of creation. Like the Platonic/Stoic *anima mundi* it is the on-going power which continues to sustain the created order.[2] Philo seems to find little difficulty in using such beliefs about the existence of a rational law or principle governing and sustaining the universe as a vehicle for his Jewish faith, not least because, as we have seen, Wisdom has a similar cosmic function in Judaism. Quite clearly, behind Philo's *logos* speculations lies a Jewish understanding of God's wisdom.

To the protological and cosmological Philo adds an anthropological dimension to the role of the *logos*. It is not simply the divine plan for creation, nor, as the principle of reason, does it permeate the cosmos alone. It is to be found in humanity itself. Indeed, without its presence, contact between the divine and the human would be impossible. In biblical tradition a similar conviction lies behind the assertion that humanity was made in the image of God and was animated by the divine spirit. In Philo, however, it is the *logos* which is the point of contact between humankind and God.[3] Philo expresses the presence of

---

1. *Op. Mund.* 20; *Conf. Ling.* 63; *Cher.* 49; *Spec. Leg.* 1.47-48.

2. *Plant.* 8-9; *Somn.* 1.241. Yet note that God Himself can perform the same sustaining function. Cf. *Rer. Div. Her.* 23, 36; *Mut. Nom.* 256; *Conf. Ling.* 170; *Spec. Leg.* 4.200.

3. The Spirit (πνεῦμα) also has this function in Philo. See Isaacs, *Concept of Spirit*, pp. 43-48.

the *logos* in two different ways: either (1) the human mind/soul receives the impress or stamp (χαρακτήρ) of the divine power;[1] or (2) the human mind/soul is the reflection/radiance (ἀπαύγασμα)[2] of the *logos*.[3] The Wisdom of Solomon had already used similar language of God's Wisdom.

> For she is a reflection (ἀπαύγασμα) of eternal light, a spotless mirror of the working of God, and an image (εἰκών) of his goodness (Wis. 7.26).

Philo can also describe the *logos* as God's image[4] in whose likeness humanity was created.[5] There is no real distinction, therefore, between the way he uses 'impress' and 'image'. Both are employed to express the likeness of the copy to its prototype or mould.

The *logos* is thus the mind of God expressed in the created order. In spite of the fact that he sometimes uses language which makes the *logos* sound as if it is a separate hypostasis, for Philo it is neither an intermediary nor a self-existent being (see pp. 130-32). Rather, it is the face which God shows to the world.[6] Philo's development of Jewish Wisdom traditions in terms of *logos* allows him at once to affirm the transcendence of the creator and His accessibility to the world He has made.

Given this background it is not difficult to see parallels between the prologue of the Epistle to the Hebrews, Jewish Wisdom speculations in general, and their appearance in the guise of the *logos* in Philo in particular.[7] Thus in Hebrews the son is: (1) given an active role in creation—'through whom he created the world' (1.2c); (2) described as the reflection (ἀπαύγασμα) of the glory of God, and the imprint[8]

---

1. *Leg. All.* 1.161; *Sacr.* 60; *Det. Pot. Ins.* 77; *Rer. Div. Her.* 38, 181, 294.

2. ἀπαύγασμα can be understood either passively as 'reflection' (RSV) or actively as 'radiance' (NEB).

3. *Op. Mund.* 146; *Spec. Leg.* 4.27.

4. *Conf. Ling.* 97; *Somn.* 2.45; *Spec. Leg.* 1.81.

5. *Op. Mund.* 139, 146.

6. *Congr.* 97; *Migr. Abr.* 173-75.

7. See Moffatt, *Hebrews*, pp. 5-8; Michel, *Hebräer*, pp. 94-100; Williamson, *Philo and Hebrews*, pp. 36-41, 74-80, 95-103; Dey, *Intermediary World*, pp. 127-54; Dunn, *Christology*, pp. 220-28; *et al.*

8. Since the two phrases are probably intended as synonymous parallelism, the passive sense of ἀπαύγασμα, 'reflection' is to be preferred. If we read them as antithetical then the active 'radiance' would be better. In the particular context it is impossible to be certain and therefore, not surprisingly, commentators differ. See

(χαρακτήρ) of God's fundamental reality (ὑπόστασις)[1] (1.3a); and
(3) shown as continuing to sustain (φέρων) everything by his
powerful word (τῷ ῥήματι τῆς δυνάμεως αὐτοῦ) (1.3b). Although
similar, what is predicated of the son is by no means identical to what
Philo says of the *logos*, however, and is insufficiently close to prove
direct dependence.[2] 'Stamp' and 'reflection' are words more often
used by Philo to describe the relationship of the human mind/soul to
the *logos*, rather than that of the *logos* to God (τὸ ὄν).[3] The principal
difference between Hebrews' son and Philo's *logos* lies in the fact that
the latter remains wholly within the realms of abstraction and is never
personalized. As an aspect of the transcendent being of God it could
not by definition, for Philo, become incarnate.

Has the author of our Epistle, like the prologue of the Fourth
Gospel, taken that definitive step whereby Jesus of Nazareth is proclaimed as the incarnation of the divine *logos*? Graham Hughes thinks
that we find in Hebrews an 'all-but explicit Logos Doctrine'.[4] Ronald
Williamson's judgment is that, 'This almost but not quite states that the
Son is God's Logos or Word. It certainly implies such a view of
him.'[5] Although Williamson is obliged to admit that the word λόγος is
not to be found in the opening verses of the Epistle, nonetheless he is
convinced that its author had the incarnation of the pre-existent Son of
God/Logos in mind. To strengthen his argument he takes instances

Attridge, *Hebrews*, pp. 42-43.

1. ὑπόστασις was originally a medical or scientific term used to describe the
sediment left behind at the bottom of a flask. It was introduced into philosophy by
the Stoics as a reference to underlying existence. See H. Koester, 'ὑπόστασις',
TDNT, VIII (1972), pp. 572-89.

2. It is more likely that our author has been influenced by Wisdom speculation
common to both, rather than directly by Philo. See Williamson, *Philo and Hebrews*,
pp. 36-41, 74-80, 95-103.

3. *Plant.* 18, which describes the *logos* as the impress (χαρακτήρ) of the divine
power, is a rare exception. Although Philo can describe the *logos* as light (*Fug.* 97;
cf. *Migr. Abr.* 40 where Wisdom is light), he does not refer to it as the ἀπαύγασμα
of God. He speaks of either the human mind as the ἀπαύγασμα of the divine *logos*
(*Op. Mund.* 146; *Somn.* 1.72, 239; *Spec. Leg.* 4.123), or the world as the reflection
of the original plan (*Plant.* 50).

4. G. Hughes, *Hebrews and Hermeneutics*, p. 5.

5. R. Williamson, 'The Incarnation of the Logos in Hebrews', *ExpTim* 95
(1983), p. 7.

where Hebrews does use λόγος and seeks to give them a christological interpretation. He paraphrases 2.2 thus:

> Now, a fortiori, if the 'message' of God enshrined in the Law is 'logos', how much more is the 'message' conveyed to mankind 'by a son', *the* Logos.[1]

Yet this is surely reading far too much into the text? The very next verse makes plain that the Lord (i.e. Jesus) is not himself the 'message' but its proclaimer.

Equally unlikely is Williamson's translation of πρὸς ὅν ἡμῖν ὁ λόγος at Heb. 4.13 as, 'with whom the Logos is present on our behalf'.[2] Here he takes λόγος to refer to the exalted son who now represents his people before God. Williamson partly justifies this reading by citing Jn 1.1 where the *logos* is 'in the presence of God' (πρὸς τὸν θεόν). He does not point out, however, that in the Gospel this refers to the pre-incarnate *logos*, whereas, if we accept his translation of Heb. 4.13, here we have the *logos* who has now returned to God. The parallel is far from exact and certainly not enough to justify understanding πρός in its Johannine sense. In the previous verse our author has warned his readers of the penetrative power of God's word:

> For the word (λόγος) of God is living and active, sharper than any two-edged sword, piercing to the division of soul and spirit, of joints and marrow, and discerning the thoughts and intentions of the heart (4.12).

Here the *logos* is not the son, but God who speaks through the Scripture which our author has been expounding (i.e. Ps. 95) in chs. 3 and 4.

That the word is the vehicle of divine judgment is an Old Testament idea.[3] Here it is also likened to a sword[4]—a simile which by the first century seems to have become a commonplace. We find it, for example, in Philo, who uses the sword as a symbol of the *logos*.[5] Of more interest to our particular study is Philo's 'cutting logos' (λόγος

---

1. Williamson, 'Incarnation', p. 7.
2. Williamson, 'Incarnation', p. 8.
3. E.g. Amos 1.2; Isa. 51.16; Jer. 7.1-3.
4. For judgment as God's sword see Isa. 34.5-6; 66.16. Wis. 18.14-16 depicts the word as a warrior wielding God's sword of judgment against the Egyptians at the time of the Exodus.
5. *Cher.* 28, 30.

τομεύς), which, like the word of God in Heb. 4.12 has a dividing function. One of the functions of the Philonic *logos* is to separate God's creation into categories. Thus it divides the soul into the rational and the irrational.[1] Philo attributes to Heraclitus the authorship of the view that there is such a principle at work in the universe, dividing into opposites and equals,[2] although for the Alexandrian rabbi it is 'God alone who is exact in judgment and alone able to divide in the middle'.[3] The author of Hebrews here expresses a similar sentiment when he states that God's judgment can penetrate even the most impenetrable regions of human existence.[4]

According to Williamson's reading, the *logos* of v. 12, which is God speaking through the psalmist, changes its referent in v. 13c to become the ascended Christ. The son of God is indeed the subject of the following verses (14-16), but has that shift taken place in the very last phrase of the preceding verse, 'with whom the logos is present on our behalf'? I think not. The more usual translation of πρὸς ὃν ἡμῖν ὁ λόγος is, 'with whom we have to do' (RSV), or better, 'with whom we have to reckon' (NEB). We can find λόγος used in the commercial sense of 'account' or 'reckoning' in pagan Greek sources.[5] More importantly, the author of Hebrews himself uses the noun in this way in 13.17 where it refers to the accountability which Christian leaders owe to God. The only ambiguity is that in 4.13 the verb is left unexpressed.[6] This should not preclude its meaning 'account' here. It makes more sense in the context than does Williamson's suggestion. In which case λόγος does not refer to the son.

In seeking further to buttress his argument, Williamson claims that there are other passages in Hebrews which imply a notion of pre-existence. Here he is in good company since a number of scholars, both past and present, have drawn the same inference even though they have not necessarily claimed that our author was utilizing a *logos*

1. *Rer. Div. Her.* 132.
2. *Rer. Div. Her.* 214.
3. *Rer. Div. Her.* 143.
4. It is unlikely that here a distinction is intended between the rational (πνεῦμα) and irrational (ψυχή) within human nature. 'Spirit and soul', 'joints and marrow', 'thoughts and intentions' are better understood as pairs of synonyms, used to emphasize that God's judgment can penetrate even what is seemingly inseparable.
5. See Moffatt, *Hebrews*, p. 58.
6. See Heb. 13.17; Mt. 12.36; Lk. 16.2; 1 Pet. 4.5 where the verb ἀποδίδωμι (render) is used. Mt. 18.23; 25.19 has συναιρέω (settle).

doctrine. Heb. 7.3 is one such passage. Here the son of God is the model for Melchizedek rather than vice versa. Yet as we have already seen (pp. 153-54), Melchizedek is not used principally to reinforce a doctrine of pre-existence but to emphasize that Jesus' is a priesthood which does not come to an end, since his resurrection proclaims the power of an indestructible life (cf. 7.16). Undoubtedly the son is the superior type of all previous mediatorial figures. Yet this is not so much by virtue of his prior existence as by his present status in heaven. The main thrust of our author's exposition is that he is 'without end', rather than that he is without 'beginning of days'. The latter statement is not pursued.

I have already maintained (*contra* Williamson *et al.*) that we should not read ῥῆμα τοῦ θεοῦ in 11.3 as other than an allusion to the traditional biblical motif of God's creative word, through whose utterance the universe came into being.[1] Unlike 1.3, here there is nothing to suggest the protological agency of the son. More tentatively, Williamson sees in 'Jesus Christ is the same yesterday (ἐχθές), today and forever' (13.8) a reference to the pre-existent son. Yet surely for our author 'yesterday' refers to the events in the life of the earthly Jesus (notably his death and ascension) to which he has been appealing throughout the homily, not to his existence from all eternity?[2]

The same can be said of 10.5-7:

> Consequently, when Christ came into the world (εἰσερχόμενος εἰς τὸν κόσμον) he said, 'Sacrifices and offerings thou hast not desired, but a body thou hast prepared for me (σῶμα δὲ κατηρτίσω μοι); in burnt offerings and sin offerings thou hast taken no pleasure. Then I said, "Lo, I have come into the world to do thy will, O God", as it is written of me in the roll of the book'.

Here, with minor variants,[3] our author is citing the LXX of Ps. 40.6-8. In the Greek version the obscure Hebrew phrase 'ears thou hast dug for me' (freely rendered in the RSV as 'thou hast given me an open

---

1. Cf. Gen. 1.3; Ps. 33(LXX 32).6; etc.
2. See F.F. Filson, *'Yesterday'—A Study of Hebrews in the Light of Chapter 13* (SBT, 4; London, 1967), pp. 30-34; *contra* Montefiore, *Hebrews*, p. 242.
3. Hebrews reads οὐκ εὐδόκησας (you were not pleased) in v. 6 in place of the LXX οὐκ ἐζήτησας (you did not seek); puts the nominative ὁ θεός (O God; the LXX reads ὁ θεός μου [my God]) in v. 7 before τὸ θέλημά σου (thy will) instead of after it, and omits ἠβουλήθην (I have resolved) at the end of the citation.

ear') has been interpretatively paraphrased as 'a body thou hast prepared for me'. Either way, it is the human person, whether in part ('ears') or whole ('body'), who is called upon to do God's will. For the psalmist, such willing, personal obedience to the Law[1] is superior to the sacrificial offerings of the cult.

The author of Hebrews puts the psalmist's words on the lips of Jesus, not in order to claim his personal pre-existence,[2] but to identify the death of Christ with the superior self-offering mentioned in Psalm 40. This, he argues, is not only more efficacious than the sacrifice of animals (cf. 9.11-14, 25; 10.4); it abrogates the whole sacrificial system (10.8-10). We have seen throughout our study of Hebrews that such an appeal to Scripture is typical of its author's attitude to God's earlier revelation. Scripture witnesses to Jesus, who may therefore be said to speak through it.

Undoubtedly it is the life of Jesus which is seen by our author as the fulfilment of the psalmist's call to a life lived in radical obedience to God. The language of 'coming (εἰσερχόμενος) into the world',[3] however, should no more be read as indicating the emergence into the world of a pre-existent being, than 'a body thou hast prepared for me' be interpreted as Jesus' ready-made human body, awaiting occupation! Equally misguided are attempts to pinpoint the moment at which Jesus' obedience begins. In this connection Harold Attridge rightly states

> Although the incarnation is clearly in view the introductory verse is important not because it stresses a particular moment when Christ's act of obedience to the divine will was made, but because it indicates that the cosmos is the sphere of the decisive sacrifice of Christ.[4]

At 2.12-13 we find another instance of Scripture (Ps. 22.22 and Isa. 8.17-18) being put into the mouth of Jesus. This does not mean,

---

1. In Ps. 40.8 ἡ κεφαλὶς βιβλίου (in the scroll of the book) refers to the Law (cf. Ps. 40.9). Hebrews, however, uses the phrase to refer to Scripture as a whole.

2. *Contra*, Westcott, *Hebrews*, p. 315, who sees here the pre-existent Christ speaking through the psalmist. See also Hanson, *Living Utterances*, p. 108, who regards these words as the address of the pre-existent son to the Father at the moment of his incarnation.

3. εἰσέρχομαι at 10.5 only implies pre-existence if read in the light of Jn 1.9 (cf. Jn 6.14; 11.27). Michel (*Hebräer*, p. 336), on the other hand, cites examples of the verb being used simply to mean 'to be born'.

4. Attridge, *Hebrews*, p. 273.

however, that it is the pre-existent Christ who is speaking, nor that the
following verses (14-16) have as their subject the pre-existent son's
considered choice to adopt the limitations of an incarnate existence.[1]
The following verse, 'Since therefore the children share (κεκοινώνηκεν) in flesh and blood,[2] he himself likewise partook (μετέσχεν)[3]
of the same nature' (2.14a), certainly stresses Jesus' solidarity with
humankind in its frailty. It is only possible to see in v. 16 ('For surely
it is not with angels that he is concerned [ἐπιλαμβάνεται] but with
the descendants of Abraham') a reference to pre-existence, however,
if we take the verb ἐπιλαμβάνομαι to mean 'assume the nature of'.[4]
Yet more naturally it means 'to lay hold of', and in this context is used
in its metaphorical sense[5] of Jesus' activity of keeping and guiding
those who follow him. Human frailty remains our lot (note the perfect
tense κεκοινώνηκεν). In the case of Jesus, however, that weakness
was but for the span of his earthly life (see the aorist μετέσχεν). As
exalted son he is no longer subject to human limitations (see 2.5-9).

In none of these passages, therefore, do we find a depiction of Jesus
as the incarnation of a pre-existent being. Indeed, on occasion our
author uses language which suggests that Christ's status as son of God
was one to which he was appointed, either before his Passion, or at his
exaltation (see 1.4, 5; 5.1-10). Like the language of 'perfection',
which we have seen (pp. 101-107) encompasses the whole process by
which Jesus entered the presence of God, that of sonship is not used of
one moment, within or beyond time, when its status was conferred.
Rather 'son' is used by the author of Hebrews to characterize Jesus'
life of obedience which culminated in the cross and ascension. In all
but the prologue it refers either to Jesus' earthly ministry or to his

1. So Hickling, 'John and Hebrews', p. 113.
2. The RSV translation here inverts the Greek 'blood and flesh'. This is an
unusual word order for what is otherwise a commonplace phrase. It may be due to
the fact that the death of Jesus is uppermost in our author's mind.
3. κοινωνέω and μετέχω are here used as synonyms. Cf. 1 Cor. 10.17-21; 2
Cor. 6.14.
4. So most Greek and Latin fathers. Among its modern proponents are Spicq,
Hébreux, II, pp. 45-46 and P.E. Hughes, *Hebrews*, pp. 117-19. For a refutation
of the suggestion that it means 'come to the aid of' (so Westcott, Moffatt, Windisch,
Bruce *et al.*) see P.E. Hughes, *Hebrews*, pp. 117-18.
5. See Attridge, *Hebrews*, p. 94.

post-resurrection heavenly existence. Attempts to see references to the son's pre-existence throughout the Epistle are unconvincing.

However atypical of the rest of the work, we do find the idea of pre-existence in the prologue. It is implicit in our author's christological appropriation of Wisdom's creating and sustaining functions. J.D.G. Dunn believes that the author of Hebrews is the first New Testament writer to introduce a notion of the son's pre-existence,[1] although he thinks that what pre-exists for our author is not a personal being but the salvific purpose in the mind of God which finds expression in Jesus. He writes:

> The thought of pre-existence is present, but in terms of wisdom christology it is the act and power of God which properly speaking is what pre-exists; Christ is not so much the pre-existent act and power of God as its eschatological embodiment.[2]

The mode of Christ's pre-existence was to become a topic of debate in subsequent Christian theology. It is not, however, the concern of the author of Hebrews. Although he may briefly allude to an existing Christian hymn or confession in which Christ had been given a protological role, his own principal portrayal of the son's activity is soteriological. Hence he quickly moves to the major affirmation of his homily:

> When he had made purification for sins, he sat down at the right hand of the Majesty on high (1.3b).

It is not the son's pre-existence but his death, viewed as the means whereby he became exalted in heaven, which is the theme which dominates the rest of his exposition. Even the following catena of scriptural quotations (1.5-13), as we have seen (pp. 167-72) is used as testimony to his post-resurrection status rather than to his protological pre-existence.[3] Jesus' session in heaven may be both his end and his beginning, but for our author it is the end which is principally his beginning rather than vice versa.

---

1. Dunn, *Christology*, pp. 51-56.
2. Dunn, *Christology*, p. 209.
3. *Contra* R.G. Hammerton-Kelly, *Pre-Existence, Wisdom and the Son of Man* (SNTSMS, 21; Cambridge: Cambridge University Press, 1973), pp. 243-58. Hammerton-Kelly, however, assumes that Hebrews is combating an angel-Christology.

3. *Heaven as the Eschatological Goal of the People of God*

We have seen that the author of Hebrews begins and ends with the theme of heaven. What opens with an affirmation of Jesus' session in heaven continues and ends with an exhortation to his audience to make heaven their goal also. The motif of Christ's present exaltation in heaven recurs throughout the homily, and is held out as encouragement to a Christian community who are feeling weighed down by the circumstances of their present terrestrial existence. They are exhorted not to lose confidence in that celestial reality which is the son's present abode, since if they do not waver, it will soon be theirs.

So much is clear. But what does Hebrews mean by 'heaven'? This is not easy to answer, not least because in the Judaeo-Christian tradition in which our author stands, heaven is not so much a geographical location as a symbol of the divine. Even within pagan Greek thought the 'firmaments' (οὐρανοί)[1] not only constitute the arch which stretches above the earth; they can also designate that which is above the firmament—the divine, which embraces everything. The cosmological and the theological, therefore, are inseparable, and both are part of what is meant by 'heaven'.[2] Similarly in Old Testament tradition[3] heaven is both part of the created order[4] and above it. It can be spoken of as God's dwelling place.[5] Yet God can choose to make any space 'holy' by gracing it with His presence, whether on earth (e.g. Mt Sinai, the sanctuary, the ark) or in heaven. Therefore to say that God is present in heaven is not to confine Him to a particular location, even in the celestial sphere.[6] He is above the firmaments He has created. In Jewish apocalyptic literature this finds its expression in the idea that

---

1. 'Heaven' should more properly be translated 'heavens', since it is usually in the plural in both Hebrew (*shamayim*) and Greek (οὐρανοί).

2. For heaven in pagan Greek thought see H. Taub, 'οὐρανός', *TDNT*, V (1967), pp. 497-501.

3. For heaven in the Old Testament see G. von Rad, 'οὐρανός', *TDNT*, V (1967), pp. 502-509.

4. Gen. 1.8; 14.19; Ps. 121.2; etc. Cf. Heb. 1.10 (= Ps. 102 [MT 101].26).

5. 1 Kgs 8.30, 39, 43; 2 Chron. 6.33.

6. 1 Kgs 8.26; 2 Chron. 2.6; 6.18.

there is more than one heaven,[1] with God inhabiting only the last and highest. In the talmudic *Hekhalot* writings[2] this was to develop into seven divine rooms or palaces through which the visionary had to pass in order to reach God's dwelling place, which was the seventh. In our Epistle it lies behind the affirmation that Jesus is now 'higher than the heavens' (ὑψηλότερος τῶν οὐρανῶν) (7.26). As we shall see, above all in Hebrews 'heaven' symbolizes the sphere of divine sovereignty.

The Old Testament has numerous poetic images of heaven as a place. It can be a tent stretched out over the earth;[3] a scroll which can be rolled up;[4] or a chamber housing snow and hail,[5] winds[6] and water.[7] These few examples should serve to remind us that the language of 'heaven'—including that used by our author—is essentially religious metaphor and, as such, defies all attempts at systematization. This is certainly evident when we look at the depiction of heaven in Hebrews. Here we find four different images of heaven as 'place'. It is: (1) the throne room of a royal court, (2) a country, (3) a city or kingdom, and (4) a shrine. Our author moves freely from one simile to another without any attempt to harmonize the diverse images. Clearly they are closely related to the various models of salvation (dominion, inheritance, entry into the holy of holies) which he employs in his presentation of the death of Jesus as the means whereby that 'heaven' is attained.

Our author has adopted the first from the Old Testament where heaven is portrayed as the courtroom of a royal palace in which the throne of God the King is located.[8] Heaven thus symbolizes the reign of God. This image of heaven lies behind the depiction of Jesus' ascension as his enthronement as the son of God, by virtue of which

---

1. In Jewish apocalyptic and later rabbinic writings the number of heavens varied. There can be two (*2 En.* 7.1), three (*2 En.* 8.1; cf. 2 Cor. 12.2-4), five (*3 Bar.* 11.1), seven (*3 En.* 1-2; 17.1-3; *b. Hag.* 12b) or ten (*4 En.* 20). See Strack–Billerbeck, III, pp. 531-33.
2. See p. 61 and notes.
3. Isa. 40.22; Ps. 104.2.
4. Isa. 34.4
5. Job 38.22.
6. Jer. 49.36; Job 37.9.
7. Ps. 33.7; Job 38.7.
8. Ps. 10(MT 11).5; Isa. 66.1, etc. Cf. also Rev. 4.2–5.2 where heaven is also depicted as a throne room.

he now shares divine sovereignty. As we have seen (pp. 167-77) this is the dominant theme of Heb. 1.4–2.18. It is also present wherever Ps. 110.1 is alluded to, since the posture of being 'seated at the right hand of the throne of the Majesty in heaven' (8.1) is one which indicates that the son shares God's dominion.

Heaven as the promised land of 'rest' is the dominant image of chs. 3 and 4, although the word 'heaven' (οὐρανοί) does not occur here. The section begins, however, with the author addressing his audience as those 'who share in a heavenly call' (κλήσεως ἐπουρανίου μέτοχοι, 3.1a). An appeal to divine election is, of course, a biblical commonplace, but this address stresses not only the heavenly (ἐπουράνιος) origin of the Christian's call, but heaven as the destination to which he or she is called. Therefore the verse continues, 'consider Jesus, the apostle and high priest of our confession' (3.1b). The focus here is not upon heaven as the origin of his call but upon heaven as the goal which he has achieved. His followers, therefore, are addressed as those who are embarked upon a journey to the self-same destination. Language of heaven as the promised land can quickly give way to the image of heaven as a cult place, as we see in the bridge passage (4.14-16) which concludes the section on the wilderness wanderings and begins the main exposition of the work of Jesus in priestly terms. Our author returns once more to the theme of heaven as the promised land near the end of his homily. Thus in ch. 11 the land of promise (v. 9), the better country looked forward to in faith by the heroes and heroines of old, is in fact 'a heavenly one' (τουτ' ἔστιν ἐπουρανίου, 11.16).

Elsewhere in the same chapter the land becomes a city 'whose builder and maker is God' (11.10), and at 12.22 that city is identified as the 'heavenly Jerusalem' (Ἰερουσαλὴμ ἐπουρανίῳ), which in the future will become not only the abode of angels but of the whole assembly of God's faithful people (see pp. 86-88). By the time we reach the end of the chapter the city has taken on the dimensions of a city-state, a kingdom (βασιλεία) which is unshakeable (ἀσάλευτος) (12.28). Just as in 1.10-12 our author has cited Scripture (Ps. 101 [MT 102].26-28) as proof of the transient nature of the whole created order (heaven included) and contrasted this with the eternal reign of God, so in 12.25-29 he makes a similar point. Here he sees in the words of Hag. 2.6 (LXX: 'Yet once more I will shake [σείσω] not only the earth but also the heaven' [12.26]) God's promise to replace the present created order which is impermanent[1] (cf. v. 27 σαλεύω) with the unshakeable kingdom of God. The most obvious source of this imagery is not that of Platonic cosmology with its distinction between the inferior world of sense perception and the superior immaterial world of Ideas,[2] but Jewish notions of heaven as both part of and beyond the created order. The image of an earthquake, used to depict the irruption of the Day of the Lord, can be found in both biblical[3] and extrabiblical[4] sources, and seems to have become an accepted part of Jewish eschatological discourse, especially in apocalyptic circles. The same can be said of language of the kingdom (βασιλεία) of God. The book of Daniel promises that the righteous shall inherit an eternal kingdom (βασιλεία αἰώνιος):[5]

> But the saints of the most high shall receive (LXX παραλήψονται) the kingdom (LXX βασιλεία), and possess the kingdom for ever and ever (Dan. 7.18).

What is a future prophecy in Daniel is, in Hebrews, a process which is already taking place (see the present participle παραλαμβάνοντες in 12.28), since the earth's 'shaking' has already occurred. Unlike Matthew's Gospel (27.51, 54) here we find no earthquake coinciding with Jesus' crucifixion; our author does not overtly identify the moment when that 'shaking' of the earth took place. We may reasonably infer from the rest of the Epistle that for him also it is the death of Jesus which has shaken the earthly order, and his ascension which signals its replacement by a heavenly one.

Images of heaven as both palace and temple had already been brought together by the psalmist, no doubt influenced by the proximity of both establishments in Jerusalem:

1. Cf. *4 Ezra* 7.21 which also looks forward to the disappearance of the visible universe.
2. See pp. 57-58 and notes.
3. See Hag. 2.6 which is cited in Heb. 12.26. Cf. also Joel 2.30; 3.16. Although the Exodus account does not mention an earthquake, it is introduced elsewhere in biblical tradition (see Ps. 68 [LXX 67].8; 77 [LXX 76].18; 114 [LXX 113].7). Theophanies in general are sometimes accompanied by an earthquake (e.g. Isa. 6.4; Ps. 18 [LXX 17].7; Amos 9.5).
4. *1 En.* 60.1; *4 Ezra* 6.11, 17; 8.18; 10.25-28; *Sib. Or.* 3.675; *2 Bar.* 32.1; 59.3. Cf. Mt. 24.29.
5. Dan. 7.14; 18.27.

> The Lord is in his temple,
> the Lord's throne is in heaven (Ps. 11 [LXX 10].4).

The author of Hebrews also depicts heaven in terms of Israel's cult place, although his sermon concentrates upon the period in Israel's history when it worshipped in the 'tent of meeting' rather than in the Jerusalem Temple. To describe heaven itself as a shrine, as does Psalm 11 and our Epistle, is not the same as to claim that the earthly sanctuary had been planned by God prior to its construction. The latter view is expressed in Exod. 25.40 (cf. Wis. 9.8). We have discussed how Philo interprets this passage in terms of heaven as the home of Platonic archetypes (pp. 53-56). Thus Philo writes of Moses:

> He saw with the soul's eye the immaterial forms of the material objects about to be made. . . So the shape of the model was stamped upon the mind of the prophet, a secretly painted or moulded prototype, produced by immaterial and invisible forms (*Vit. Mos.* 2.74-76).

In a later rabbinic text, *Num. R.* 12.12, we find a tradition according to which God, at the same time as instructing Moses to erect the tabernacle in the wilderness, commanded the angels to erect a tabernacle in heaven. There Metatron,[1] the first among the angels, offers up the souls of the righteous upon the heavenly altar for Israel's sins.[2] There is nothing to suggest, however, that such speculations have contributed to the thought of Hebrews. Here 'heaven as sanctuary' does not parallel an earthly counterpart;[3] it is the superior reality which replaces the earthly shrine. As we shall see, moreover, for our author there can be no altar of sacrifice in heaven's sanctuary, since the death of Jesus is that 'altar', and that was located on earth.

---

1. In *3 Enoch* Metatron is the 'prince of the presence' (8.1), the lesser YHWH (12.5) who guides Ishmael through the heavenly palaces to the throne of God. In its present form *3 Enoch* is not earlier than the fifth century CE, however. See P. Alexander, '3 (Hebrew Apocalypse of) Enoch', in *The Old Testament Pseudepigrapha*, I (ed. J.H. Charlesworth; London: Darton, Longman & Todd, 1983), pp. 223-53.

2. See J. Johannson, *Parakletoi* (Lund: Gleerup, 1940), p. 145.

3. In Revelation, on the other hand, the temple in heaven (Rev. 11.19; 14.17-18) is contemporary with the one on earth (Rev. 11.1-2). The former is inhabited not only by angels (5.2; 7.11), the cherubim (4.6, 8, 9) and the 24 elders (4.4, 10; 5.8), but also by the martyrs (6.9-11). Together they are engaged in a heavenly liturgy of praise (4.8, 11; 5.9-14). In the new Jerusalem, however, there will be no temple, since it will be replaced by the presence of the Lord (21.22).

Therefore it would be more accurate to say that, in Hebrews, heaven is portrayed principally as the inner sanctum of the shrine rather than as the sanctuary *in toto*. Although our author can describe heaven as a tabernacle (σκηνή), the analogy he draws between the ascension of Jesus and the entry of the high priest into the holy of holies (τὰ ἅγια[1] or ἅγια ἁγίων[2]) on the Day of Atonement demands that heaven be more than the tabernacle in general. Christ has entered the sanctuary's most sacred enclave. This point is clearly made in 8.1-6, where our author identifies the true tent (σκηνὴ τῆς ἀληθινῆς) with the holy of holies (τὰ ἅγια) which is heaven (literally 'heavenly' [ἐπουράνιος]) itself. The earthly tabernacle is but a mere shadow or copy. In 9.1-7 our attention is drawn to the distinction between the two main divisions of the wilderness tabernacle: (1) the first, outer enclosure (σκηνὴ ἡ πρώτη)[3] in which the priesthood in general serve; and (2) the holy of holies (ἅγια ἁγίων) which is the exclusive domain of the high priest. As the Melchizedekian high priest, Jesus' entry into heaven is the definitive entry into the innermost shrine (see 9.12). *En route* he has come (παραγενόμενος) through (διά) 'the greater and more perfect tent (σκηνή)[4] not made with hands, that is not of this creation' (9.11). This would suggest that heaven also has more than one compartment; that like the high priest on the Day of Atonement, Jesus also has to pass through the outer sanctuary in order to reach the holy of holies. We can see a similar idea in 4.14 where Jesus is described as the high priest, 'who has passed through the heavens' (διεληλυθότα τοὺς οὐρανούς). Neither passage, however, reflects an understanding of the ascension as Christ's journey through numerous celestial spheres, defeating the hostile forces at each stage,

---

1. Heb. 8.2.
2. Heb. 9.3.
3. As we have seen (pp. 42-43) in 9.8-9a σκηνή ἡ πρωτή changes its referent to become the first, i.e., the Mosaic tabernacle, which is contrasted with that in which Christ is now enthroned.
4. This is to understand διά as locative rather than instrumental, and to take σκηνή as referring to the heavenly tabernacle. So, Moffatt, *Hebrews*, p. 120; Spicq, *Hébreux*, II, p. 256; Michel, *Hebräer*, p. 310; Peterson, *Hebrews and Perfection*, pp. 140-44; Williamson, 'Eucharist', pp. 204-206; Attridge, *Hebrews*, pp. 245-47.

in order finally to reach the highest heaven.[1] Our author is indebted to Judaism's Day of Atonement rituals, not Gnostic mythology. Just as the climax of those ceremonies occurs with the entry of the high priest into the holy of holies, so in Hebrews, Jesus' life reaches its consummation in his entry into the very presence of God in that most sacred of all space—heaven.

Sacrifice is the means whereby entry into the holy of holies can be effected. On the Day of Atonement that expiatory sacrifice was made by the high priest on the altar of burnt offerings (LXX θυσιαστήριον). Obviously, since sacrifice was the prerequisite of that entry, the altar upon which the animal was slain had, of necessity, to be located outside the inner shrine.[2] On this analogy the locus of Jesus' sacrifice must similarly be located on earth and not in heaven. The only suggestion that there might be an altar in heaven is in 9.4, where, summarizing the contents of the Mosaic tabernacle, the author of Hebrews places the altar of incense (θυμιατήριον)[3] inside rather than outside the inner sanctum. This is contrary to biblical tradition (Exod. 30.1-10; 38.25-28).[4] Harold Attridge, however, claims that such an understanding can be found in Jewish tradition. He suggests that it may have arisen from the ambiguity of the septuagintal translation of 'opposite the curtain' (LXX ἀπέναντι τοῦ καταπετάσματος) at Exod. 30.6, which could have been understood as 'inside the curtain'. In which case the following verse (Exod. 30.7) in which the 'daily' offerings of the priests on the altar of incense, which in Greek is rendered πρωΐ πρωΐ—'early', would have been taken to refer to the time at which the high priest entered the holy of holies on the Day of Atonement.[5] Be that as it may, the author of the Epistle to the

---

1. Such an understanding of the ascension may lie behind Eph. 4.8-10. Col. 2.15, on the other hand, sees the crucifixion rather than the ascension as the occasion of the 'disarming' of the hostile forces.

2. See Exod. 27.1-8; 38.1-7.

3. At Exod. 30.1-10; 38.25-28 the LXX has θυσιαστήριον θυμιάτος for the altar of incense. θυμιατήριον in the LXX (cf. 2 Chron. 26.19; Ezek. 8.11) usually refers to the censer. It is, however, possible that here Hebrews may be using a Greek version closer to that of Symmachus and Theodotion, since both read θυμιατήριον at Exod. 30.9.

4. Cf. also Philo, *Rer. Div. Her.* 226; *Vit. Mos.* 2.101-104; Josephus, *War* 1.152; *Ant.* 3.139-50.

5. Attridge, *Hebrews*, pp. 234-38.

Hebrews gives no indication of the presence of the altar of incense in heaven. The only thing he puts there is God's throne from which mercy is dispensed (4.16).[1] It is possible (see pp. 90-91) that in our author's mind this had become assimilated to the ark of the covenant (cf. 9.5, ἱλαστήριον) which was situated in the holy of holies of the Mosaic tabernacle. More likely is the suggestion that, as he moves back and forth between his models of royal court and the sanctuary's inner sanctum, heaven's one furnishing[2] becomes either a throne or the ark.

What then of the altar (θυσιαστήριον) in Heb. 13.10? This question cannot be answered without reference to a number of others which confront us in 13.9-16. This passage has long been recognized by scholars as one which is fraught with exegetical problems. Helmut Koester has placed it 'among the most difficult passages of the entire New Testament'.[3] We find no help in its immediately preceding section, since vv. 9-16 are introduced parenthetically into a chapter appended by our author to the end of his sermon proper.[4] Apart from

---

1. Heb. 4.16.
2. To my knowledge no scholar has suggested that the heavenly things (τὰ ἐπουράνια) which require better sacrifices (9.23) are the contents of heaven. Some (e.g. Michel, *Hebräer*, pp. 213-14; Héring, *Hebrews*, p. 82) see in this verse an echo of the myth of Satan's expulsion from heaven (cf. Isa. 14.12-21; Lk. 10.18; Jn 12.31; Rev. 12.7-9). Alternatively, others (e.g. Spicq, *Hébreux*, II, p. 267) have suggested that it refers, by analogy with the Mosaic tabernacle, to the inauguration of the heavenly sanctuary by the sacrifice of Jesus. This is to understand καθαρίζειν (to cleanse) in 9.23 as synonymous with ἐγκαινίζειν (to inaugurate) in 9.18. The attempt to give an ecclesiological interpretation to τὰ ἐπουράνια by understanding it to refer to the church as the new temple which stands in need of cleansing (so Bruce, *Hebrews*, pp. 218-19) is even less successful. Such an identification goes wholly against Hebrews' eschatology and soteriology. The best solution (see F.-J. Schierse, *Verheissung und Heilsvollendung: zur theologischen Grundfrage des Hebräerbriefes* [Munich: Zink, 1955], p. 48; Attridge, *Hebrews*, pp. 260-62) is to understand 'heavenly' in 9.23 as a metaphor for the interior conscience, cleansed by the superior sacrifice of Jesus. It thus picks up the theme of 9.11-14.
3. H. Koester, '"Outside the Camp": Hebrews 13.9-14', *HTR* 55 (1962), p. 299.
4. The ending of ch. 12, together with the abrupt change in style and tone at 13.1 suggest that the sermon ends at 12.29. This is not to say (*contra* E.D. Jones, 'The Authorship of Hebrews XIII', *ExpTim* 46 [1934–35], pp. 562-67; Theissen, *Untersuchungen*, p. 14; Buchanan, *Hebrews*, pp. 243-45, 267-68; *et al.*) that ch. 13 has been added by another hand. 13.22-25 may be a later addition (see

this parenthesis the rest of the chapter is mostly a list of practical and specific instructions on how his audience should conduct their lives (see vv. 1-6, 17-19). Mid-way through this list a note of warning is sounded which harkens back to the theme of Jesus' sacrificial death:

> Do not be led astray by diverse and strange teachings (διδαχαὶ ποικίλαι καὶ ξέναι): for it is well that the heart be strengthened by grace, not by foods (βρώματα) which have not benefited their adherents. We have an altar (θυσιαστήριον) from which those who serve the tent (οἱ τῇ σκηνῇ λατρεύοντες) have no right to eat. For the bodies of those animals whose blood is brought into the sanctuary (εἰς τὰ ἅγια) by the high priest as a sacrifice for sin (περὶ ἁμαρτίας) are burned outside the camp (ἔξω τῆς παρεμβολῆς). So Jesus also suffered outside the gate (ἔξω τῆς πύλης) in order to sanctify the people through his own blood (13.9-11).

Yet just exactly what are these teachings his readers should avoid? How, if at all, are they related to the 'foods' which have not benefited their adherents? Who are these adherents who serve the tent and are excluded from the altar? Our answers will depend upon what we understand the altar to refer to. Since that in turn depends upon our answers to these other questions, inevitably it becomes a circular argument. Any satisfactory interpretation of this passage, however, must take all these questions into account. Above all it should be consistent with the whole tenor of the rest of the Epistle.[1]

Three major alternatives have been proposed vis-à-vis the altar in v. 10: (1) that it refers to an altar situated in the heavenly rather than the earthly sanctuary, where Jesus offers his sacrifice;[2] (2) that it designates the table used by Christians in their celebration of the Lord's Supper;[3] (3) that it is either Golgotha, the place of Jesus' sacrifice,[4] or

Héring, *Hebrews*, p. 119; Vanhoye, *La Structure*, pp. 219-21) but the rest of the chapter is better understood as the author's own epistolary appendix (see Kümmel, *Introduction*, p. 398 n. 37).

1. Buchanan (*Hebrews*, pp. 233-38) requires no such consistency since he believes that the whole of ch. 13 was written by a different author to a different audience from that of 1–12.

2. So J. Cambier, 'Eschatologie ou hellénisme dans l'épître aux Hébreux: Une étude sur μένειν et l'exhortation finale de l'épître', *Salesianum* 11 (1949), p. 69; Schierse, *Verheissung*, p. 191; Theissen, *Untersuchungen*, p. 78; Williamson, 'Eucharist', pp. 307-308; Thompson, *Beginnings*, pp. 146-47.

3. So Moffatt, *Hebrews*, pp. 233-38; P. Andriessen, 'L'Eucharistie dans l'épître aux Hébreux', *NRT* 3 (1972), pp. 275-76.

4. So Bruce, *Hebrews*, pp. 399-401; Montefiore, *Hebrews*, p. 244; Braun,

is an image used of the sacrifice of Christ in general.[1]

J.W. Thompson[2] is to be numbered among those contemporary scholars who seek to uphold the first interpretation. He maintains that βρώματα is a metaphor for any teaching which would claim that stability is to be found on earth. Against this the author of Hebrews maintains that the only unchanging reality is heaven. Therefore he calls upon his readers to leave the world of the flesh (= σκηνή) with all its transience, and to look to the heavenly realm (= ἔξω τῆς παρεμβολῆς) before whose altar Christ now offers his sacrifice. Thompson thus sees this passage as an elaborate allegorization of Exod. 33.7 which locates the Mosaic tabernacle 'outside the camp', similar to that used by Philo in his treatment of this verse.[3] For Philo 'outside the camp' represents Moses' departure from the world of sense perception and his entry into the mysteries of the invisible, heavenly world. Exod. 33.7, thus interpreted, becomes a means to extol Moses as the supreme mystagogue. It is doubtful, however, *contra* Thompson, whether Philo throws any light on Heb. 13.9-16, where the principal frame of reference is historical and eschatological rather than metaphysical or mystical. The most telling fact against any interpretation which would locate the altar of sacrifice in heaven is that our author, in using the wilderness tabernacle as a model for heaven, remains true to the typology; the holy of holies contains no such altar. As we have seen, our author does place an altar—that of incense (θυμιατήριον)—in the inner shrine (9.4), but at 13.10 it is the altar of sacrifice (θυσιαστήριον) which is under discussion. Had our author intended this as a reference to an altar in heaven it would have completely cut across his interpretation of the death of Jesus as the expiatory sacrifice by means of which he was able to enter heaven's holy of holies.

In spite of F.D.V. Narborough's confident assertion that this passage 'must imply, in the eyes of unprejudiced criticism, some reference to the Holy Communion',[4] the identification of the altar with the eucharistic table is equally unconvincing. Perhaps the most plausible

Hebräer, p. 463; Wilson, *Hebrews*, p. 243.
1. So P.E. Hughes, *Hebrews*, p. 577; Attridge, *Hebrews*, p. 398.
2. Thompson, *Beginnings*, pp. 141-51.
3. *Gig.* 54. Cf. *Leg. All.* 2.54; 3.46.
4. Narborough, *Hebrews*, p. 150.

attempt to do so can be seen in James Moffatt's commentary. He understands Heb. 13.9-16 as a polemic on the part of the author of the Epistle against those Christians who would understand the Last Supper as a sacrificial meal. Against them our author argues that just as the Day of Atonement victim was not consumed by the worshippers but was taken outside the camp and there burned, so for the Christian there can be no consumption of the body (= βρώματα) of Jesus, since that too was an expiatory sacrifice.[1] There are a number of obstacles to this reading, however:[2] (1) the vocabulary is not what we should expect if this were the topic under discussion. There is no evidence prior to the second century of the term 'altar' (θυσιαστήριον) being used of the Lord's 'table' (τράπεζα).[3] Nor is βρῶμα used elsewhere in the New Testament of the eucharistic bread (ἄρτος). The only possible exception is Jn 6.55, 'For my flesh is food (βρῶσις) indeed, and my blood is drink indeed', although it is far from certain that the Johannine passage is itself a reference to the Eucharist.[4] More likely, there 'food' and 'drink' are used figuratively of Jesus, the new manna, who bestows life which is eternal (cf. Jn 6.27). (2) We have already noted that one of the more striking features of our Epistle is that it displays no interest whatsoever in the Eucharist[5]—even when dealing with Jesus' Melchizedekian high priesthood, where we would expect at least some echo. Were the author engaged in a debate about the interpretation of the Lord's Supper this silence would be all the more 'defeaning'. As Harold Attridge comments:

> That our author found questionable what later came to be regarded as orthodox Christian sacramentalism is certainly possible, although it cannot be finally established.[6]

1. Moffatt, *Hebrews*, pp. 223-38. Cf. Robinson, *Hebrews*, p. 201; Theissen, *Untersuchungen*, pp. 76-79.

2. See especially the refutations in Koester, 'Outside the Camp', pp. 299-315, and Williamson, 'Eucharist', pp. 300-12.

3. The earliest instance of this is Ignatius of Antioch, *Phld.* 4; cf. *Magn.* 72.

4. Modern scholars are divided with regard to Jn 6.51c-58. (1) Is this section redactional or integral? (2) Does it contain eucharistic teaching? (3) If so, (a) is the Eucharist the principal or peripheral theme and (b) was such teaching intended as corrective and if so, of what? For a brief discussion of some of these issues, see R. Kysar, *The Fourth Evangelist and this Gospel: An Examination of Contemporary Scholarship* (Minneapolis: Augsburg 1975), pp. 252-55.

5. So Williamson, 'Eucharist', *contra* Andriessen, 'L'Eucharistie'.

6. Attridge, *Hebrews*, p. 396.

Sacred Space

Such a possibility cannot simply be dismissed as mere 'prejudice'! Yet neither can this particular passage be used as evidence of our author's anti-sacramental view of the Eucharist—not least because it is not about the Lord's Supper. (3) What can be said from the rest of the Epistle, however, is that it is the death of Jesus, not a ritual meal, which is the means of access to God. To speak of the Eucharist as an altar present in the Christian community would therefore go against the grain of the whole argument,[1] which likens the death of Jesus to the Day of Atonement sacrifice—which is not consumed. Thus Attridge is right when he goes on to stress that what we find in 13.9-16:

> is a piety that is not grounded in sacramental practice, but that draws directly from the sacrificial death of Christ implications for Christian life.[2]

All of which leads us to the conclusion that the altar is located neither in heaven, nor on earth at the Eucharist, but represents the sacrifice of Jesus. Despite the extremely dense nature of the argument in this passage, that much is clear. However, some of the referents are either cryptic and/or have more than one subject. Therefore the passage requires careful 'unpacking'. It begins (v. 9) with a general warning against false teaching, which our author describes pejoratively as multiple (ποικίλος)[3] and alien (ξένος).[4] What follows is not a piece of polemic,[5] however, but positive exhortation advanced initially by way of negative argument. Thus 'grace' (χάρις) is contrasted with 'foods' (βρώματα), that is, the death and resurrection of

---

1. See Michel, *Hebräer*, p. 342.

2. Attridge, *Hebrews*, p. 396. Cf. Williamson, 'Eucharist', p. 309.

3. For a pejorative use of ποικίλος as multiple and thereby at variance with the truth see Tit. 3.3.

4. Josephus (*War* 2.414) also describes false teaching within Judaism as ξένος.

5. Among those who read this passage as polemical there is no agreement as to who the opponents are. Some (e.g. Moffatt, *Hebrews*, p. 234) think it is aimed at Christian sacramentalists. Others see it as an attack on those Christians who want to keep the Jewish food laws (Montefiore, *Hebrews*, p. 243) or take part in the Passover *seder* (Spicq, *Hébreux*, II, p. 423). Alternatively it has been suggested that the danger facing the addressees is their desire to return to the worship of Judaism, either by taking part in the cultic rites of a still-operative Jerusalem Temple (Guthrie, *Hebrews*, p. 273; Lindars, 'Rhetorical Structure', pp. 387-88), or via the reconstruction of the cult based on the wilderness tabernacle (Brown, *Antioch and Rome*, pp. 152-56).

Jesus as the gracious act of God (cf. Heb. 2.9; 10.29) is superior to all the cultic arrangements legislated for under the Mosaic covenant. We find βρῶμα listed among the regulations concerning the first tabernacle in 9.9-10. In the same vein βρώματα here symbolize all such cultic ordinances[1] which have now been superseded by the death of Jesus. Christians do indeed have an 'altar', namely an expiatory sacrifice, which, like that of the Day of Atonement, is not consumed (v. 10) but disposed of 'outside the camp' (v. 11). In this phrase from Lev. 16.27 our author sees a reference, not only to the fate of the expiatory victim, but to the place where Christ was crucified, that is, beyond Jerusalem's walls,[2] 'beyond the gate' (v. 12).

Our author concludes this section with an exhortation which sums up what has been his major paraenetic purpose throughout the homily, namely, to direct his community's focus away from the fate of Jerusalem and its sanctuary, and to point them along the road of pilgrimage which Jesus himself took:

> Therefore let us go forth to him outside the camp, and bear the abuse (ὀνειδισμόν) he endured. For here we have no lasting (μένουσαν) city but seek the city which is to come (μέλλουσαν) (13.13-14).

Abuse (ὀνειδισμός), as the lives of both Moses (11.26) and Jesus demonstrate, is the necessary lot[3] of those who would embark upon the journey from the earthly to the heavenly Jerusalem of the future (μέλλουσαν). Endurance has been the dominant theme from 10.19 onwards. Here the preacher exhorts his congregation to look beyond their present plight to the future city of God. No expiatory sacrifice is necessary to gain access into this sacred territory, since, in the death

1. So Koester, 'Outside the Camp', pp. 304-307.
2. For the place of execution 'outside the camp' see Lev. 24.14, 23; Num. 15.36. Deut. 22.24 has 'outside the gate'. Only Jn 19.20 states that Jesus was crucified 'near the city'. Mk 15.20 and Mt. 27.31 imply that Golgotha was outside the city walls when they state that Jesus was 'led out' (cf. Lk. 23.2 'led away').
3. Cf. also 12.13-17 where, via a citation from LXX Prov. 3.11-12 in vv. 5-6, suffering is explained in terms of a father disciplining his children. Parental discipline as educative is a common theme in Jewish Wisdom tradition (e.g. Prov. 13.24; Ecclus 30.1; 18.14). See Attridge, *Hebrews*, p. 361. God's discipline (Deut. 8.5; 2 Kgdms 7.14; Jer. 2.30; 5.3) is similarly depicted as a sign of His parental love (Ps. 94 [LXX 93].12; Job 5.17).

of Jesus, that necessity has already been met. Therefore there is no
need to look to the Jerusalem cult. Whether that remains or continues
is of no further significance, since the work of Jesus has made it
redundant. The worship which is now required is 'a sacrifice of praise
to God,[1] the fruit of lips that acknowledge his name' (13.15). The language of cult has now become wholly metaphorical. 'Sacrifice' for the
Christian is the praise of God in worship and the performance of good
works in the world (13.15-16).

What emerges from our study of Hebrews is that, for all the spatial
character of the images it uses to depict heaven (promised land, holy
city, royal court, sacred shrine), they always have simultaneously a
time reference. This merging of spatial and temporal is a feature of
some Jewish apocalyptic works. So *2 Bar.* 51.8-10a:

> For they shall see that world which is now invisible to them, and they will
> see a time which is now hidden to them. And time will no longer make
> them older. For they will live in the heights of that world and they will be
> like the angels.

Here the invisible world and hidden time have become one. In our
Epistle, 'heaven' has the character of both since it is its author's symbolic term for salvation. His message to his readers is that only Jesus
has fully achieved such a state; that where he has gone others may
follow. But in the meantime salvation is not to be located in this place
nor identified with this time. There is nothing to suggest that this particular congregation believed the latter. There is no hint of the
triumphalism born of an over-realized eschatology with which the
apostle Paul had to contend.[2] By contrast, this particular group seems
to have lacked confidence in the promise of the reign of God. Hence
they were in danger of losing hope. I have suggested that the fall of
Jerusalem may have played a major part in this failure of nerve. With
the desecration of such sacred space how were they to understand
God's promises of land and sanctuary as the *locus* of salvation?

Our author calls his audience to see in Jesus' session in heaven the
assurance of that salvation, and its re-location. In exhorting them to
look to heaven he is not inviting them to abandon the world, either in

---

1. See Philo, *Spec. Leg.* 1.272. Cf. 1 Pet. 2.5.
2. See A.C. Thiselton, 'Realized Eschatology at Corinth', *NTS* 24 (1978),
pp. 510-26.

some mystical experience achieved through worship, or in a life beyond the grave. In Hebrews, heaven is not depicted as the home of the dead[1] but the state promised to the elect when Jesus returns to gather his faithful of all ages. In the meantime heaven is inhabited only by God, His son and the angels. Thus, for humanity, salvation lies not in the present but in the imminent future. Neither, despite the depiction of heaven with its throne and angelic hosts, is there any hint of a mystical understanding of salvation in Hebrews.[2] Not surprisingly in a work which draws heavily upon the cultic paradigm of the entry of the high priest into the holy of holies for Jesus' entry into heaven, we find that his followers are encouraged to draw near to God via worship. Thus προσέρχομαι, a verb which in the cult had almost become a technical term for worshipping God, is used of the Christian's access to God (4.16; 7.25; 10.22; 12.18). Yet it remains the language of approach rather than attainment. Only Jesus has entered (εἰσέρχομαι, 6.20; 9.12, 24, 25) the presence of God. As yet for the people of God that entry remains in the future (4.1, 3, 4, 9).

For the present the gospel of promise is experienced only as hope[3] since salvation, the time and space of heaven, has yet to be attained by the believer. No more now, therefore, than in the Mosaic age does the path to glory (cf. 2.9) lie in withdrawal from the world. The people of God must pass through the wilderness, not seek refuge within the supposedly safe enclaves of an earlier generation's sacred territory.[4] The goal of their pilgrimage is nothing less than the reign of God, which Jesus now shares, and which he holds out to his followers as their inheritance.

---

1. In Heb. 2.14-15 Jesus has overcome death's power (the devil) so that his followers need no longer live in fear of death. He does not, however, teach that the Christian dead are even now in heaven. Like the apostle Paul (1 Cor. 15.20-23; 1 Thess. 4.13-18), our author believes that that will only take place at the eschaton.

2. *Contra* H.-M. Schenke, 'Erwägungen', who claims that Hebrews has been influenced by *Merkavah* mysticism.

3. So Käsemann, *Wandering People*, p. 19.

4. Koester ('Outside the Camp', pp. 301-303) sees the author's call as one to a life of secularity. I, on the other hand, have argued throughout this study that the author of Hebrews does not abolish the notion of sacred time/space; he relocates it.

It is chiefly the responsibility of the theologian rather than the historical exegete to relate the insights of the biblical text to the experience
of the contemporary community of faith. The implications (if any) of
this study for that particular enterprise, therefore, remain for others
to pursue.

Which is not to say that my own Christian understanding has gone
unchallenged by Hebrews. As a result of my encounter with the text I
have had to rethink a number of issues, not least that of the relationship between contemporary experience and inherited religious
tradition—including Scripture. When I began this study one of the
questions I asked of the author of the Epistle was, 'How do you use the
Old Testament?' From the viewpoint of a Christianity whose
Scriptures include the New Testament this is a perfectly valid question. Yet was it the right question to ask of a first-century Christian
author who had no New Testament as part of his canon? True, he
would have had to hand traditional material, both written and oral,
about Jesus and the movement which he had inspired. This, however,
was a long way from becoming 'Scripture'. From the point of view of
the author of Hebrews, those Christian traditions which were available
to him would have been regarded as inspired contemporary insights
rather than canonized Scripture. In which case it follows that what he
was attempting was not to relate the two parts of what was subsequently to become the Christian canon, but to understand Scripture in
the light of Christian experience. The better way to phrase the question, therefore, is, 'How does the author of Hebrews use Scripture?'

Put that way, the answers we get may well challenge some of our
own presuppositions—not least if we were to take our author's
approach as paradigmatic for contemporary use of the Christian
Scriptures. One of the implications of so doing would be a recognition
that the beliefs and institutions of the New Testament, as surely as
those of the Old Testament, also need to be put to the christological

test. Since the author of Hebrews accepts all Scripture as the inspired word of God, none of it can be ignored. Nonetheless, its authority subsists wholly in its witness to Jesus, the Son. He alone is God's definitive, last Word, before whom all revelation is relative. He is therefore the norm by which all Scripture is judged. Subsequent Christianity has understood this to mean that the written word of the New Testament reigns supreme over the Old Testament. Yet within our author's context it was the unique and definitive character of the life and work of Jesus of Nazareth, not a set of writings, which was the norm by which all inherited religious traditions were to be judged. Some will be found wanting and should be declared redundant for the present age, whereas others will have an on-going validity. The author of the Epistle to the Hebrews provides us with no sure litmus test by which we can invariably tell which falls into what category. What he does do, however, is attempt to hold together an understanding of God's revelation in Scripture, in Jesus, and in the contemporary events of his own time, and to create from them a living word which would speak to his own generation.

Another important difference between a first- and twentieth-century reading of Hebrews is that, for us, Judaism and Christianity have long since gone their separate ways, whereas for our author they had yet to become different religions. As far as he was concerned the issue was between the faithful and the faithless among the people of God in every generation, rather than the Christian faithful over against the faithless Jew. Much as I would take issue with Ernst Käsemann's Gnostic reading of Hebrews, he was surely right to criticize those commentators who saw an anti-Jewish polemic at work in this Epistle:

> It is a product of fantasy to read from our letter a Judaizing disintegration threatening the Christian community or the danger of apostasy toward Judaism.[1]

Jewish–Christian relations have enough genuine tensions which arise from the 'scandal' of their respective particularities, without adding to them by erroneously enlisting the Epistle to the Hebrews on the side of a thinly disguised anti-Semitism. If anything, our author's understanding of Israel as the people of God, past and present, who have been granted a proleptic vision of 'the good things to come', could

---

1. Käsemann, *Wandering People*, p. 24.

offer something constructive in the dialogue between what have long since become two, separate communities of faith.

The possibility of such dialogue has not been made easier by Christian claims to salvation which smack of a glib triumphalism. Speaking for Judaism Martin Buber has said:

> There are no knots in the mighty cord of our Messianic belief, which fastened to a rock on Sinai, stretches to a still invisible peg anchored in the foundations of the world. In our view, redemption occurs forever, and none has yet occurred. Standing bound and shackled in the pillory of mankind we demonstrate with the bloody body of our people the unredeemedness of the world.[1]

Writing as a Christian, the author of Hebrews would not agree that no redemption has occurred. He believed that in Jesus, through his death and ascension to heaven, it had. Nonetheless, I think he would agree with Buber that salvation 'stretches to a still invisible peg' yet to be attained by the people of God. To understand Christianity wholly in terms of the present experience of salvation not only flies in the face of what is demonstrably the unredeemedness of the world; it limits the transcendent to the here and now. No doubt in reaction to a wholly future and otherworldly orientation, much modern theology has concentrated upon the attainment of the kingdom of God (or as our author would say, 'heaven') in our present, earthly structures. That too is a dimension of the gospel I would personally wish to affirm. Yet, just as in the past, so the prophet of today quickly becomes tomorrow's church functionary. The author of Hebrews, on the other hand, challenges all our attempts to 'localize' God in our own religious institutions or to confine Him to the 'today' of human history. He expresses this future dimension largely in spatial terms. Yet, as we have seen, his language of 'heaven' represents more than geographical location. It conjures up a reality which at once both encompasses and transcends the world. Surely an adequate articulation of Christian faith can aim at no less?

We should not, of course, look to our Epistle for a balanced and complete presentation of Christianity, as if it were a piece of systematic theology. Like all good sermons Hebrews does not aim at 'coverage' but concentrates upon those aspects of inherited belief

1. M. Buber, quoted in Ernst Simon, 'Martin Buber: His Way between Thought and Deed', *Jewish Frontier* 15 (1948), p. 26.

which have specific bearing upon the present situation of its audience. Hence, the author of Hebrews largely confines himself to traditions concerning Jesus' death and heavenly session—to the virtual exclusion of all else, and this, I have suggested, because the issue he needed to address was the loss of Israel's most sacred site, the Temple in Jerusalem. By emphasizing Jesus' present location in heaven, the most sacred of all space, he effectively relativizes biblical traditions concerning the divinely appointed places of rendezvous between God and His people. By drawing an analogy between the death and ascension of Jesus and the Day of Atonement rites, he is able to claim that the cult is now defunct, because its intended purpose has been fulfilled.

Since, on my reading, it was the fall of Jerusalem in 70 CE which was the occasion of Hebrews, it is not surprising that its author drew so heavily upon Israel's cult in his presentation of the Christian faith. This does not mean that it is necessarily a language which is appropriate for a contemporary understanding of the work of Christ. One of the major differences between now and then is that in its first-century context 'sacrifice' would have referred principally to a concrete act, whereby an animal was slaughtered and offered to the deity as part of a religious ritual. From the time of the fall of the Temple, however, for both Judaism and Christianity 'sacrifice' has come to have a wholly metaphorical connotation. The Epistle to the Hebrews itself has contributed to this shift in meaning in as much as it described the death of Christ as a sacrifice, and his offering as that of the work of the high priest. Clearly the language of priest and victim when applied to Jesus is metaphorical, since he was literally neither. Coming from the tribe of Judah he would have been ineligible for the priesthood—a thought which may be of some consolation to those women who, by virtue of their sex, are barred from ordination in those churches which perpetuate the priesthood in their model of Christian ministry. The author of Hebrews, however, in placing the work of Christ within a wholly unique priestly category, 'after the order of Melchizedek', at once signals the metaphorical status of the term 'priest' applied to Jesus, and affirms that for Christians the literal Levitical order is no longer operative. What would be the implications of that particular insight for the contemporary debate about ordination?

If the language of priesthood applied to Jesus is metaphorical, so too is that of sacrificial victim. All too often its analogical character has been ignored, especially by those who have propounded 'theories' of the atonement written on the twin tablets of logical explanation and divine necessity. Ironically, the Epistle to the Hebrews has often been utilized in this enterprise. Yet, as we have seen in this study, the sacrificial system appealed to by its author offered no causal explanation of the connection between action and result. Certain rites were thought to be the God-given means whereby the barrier between the human and the divine could be overcome, but we are given no 'how?' or 'why?'. Furthermore, in neither Judaism's cult nor in Hebrews' use of it are there the notions of 'ransom' or 'just penalty', which were later added to the sacrificial register to produce that dogmatic hybrid, 'the penal substitutionary view of the atonement'. Unlike the Western church, moreover, the preoccupation of Hebrews is not with the death of Christ, but with his present enthronement in heaven, with the affirmation that, 'He reigns'. The cross is seen as but the means whereby that end was achieved. If, therefore, 'sacrifice' is neither an end in itself nor the principal aim of Christian living, this surely calls for a shift, not only in our soteriology, but in much of the contemporary church's spirituality.

Above all, an exposition of the theology of the Epistle to the Hebrews in its original context recalls us to the metaphorical nature of all language about God. In bringing together the death and session of Jesus and the Day of Atonement our author has gone beyond simile, or, for that matter, the straightforward substitution of one set of terms for another. What we find here rather is a 'transaction between contexts',[1] an interaction which issues in new insight.[2] My hope is that

---

1. I.A. Richards, *The Philosophy of Rhetoric* (Oxford: Oxford University Press, 1936), p. 94.

2. For an interactive view of the function of metaphor see Richards, *Rhetoric*, pp. 89-138. Max Black (*Models and Metaphors: Studies in Language and Philosophy* [Ithaca, NY: Cornell University Press, 1963], pp. 9-13, 14-55), noting the similarity between scientific models and metaphors, calls analogue models which generate fresh insight, 'disclosure models'.

in reclaiming the language of Hebrews as metaphor, what it has to say may be taken seriously, if not literally,[1] and that it may be allowed to generate new meaning and open up fresh vistas for today's community of faith.

1. See I.G. Barbour, *Myths, Models and Paradigms: The Nature of Scientific and Religious Language* (London: SCM Press, 1974), who makes the point that a model, whether in religion or science is:

> a symbolic representation of selected aspects of the behaviour of a complex system for particular purposes. It is an imaginative tool for ordering experience, rather than a description of the world (p. 6).

Nonetheless it is to be taken seriously, if not literally (pp. 7, 34-37, 50). I would add that the same can be said of religious metaphor.

BIBLIOGRAPHY

Aalen, S., ' "Reign" and "House" in the Kingdom of God in the Gospels', *NTS* 8 (1961), pp. 215-40.

Abelson, J., *The Immanence of God in Rabbinical Literature* (London: Macmillan, 1912).

Adams, J.C., 'Exegesis of Heb. 6.1ff.', *NTS* 13 (1967), pp. 378-85.

Alexander, P., '3 (Hebrew Apocalypse of) Enoch', in *The Old Testament Pseudepigrapha*, I (ed. J.H. Charlesworth; London: Darton, Longman & Todd, 1983), pp. 223-53.

Anderson, A.A., *Psalms*, I (NCB; London: Oliphants, 1972).

Anderson, C.P., 'The Epistle to the Hebrews and the Pauline Letter Collection', *HTR* 59 (1966), pp. 429-48.

—'Hebrews among the Letters of Paul', *SR* 5 (1975–76), pp. 258-66.

Andriessen, P., 'L'Eucharistie dans l'épître aux Hébreux', *NRT* 3 (1972), pp. 275-76.

Armstrong, A.H., 'Plotinus', in *The Cambridge History of Later Greek and Early Medieval Philosophy* (ed. A.H. Armstrong; Cambridge: Cambridge University Press, 1967), pp. 195-271.

Attridge, H.W., ' "Heard Because of his Reverence" (Heb. 5.7)', *JBL* 98 (1979), pp. 90-93.

—'Historiography', in *Jewish Writings of the Second Temple Period* (CRINT, 2.2; ed. M. Stone; Assen: Van Gorcum, 1984), pp. 160-75.

—*The Epistle to the Hebrews* (Hermeneia; Philadelphia: Fortress Press, 1989).

Barbour, I.G., *Myths, Models and Paradigms: The Nature of Scientific and Religious Language* (London: SCM Press, 1974).

Barrett, C.K., 'The Eschatology of the Epistle to the Hebrews', in *The Background of the New Testament and its Eschatology* (ed. W.D. Davies and D. Daube; Cambridge: Cambridge University Press, 1956), pp. 363-93.

—*From First Adam to Last: A Study in Pauline Theology* (London: A. & C. Black, 1962).

—*The Second Epistle to the Corinthians* (BNTC; London: A. & C. Black, 1973).

Barth, M., 'The OT in Hebrews: An Essay in Biblical Hermeneutics', in *Current Issues in New Testament Interpretation: Essays in Honour of O.A. Piper* (ed. W. Klassen and G.F. Snyder; New York: Harper, 1962), pp. 263-73.

Barthélemy, R.P.D., 'Redécouverte d'un chainon manquant de l'histoire de la Septante', *RB* 60 (1953), pp. 18-29.

Behm, J., 'παράκλητος', *TDNT*, V (1968), pp. 800-14.

Black, M., *The Scrolls and Christian Origins* (London: Nelson, 1961).

—*Romans* (NCB; London: Oliphants, 1973).

Black, Max, *Models and Metaphors: Studies in Language and Philosophy* (Ithaca, NY: Cornell University Press, 1963).

Blass, F., *Der Brief an die Hebräer* (Halle: Niemeyer, 1903).

Borgen, P., *Bread from Heaven: An Exegetical Study of the Concept of Manna in the Gospel of John and the Writings of Philo* (Leiden: Brill, 1965).

Bornhäuser, K., *Empfänger und Verfasser des Briefes an die Hebräer* (Gütersloh: Bertelsmann, 1932).

Bornkamm, G., 'Das Bekenntnis im Hebräerbrief', in *Studien zu Antike und Christentum* (Munich: Kaiser, 2nd edn, 1963), pp. 188-203.

Brandenburg, S., 'Text Vorlagen von Hebr. V.7-10', *NovT* 11 (1969), pp. 190-224.

Braun, F.M., 'L'arrière-fond judaïque du quatrième évangile et la communauté de l'alliance', *RB* 62 (1955), pp. 5-44.

Braun, H., *Qumran und das Neue Testament* (2 vols.; Tübingen: Mohr [Paul Siebeck], 1965).

—*An die Hebräer* (HNT, 14; Tübingen: Mohr [Paul Siebeck], 1984).

Bright, J., *Jeremiah* (AB; New York: Doubleday, 1965).

Brown, R.E., 'The Messianism of Qumran', *CBQ* 19 (1959), pp. 53-82.

—'Does the NT call Jesus God?', *TS* 26 (1965), pp. 545-73.

—*The Community of the Beloved Disciple* (London: Geoffrey Chapman, 1979).

Brown, R.E., and J.P. Meier, *Antioch and Rome* (London: Geoffrey Chapman, 1983).

Bruce, F.F., ' "To the Hebrews" or "To the Essenes"?', *NTS* 9 (1962–63), pp. 217-32.

—*The Epistle to the Hebrews* (NLC; London: Marshall, Morgan & Scott, 1965).

—*1 and 2 Corinthians* (NCB; London: Oliphants, 1971).

Buchanan, G.W., 'The Samaritan Origin of the Gospel of John', in *Religions in Antiquity: Essays in Memory of E.R. Goodenough* (ed. J. Neusner; Leiden: Brill), pp. 149-75.

—*To the Hebrews* (AB; New York: Doubleday, 1972).

—'The Present State of Scholarship on Hebrews', in *Christianity, Judaism and other Greco-Roman Cults: Studies for Morton Smith at 60*, I (ed. J. Neusner; Leiden: Brill, 1975), pp. 299-330.

Bultmann, R., 'εὐλαβής', *TDNT*, II (1964), pp. 751-54.

Caird, G.B., 'The Exegetical Method of the Epistle to the Hebrews', *CJT* 5 (1959), pp. 44-51.

—*The Language and Imagery of the Bible* (London: Gerald Duckworth, 1980).

Cambier, J., 'Eschatologie ou hellénisme dans l'épître aux Hébreux: Une étude sur μένειν et l'exhortation finale de l'épître', *Salesianum* 11 (1949), pp. 62-86.

Camp, C.V., *Wisdom and the Feminine in the Book of Proverbs* (Sheffield: JSOT Press, 1985).

Chadwick, H., 'St Paul and Philo of Alexandria', *BJRL* 48 (1966), pp. 286-307.

—'Philo', in *The Cambridge History of Later Greek and Early Medieval Philosophy* (ed. A.H. Armstrong; Cambridge: Cambridge University Press, 1967), pp. 137-57.

Charles, R.H. (ed.), *The Apocrypha and Pseudepigrapha of the Old Testament in English* (2 vols.; Oxford: Clarendon Press, 1913).

Charlesworth, J.H. (ed.), *The Old Testament Pseudepigrapha* (London: Darton, Longman & Todd, 1983).

Childs, B.S., *Myth and Reality in the Old Testament* (SBT, 27; London: SCM Press, 1960).

—*Exodus: A Commentary* (London: SCM Press, 1974).

Chilton, B.D., and P.R. Davies, 'The Aqedah: A Revised Tradition History', *CBQ* 40 (1978), pp. 514-46.

Clark, K.W., 'Worship in the Jerusalem Temple after AD 70', *NTS* 6 (1969–70), pp. 269-80.

Clifford, R.J., *The Cosmic Mountain in Canaan and the Old Testament* (Cambridge, MA: Harvard University Press, 1972).

Colson, F.H., G.H. Whitaker and J.W. Earp (eds.), *Philo* (LCL; 10 vols.; Cambridge, MA: Harvard University Press, 1928–62).

Conzelmann, H., *1 Corinthians* (Hermeneia; Philadelphia: Fortress Press, 1975).

Coppens, J., 'Les affinités qumraniennes de l'épître aux Hébreux', *NRT* 84 (1962), pp. 128-41, 257-82.

Cosby, M.R., 'The Rhetorical Composition of Hebrews 11', *JBL* 107 (1988), pp. 257-73.

Cullmann, O., 'The Significance of the Qumran Texts for Research into the Beginnings of Christianity', in *The Scrolls and the New Testament* (ed. K. Stendahl; London: SCM Press, 1958), pp. 18-32.

—*The Christology of the New Testament* (London: SCM Press, 2nd edn, 1963).

—*The Johannine Circle* (London: SCM Press, 1975).

Dahl, N.A., 'A New and Living Way: The Approach to God according to Heb. 10.19-25', *Int* 5 (1951), pp. 401-12.

—'Eschatology and History in the Light of the Qumranic Texts', in *The Crucified Messiah* (Minneapolis: Augsburg, 1974), pp. 129-45.

Dan, J., 'Shekhinah', *EncJud* 14 (Jerusalem: Keter Publishing House, 1971), pp. 1349-54.

D'Angelo, M.R., *Moses in the Letter to the Hebrews* (Missoula, MT: Scholars Press, 1979).

Danielou, J., *The Dead Sea Scrolls and Primitive Christianity* (Baltimore: Helicon, 1958).

Davenport, G.L., 'The "Anointed of the Lord" in the Psalms of Solomon 17', in *Ideal Figures in Ancient Judaism* (ed. G.W.E. Nickelsburg and J.J. Collins; Chico, CA: Scholars Press, 1980), pp. 67-92.

Davies, W.D., *Paul and Rabbinic Judaism* (London: SPCK, 3rd edn, 1970).

—*The Gospel and the Land: Early Christianity and Jewish Territorial Doctrine* (Berkeley: University of California Press, 1974).

Deichgräber, R., *Gotteshymnus und Christushymnus in der frühen Christenheit: Untersuchungen zu Form, Sprache und Stil der frühchristlichen Hymnen* (Göttingen: Vandenhoeck & Ruprecht, 1967).

Demarest, B., *A History of the Interpretation of Hebrews 7,1-10 from the Reformation to the Present* (Tübingen: Mohr [Paul Siebeck], 1976).

Dey, L.K.K., *The Intermediary World and Patterns of Perfection in Philo and Hebrews* (Missoula, MT: Scholars Press, 1975).

Dibelius, M., *Der Verfasser des Hebräerbriefes* (Strasbourg: Heitz, 1910).

—*Geschichte der urchristlichen Literatur*, II (Berlin: de Gruyter, 1926).

Douglas, M., *Purity and Danger: An Analysis of Concepts of Pollution and Taboo* (London: Routledge & Kegan Paul, 1966).

Dunn, J.D.G., *Baptism in the Holy Spirit* (SBT, 15; London: SCM Press, 1970).

—'Prophetic "I" Sayings and the Jesus Tradition: The Importance of Testing Prophetic Utterances within Early Christianity', *NTS* 24 (1977–78), pp. 175-98.

—*Christology in the Making: An Inquiry into the Origins of the Doctrine of the Incarnation* (London: SCM Press, 1980).

Ehrhardt, A., *The Framework of the New Testament Stories* (Manchester: Manchester University Press, 1964).

Eliade, M., *The Sacred and the Profane: The Nature of Religion* (New York: Harcourt, Brace, 1959).

Ellingworth, P., 'The Unshakable Priesthood: Hebrews 7.24', *JSNT* 23 (1985), pp. 125-26.

Elliott, J.K., 'When Jesus was apart from God: An Examination of Heb. 2.9', *ExpTim* 83 (1972), pp. 339-41.

Ellis, E.E., 'Midrash, Targum and New Testament Quotations', in *Neotestamentica et Semitica: Studies in Honour of Matthew Black* (ed. E.E. Ellis and M. Wilcox; Edinburgh: T. & T. Clark, 1969), pp. 61-69.

Festugière, A.J., *La révélation d'Hermès Trismégiste*. II. *Dieu cosmique* (Paris: Gabalda, 1949).

Filson, F.F., *'Yesterday': A Study of Hebrews in the Light of Chapter 13* (SBT, 4; London: SCM Press, 1967).

Finkelstein, L., *The Pharisees: The Sociological Background of their Faith* (2 vols.; Philadelphia: Jewish Publication Society of America, 3rd edn, 1963).

Fiorenza, E.S., *In Memory of Her: A Feminist Theological Reconstruction of Christian Origins* (London: SCM Press/New York: Crossroad, 1983).

—*Bread Not Stone: The Challenge of Feminist Biblical Interpretation* (Boston: Beacon Press, 1986).

Fitzmyer, J.A., 'Further Light on Melchizedek from Qumran Cave 11', *JBL* 86 (1967), pp. 25-41.

—'The Son of David Tradition and Mt 22.41-46 and Parallels', in *Essays on the Semitic Background of the New Testament* (London: Geoffrey Chapman, 1971), pp. 113-26.

—*A Wandering Aramean: Collected Aramaic Essays* (Missoula, MT: Scholars Press, 1979).

—*The Gospel according to Luke* (AB, 1; New York: Doubleday, 1979).

Flusser, D., 'The Dead Sea Sect and Pre-Pauline Christianity', in *Scripta Hierosolymitana 4: Aspects of the Dead Sea Scrolls* (ed. C. Rabin and Y. Yadin; Jerusalem: Hebrew University, 1958), pp. 215-66.

Frankfort, H., *Kingship and the Gods: A Study of Ancient Near Eastern Religion as Interaction of Society and Nature* (Chicago: University of Chicago Press, 1948).

Fuller, R.H., *The Foundation of New Testament Christology* (London: Lutterworth, 1965).

Gärtner, B., *The Temple and the Community in Qumran and the New Testament* (Cambridge: Cambridge University Press, 1965).

Gaston, L., *No Stone on Another: Studies in the Significance of the Fall of Jerusalem in the Synoptic Gospels* (Leiden: Brill, 1970).

Gilbert, M., 'The Wisdom of Ben Sira', in *Jewish Writings of the Second Temple Period* (CRINT, 2.2; ed. M.E. Stone; Assen: Van Gorcum, 1984).

Glasson, T.F., *Moses in the Fourth Gospel* (London: SCM Press, 1963).

Glaze, R.E., *No Easy Salvation* (Zachary, LA: Insight, 1966).

Grässer, E., 'Der Hebräerbrief 1938–1963', *TRu* 30 (1964), pp. 138-256.

—*Der Glaube in Hebräerbrief* (Marburg: Elwert, 1965).

—'Hebräer 1,1-4: Ein exegetischer Versuch', in *Text und Situation: Gesammelte Aufsatz zum Neuen Testament* (Gütersloh: Gerd Mohn, 1973), pp. 183-230.

Green, H.B., 'Matthew, 1 Clement and Luke: Their Sequence and Relationship', *JTS* 40 (1989), pp. 1-25.

Gruenwald, I., *Apocalypticism and Merkavah Mysticism* (Leiden: Brill, 1980).

Guthrie, D., *Hebrews* (TNTC; Grand Rapids: Eerdmans; Leicester: Inter-Varsity Press, 1983).

Hammerton-Kelly, R.G., *Pre-Existence, Wisdom and the Son of Man* (SNTSMS, 21; Cambridge: Cambridge University Press, 1973).

Hanson, A.T., 'Christ and the OT according to Hebrews', *Studia Evangelica* 2 (1964), pp. 394-97.

—*The Living Utterances of God: The New Testament Exegesis of the Old* (London: Darton, Longman & Todd, 1983).

Harnack, A. von, 'Probabilia über die Adresse und den Verfasser des Hebräerbriefes', *ZNW* 1 (1900), pp. 16-41.

—'Zwei alte dogmatische Korrekturen im Hebräerbrief', in *Studien zur Geschichte des NT und der alten Kirche* (Berlin: de Gruyter, 1931), pp. 236-45.

Hay, D.M., *Glory at the Right Hand: Psalm 110 in Early Christianity* (SBLMS, 18; Nashville: Abingdon Press, 1973).

Helderman, J., *Die Anapausis in Evangelium Veritatis* (Leiden: Brill, 1984).

Hengel, M., *Judaism and Hellenism: Studies in their Encounter in Palestine during the Early Hellenistic Period* (2 vols.; London: SCM Press, 1974).

—'Zwischen Jesus und Paulus', *ZTK* 72 (1975), pp. 151-206.

—*The Son of God: The Origin of Christology and the History of Jewish-Hellenistic Religion* (London: SCM Press, 1976).

Héring, J., *The Epistle to the Hebrews* (London: Epworth, 1970).

Hickling, C.J.A., 'John and Hebrews: The Background of Hebrews 2.10-18', *NTS* 29 (1988), pp. 112-15.

Higgins, A.J.B., 'The Priestly Messiah', *NTS* 13 (1966–67), pp. 211-39.

Hofius, O., *Katapausis: Die Vorstellung von endzeitlichen Ruheort im Hebräerbrief* (WUNT, 2; Tübingen: Mohr [Paul Siebeck], 1970).

Holladay, C., *Theios Aner in Hellenistic Judaism: A Critique of the Use of this Category in NT Christology* (Missoula, MT: Scholars Press, 1977).

Hooker, M.D., *Jesus and the Servant: The Influence of the Servant Concept of Deutero-Isaiah in the NT* (London: SPCK, 1959).

—'Interchange in Christ', *JTS* 21 (1971), pp. 349-61.

—'Were there False Teachers at Colossae?', in *Christ and Spirit in the New Testament: Studies in Honour of C.F.D. Moule* (ed. B. Lindars and S. Smalley; Cambridge: Cambridge University Press, 1973), pp. 315-32.

—'Philippians 2.6-11', in *Jesus und Paulus: Festschrift für W.G. Kümmel zur 70 Geburtstag* (ed. E.E. Ellis and E. Grässer; Göttingen: Vandenhoeck & Ruprecht, 1975), pp. 151-64.

—'In His Own Image', in *What about the New Testament? Essays in Honour of Christopher Evans* (ed. M.D. Hooker and C. Hickling; London: SCM Press, 1975), pp. 28-44.

—'Interchange and Atonement', *BJRL* 60 (1978), pp. 462-81.

—'Interchange in Christ and Ethics', *JSNT* 25 (1985), pp. 3-17.

Hoppins, R., *Priscilla, Author of the Epistle to the Hebrews and other Essays* (New York: Exposition, 1969).

Horbury, W., 'The Aaronic Priesthood in the Epistle to the Hebrews', *JSNT* 19 (1983), pp. 43-71.

Horton, F., *The Melchizedek Tradition: A Critical Examination of the Sources to the Fifth Century A.D. and the Epistle to the Hebrews* (SNTSMS, 30; Cambridge: Cambridge University Press, 1976).

Howard, G., 'Hebrews and the OT Quotations', *NovT* 10 (1968), pp. 208-16.

Howard, W.F., 'The Epistle to the Hebrews', *Int* 5 (1951), pp. 80-91.

Hughes, G., *Hebrews and Hermeneutics: The Epistle to the Hebrews as an NT Example of Biblical Interpretation* (SNTSMS, 36; Cambridge: Cambridge University Press, 1979).

Hughes, P.E., *Commentary on the Second Epistle to the Corinthians* (NICNT; Grand Rapids: Eerdmans, 1962).

—*A Commentary on the Epistle to the Hebrews* (Grand Rapids: Eerdmans, 1977).

Hultgärd, A., 'The Ideal "Levite", the Davidic Messiah and the Saviour Priest in the Testament of the Twelve Patriarchs', in *Ideal Figures in Ancient Judaism* (ed. G.W.E. Nickelsburg and J.J. Collins; Chico, CA: Scholars Press, 1980), pp. 93-110.

Isaacs, M.E., *The Concept of Spirit: A Study of Pneuma in Hellenistic Judaism and its Bearing on the New Testament* (Heythrop Monographs, 1; London: Heythrop College, 1976).

—'The Prophetic Spirit in the Fourth Gospel', *HeyJ* 24 (1983), pp. 391-407.

Jeremias, J., *Jesus' Promise to the Nations* (SBT, 24; London: SCM Press, 1958).

—*The Eucharistic Words of Jesus* (London, 3rd rev. edn, 1966).

—*Jerusalem in the Time of Jesus* (London: SCM Press, 1969).

Jewett, R., *Dating Paul's Life* (London: SCM Press, 1975).

—*Letter to Pilgrims: A Commentary on the Epistle to the Hebrews* (New York: Pilgrim Press, 1981).

Johannson, J., *Parakletoi* (Lund: Gleerup, 1940).

Johnson, A.R., *Sacral Kingship in Ancient Israel* (Cardiff: Cardiff University Press, 2nd edn, 1967).

Johnson, M.D., 'Life of Adam and Eve', in *The Old Testament Pseudepigrpha*, II (ed. J.H. Charlesworth; London: Darton, Longman & Todd, 1985), pp. 249-95.

Johnson, W.G., 'The Pilgrimage Motif in the Book of Hebrews', *JBL* 97 (1978), pp. 239-51.

Jonge, M. de, *The Testament of the Twelve Patriarchs: A Study of their Text, Composition and Origin* (Assen: Van Gorcum, 1953).

Jonge, M. de, and A.S. van der Woude, '11Q Melchizedek and the NT', *NTS* 12 (1965–66), pp. 301-26.

Jones, E.D., 'The Authorship of Hebrews XIII', *ExpTim* 46 (1934–35), pp. 562-67.

Käsemann, E., *Das wandernde Gottesfolk: Eine Untersuchung zum Hebräerbrief* (FRLANT, 37; Göttingen: Vandenhoeck & Ruprecht, 1939); ET *The Wandering People of God: An Investigation of the Letter to the Hebrews* (Minneapolis: Augsburg, 1984).

—*Commentary on Romans* (London: SCM Press, 1977).

Kaufmann, S.S., 'On Methodology in the Study of the Targums and their Chronology', *JSNT* 23 (1985), pp. 117-24.

Kennedy, G., *The Art of Rhetoric in the Roman World: 300 BC–AD 300* (Princeton: Princeton University Press, 1972).

Kistemaker, S.J., *The Psalms Citations in the Epistle to the Hebrews* (Amsterdam: Soest, 1961).

Kittel, G., and G. Friedrich (eds.), *Theological Dictionary of the New Testament* (9 vols.; Grand Rapids: Eerdmans, 1964–74).

Knibb, M.A., *The Qumran Community* (Cambridge: Cambridge University Press, 1987).

Knox, W.L., 'The Divine Wisdom', *JTS* 58 (1937), pp. 230-37.

Koester, H., '"Outside the Camp": Hebrews 13.9-14', *HTR* 33 (1962), pp. 299-315.

—'ὑπόστασις', *TDNT*, VIII (1972), pp. 572-89.

—*Introduction to the New Testament* (2 vols.; Berlin: de Gruyter; Philadelphia: Fortress Press, 1982).

Kosmala, H., *Hebräer, Essener, Christen* (Leiden: Brill, 1969).

Kysar, R., *The Fourth Evangelist and his Gospel: An Examination of Contemporary Scholarship* (Minneapolis: Augsburg, 1975).

Kuhn, K.G., 'The Two Messiahs of Aaron and Israel', in *The Scrolls and the New Testament* (ed. K. Stendahl; London: SCM Press, 1957), pp. 54-64.

Kümmel, W.G., *Introduction to the New Testament* (London: SCM Press, 2nd edn, 1975).

Lang, B., *Wisdom in the Book of Proverbs: An Israelite Goddess Redefined* (New York: Pilgrim Press, 1986).

Laub, F., *Bekenntnis und Auslegung die paraenetische Funktion der Christologie im Hebräerbrief* (Regensburg: Pustet, 1980).

Liebermann, S., *Greek in Jewish Palestine* (New York: Jewish Theological Seminary of America, 1942).

Lightfoot, J.B., *Colossians and Philemon* (London: Macmillan, 2nd edn, 1876).

Lincoln, A.T., *Paradise Now and Not Yet: Studies in the Role of the Heavenly Dimension in Paul's Thought with Special Reference to his Eschatology* (SNTSMS, 43; Cambridge: Cambridge University Press, 1981).

Lindars, B., *New Testament Apologetic: The Doctrinal Significance of the Old Testament Quotations* (London: SCM Press, 1961).

—'The Rhetorical Structure of Hebrews', *NTS* 35 (1989), pp. 382-406.

Liver, J., 'The Doctrine of the Two Messiahs in Sectarian Literature in the Time of the Second Commonwealth', *HTR* 52 (1959), pp. 149-85.

Lloyd, A.C., 'The Later Neoplatonists', in *The Cambridge History of Later Greek and Early Medieval Philosophy* (ed. A.H. Armstrong; Cambridge: Cambridge University Press, 1967), pp. 272-325.

Lohse, E., 'χείρ', *TDNT*, IX (1974), pp. 424-34.

Longenecker, R., *Biblical Exegesis in the Apostolic Period* (Grand Rapids: Eerdmans; Exeter: Paternoster Press, 1975).

Lüdemann, G., *Paul Apostle to the Gentiles: Studies in Chronology* (London: SCM Press, 1984).

Mack, B.L., *Logos and Sophia: Untersuchungen zur Weisheitstheologie in hellenistischen Judentum* (Göttingen: Vandenhoeck & Ruprecht, 1973).

Maier, J., *The Temple Scroll: An Introduction, Translation and Commentary* (Sheffield: JSOT Press, 1985).

Manson, T.W., 'The Problem of the Epistle to the Hebrews', *BJRL* 32 (1949–50), pp. 1-17.

Manson, W., *The Epistle to the Hebrews: An Historical and Theological Reconsideration* (London: Hodder & Stoughton, 1951).

Marcus, R. (ed.), *Philo Supplement: Questions and Answers on Genesis and Exodus* (LCL; 2 vols.; London: Heinemann; Cambridge, MA: Harvard University Press, 1953).

Mason, S.N., 'Priesthood in Josephus and the "Pharisaic Revolution" ', *JBL* 107 (1988), pp. 657-61.

McCullough, J.C., 'The OT Quotations in Hebrews', *NTS* 26 (1980), pp. 363-79.

McKane, W., *Proverbs: A New Approach* (Philadelphia: Westminster Press, 1970).

McKelvey, R.J., *The New Temple: The Church in the New Testament* (Oxford: Oxford University Press, 1969).

Meeks, W.A., *The Prophet-King: Moses Traditions and the Johannine Christology* (Leiden: Brill, 1967).

Metzger, B.M., *A Textual Commentary on the Greek New Testament* (New York: United Bible Society, 1971).

—'The Fourth Book of Ezra', in *The Old Testament Pseudepigrapha*, I (ed. J.H. Charlesworth; London: Darton, Longman & Todd, 1983), pp. 519-59.

Michel, O., *Der Brief an die Hebräer* (Göttingen: Vandenhoeck & Ruprecht, 12th edn, 1966).

Milik, J.T., *Ten Years of Discovery in the Wilderness of Judea* (London: SCM Press, 1959).

—'Le travail d'édition des fragments manuscrits de Qumrân', *RB* 63 (1956), pp. 49-67.

Milstrom, J., 'Israel's Sanctuary: The Priestly "Picture of Dorian Gray"', *RB* 83 (1976), pp. 390-99.

Moffatt, J., *A Critical & Exegetical Commentary on the Epistle to the Hebrews* (ICC; Edinburgh: T. & T. Clark, 1924).

Moloney, J.F., 'The Re-Interpretation of Ps VIII and the Son of Man Debate', *NTS* 27 (1981), pp. 656-72.

Montefiore, H., *The Epistle to the Hebrews* (BNTC; London: A. & C. Black, 1964).

Moore, G.F., *Judaism in the First Centuries of the Christian Era: The Age of the Tannaim* (3 vols.; Cambridge, MA: Harvard University Press, 1927–30).

—'Intermediaries in Jewish Theology', *HTR* 15 (1962), pp. 41-85.

Moule, C.F.D., 'Sanctuary and Sacrifice in the Church of the New Testament', *JTS* 1 (1950), pp. 29-41.

Mowinckel, S., 'Die Vorstellung des Spätjudentums von Heiligen Geist als Fürsprecher und der johanneische Paraklet', *ZNW* 32 (1933), pp. 97-130.

—*He That Cometh* (Oxford: Basil Blackwell, 1956).

—*The Psalms in Israel's Worship* (Oxford: Basil Blackwell, 1967).

Murphy, F.J., 'The Temple in the Syriac Apocalypse of Baruch', *JBL* 106 (1987), pp. 671-83.

Murray, R., 'Jews, Hebrews and Christians: Some Needed Distinctions', *NovT* 24 (1982), pp. 194-208.

Nairne, A., *The Epistle of Priesthood* (Edinburgh: T. & T. Clark, 2nd edn, 1915).

Narborough, F.D.V., *The Epistle to the Hebrews* (Oxford: Clarendon Press, 1930).

Nestle, E., and K. Aland (eds.), *Novum Testamentum Graece* (Stuttgart: Deutsche Bibelgesellschaft, 26th edn, 1979).

Neusner, J., *Early Rabbinic Judaism* (Leiden: Brill, 1975).

Nickelsburg, G.W.E., *Jewish Literature between the Bible and the Mishnah* (London: SCM Press, 1981).

Nicholson, E.W., *Exodus and Sinai in History and Tradition* (Oxford: Clarendon Press, 1973).

—*Jeremiah 26–52* (CBC; Cambridge: Cambridge University Press, 1975).

—*God and his People: Covenant and Theology in the Old Testament* (Oxford: Clarendon Press, 1986).

Oepke, A., 'μεσίτης', *TDNT*, IV (1967), pp. 598-624.

Pearson, B.A., *Nag Hammadi Codices IX and X* (London, 1981).

Peterson, D., *Hebrews and Perfection: An Examination of the Concept of Perfection in the Epistle to the Hebrews* (SNTSMS, 47; Cambridge: Cambridge University Press, 1982).

Pierce, C.A., *Conscience in the New Testament* (SBT, 15; London: SCM Press, 1955).

Porter, J.R., 'Psalm XLV 7', *JTS* (1961), pp. 51-53.

Rad, G. von, *The Problem of the Hexateuch and other Essays* (Edinburgh: Oliver & Boyd, 1966).

—*Deuteronomy* (London: SCM Press, 1966).

—'οὐρανός', *TDNT*, V (1967), pp. 502-509.

—*Genesis: A Commentary* (London: SCM Press, 2nd edn, 1972).

Ramsey, I.T., *Models and Mystery* (London: Oxford University Press, 1964).

Richards, I.A., *The Philosophy of Rhetoric* (Oxford: Oxford University Press, 1936).

Ringgren, H., *Israelite Religion* (London: SPCK, 1969).

Rissi, M., *Die Theologie des Hebräerbriefs: Ihre Verankerung in der Situation des Verfassers und seiner Leser* (WUNT, 41; Tübingen: Mohr [Paul Siebeck], 1987).

Robinson, J.A.T., *Redating the New Testament* (London: SCM Press, 1976).

Robinson, J.M. (ed.), *The Nag Hammadi Library in English* (Leiden: Brill, 1977).

Robinson, T.H., *The Epistle to the Hebrews* (MNTC; London: Hodder & Stoughton, 1933).

Rowland, C., *The Open Heaven: A Study of Apocalyptic in Judaism and Early Christianity* (London, 1982).

Ruether, R.R., *Sexism and God-Talk: Towards a Feminist Theology* (Boston: Beacon Press, 1983).

Russell, D.S., *The Method and Message of Jewish Apocalyptic* (Philadelphia: Fortress Press, 1964).

Sanders, E.P., *Paul and Palestinian Judaism: A Comparison of Patterns of Religion* (London: SCM Press, 1977).

—*Jesus and Judaism* (London: SCM Press, 1985).

Sanders, J.T., *The New Testament Christological Hymns: Their Historical Religious Background* (Cambridge: Cambridge University Press, 1971).

Schaeffer, J.R., 'The Relationship between Priestly and Servant Messianism in the Epistle to the Hebrews', *CBQ* 30 (1968), pp. 359-85.

Schenke, H.-M., 'Erwägungen zum Rätsel des Hebräerbriefes', in *Neues Testament und christliche Existenz* (ed. H.D. Betz and L. Schottroff; Tübingen: Mohr [Paul Siebeck], 1973), pp. 421-37.

Schierse, F.-J., *Verheissung und Heilsvollendung: Zu theologischen Grundfrage des Hebräerbriefes* (Munich: Zink, 1955).

Schmidt, K.L., 'Jerusalem als Urbild und Abbild', *Eranos Jahrbuch* 18 (1950), pp. 207-48.

Schmidt, W.H., *The Faith of the Old Testament: A History* (Oxford: Basil Blackwell, 1983).

Schürer, E., *The History of the Jewish People in the Age of Jesus Christ*, I, II (rev. G. Vermes, F. Millar and M. Black; Edinburgh: T. & T. Clark, 1973, 1979).

Schweizer, E., 'σάρξ', *TDNT*, VII (1971), pp. 98-151.

Scobie, C.H.H., 'The Origins and Development of Samaritan Christianity', *NTS* 19 (1972–73), pp. 390-414.

Scholem, G.G., *Major Trends in Jewish Mysticism* (New York: Schocken Books, 3rd edn, 1955).

Scott, E.F., *The Epistle to the Hebrews: Its Doctrine and Significance* (Edinburgh: T. & T. Clark, 1922).

Selwyn, E.G., *The First Epistle of Peter* (London: Macmillan, 1955).

Sevenster, J.N., *Do You Know Greek? How Much Greek Could the First Jewish Christians Have Known?* (Leiden: Brill, 1968).

Bibliography 235

Skehan, P.W., 'A Fragment of the "Song of Moses" (Deut. 32) from Qumran', *BASOR* 136 (1954), pp. 12-15.

Smith, J.Z., *Map is Not Territory: Studies in the History of Religions* (Leiden: Brill, 1978).

—*To Take Place: Toward Theory in Ritual* (Chicago: University of Chicago Press, 1987).

Sowers, S.G., *The Hermeneutics of Philo and Hebrews* (Zürich: EVZ-Verlag, 1965).

Spicq, C., *L'épître aux Hébreux* (2 vols.; Paris: Gabalda, 1952–53).

—'L'origine johannique de la conception du Christ-prêtre dans l'épître aux Hébreux', in *Aux sources de la tradition chrétienne: Mélanges offerts à M.M. Goguel* (Neuchâtel: Delachaux et Niestlé, 1950).

—'L'Epître aux Hébreux, Apollos, Jean-Baptiste, Les Hellénistes et Qumrân', *RevQ* 1 (1959), pp. 365-90.

Starcky, J., 'Les quatres étages du Messianism à Qumrân', *RB* 70 (1963), pp. 481-505.

Stauffer, E., *New Testament Theology* (London: SCM Press, 1965).

Stewart, R.A., 'The Sinless High-Priest', *NTS* 14 (1967–68), pp. 126-35.

Stone, M.E. (ed.), *Jewish Writings of the Second Temple Period* (CRINT; Assen: Van Gorcum, 1984).

Stowers, S., *Letter Writing in Greco-Roman Antiquity* (Philadelphia: Fortress Press, 1985).

Strack, H.L., and P. Billerbeck, *Kommentar zum Neuen Testament aus Talmud und Midrasch* (4 vols.; Munich: Beck, 1922–28).

Swetnam, J., ' "The Greater and More Perfect Tent": A Contribution to the Discussion of Hebrews 9.11', *Bib* 47 (1966), pp. 91-106.

—'On the Literary Genre of the "Epistle" to the Hebrews', *NovT* 11 (1969), pp. 261-69.

—*Jesus and Isaac: A Study of the Epistle to the Hebrews in the Light of the Aqedah* (Rome: Pontifical Biblical Institute, 1981).

Synge, F.C., *Hebrews and the Scriptures* (London: SPCK, 1959).

Taub, H., 'οὐρανός', *TDNT*, V (1967), pp. 497-501.

Tcherikover, V., *Hellenistic Civilization and the Jews* (Philadelphia: Jewish Publication Society of America; Jerusalem: Hebrew University Press, 1959).

Thackeray, H.StJ., R. Marcus, A. Wikgren and L.H. Feldman (eds.), *Josephus* (LCL; 9 vols.; London: Heinemann; Cambridge, MA: Harvard University Press, 1926–65).

Theissen, G., *Untersuchungen zum Hebräerbrief* (Gütersloh: Gerd Mohn, 1969).

Thiselton, A.C., 'The New Hermeneutic', in *New Testament Interpretation: Essays in Principles and Methods* (ed. I.H. Marshall; Exeter: Paternoster Press, 1977).

—'Realized Eschatology at Corinth', *NTS* 24 (1978), pp. 510-26.

Thomas, K.J., 'The OT Citations in Hebrews', *NTS* 11 (1964–65), pp. 303-25.

Thompson, J., *The Beginnings of Christian Philosophy: The Epistle to the Hebrews* (CBQMS, 13; Washington, DC: Catholic Biblical Association, 1982).

Thrall, M.E., *Greek Particles in the New Testament* (Leiden: Brill, 1962).

Thyen, H., *Der Stil der Jüdisch-Hellenischen Homilie* (Göttingen: Vandenhoeck & Ruprecht, 1955).

Turner, N., *Grammatical Insights into the New Testament* (Edinburgh: T. & T. Clark, 1965).

Vanhoye, A., *La structure litteraire de l'épître aux Hébreux* (StudNeot, 1; Paris: Desclée de Brouwer, 1963).

—*L'Epître aux Hébreux texte grec: Structure* (Rome: Pontifical Biblical Institute, 1967).

Vaux, R. de, *Ancient Israel: Its Life and Institutions* (London: Darton, Longman & Todd, 1961).

Vermes, G., *The Dead Sea Scrolls in English* (Harmondsworth: Penguin, 2nd edn, 1975).

—*The Dead Sea Scrolls: Qumran in Perspective* (London: SCM Press, 1977).

Wacholder, B.Z., *The Dawn of Qumran: The Sectarian Torah and the Teacher of Righteousness* (Cincinnati: Hebrew Union College Press, 1983).

Wagner, G. (ed.), *An Exegetical Bibliography on the Letter to Hebrews and the Apocalypse of John* (Bibliographical Aids, 14; Rüschlikon-Zürich: Baptist Theological Seminary, 1979).

Wendland, P., *Die urchristlichen Literaturformen* (Tübingen: Mohr [Paul Siebeck], 1912).

Westcott, B.F., *The Epistle to the Hebrews* (London: Macmillan, 3rd edn, 1909).

Westermann, C., *The Praise of God in the Psalms* (London: SCM Press, 1965).

Whybray, R.N., *Wisdom in Proverbs* (SBT, 45; London: SCM Press, 1965).

Williamson, R., *Philo and the Epistle to the Hebrews* (Leiden: Brill, 1970).

—'Hebrews 4.15 and the Sinlessness of Jesus', *ExpTim* 8 (1974–75), pp. 4-8.

—'The Eucharist and the Epistle to the Hebrews', *NTS* 21 (1975), pp. 300-12.

—'Philo and New Testament Christology', in *Studia Biblica 1978*, III (ed. E.A. Livingstone; Sheffield: JSOT Press, 1980), pp. 439-45.

—'The Incarnation of the Logos in Hebrews', *ExpTim* 95 (1983), pp. 4-8.

—*Jews in the Hellenistic World: Philo* (Cambridge Commentaries on Writings of the Jewish and Christian World 200 BC to 200 AD, 1.2; Cambridge: Cambridge University Press, 1989).

Wilson, R.McL., *Gnosis in the New Testament* (Oxford: Basil Blackwell, 1968).

—*Hebrews* (NCC; Basingstoke: Marshall, Morgan & Scott; Grand Rapids: Eerdmans, 1987).

Windisch, H., '"Ελλην', *TDNT*, II (1962), pp. 502-16.

Wolfson, H.A., *Philo: Foundation of Religious Philosophy in Judaism, Christianity and Islam* (2 vols.; Cambridge, MA: Harvard University Press, 1947).

Yadin, Y., 'The Dead Sea Scrolls and the Epistle to the Hebrews', in *Scripta Hierosolymitana 4: Aspects of the Dead Sea Scrolls* (ed. Y. Yadin and C. Rabin; Jerusalem: Hebrew University Press, 1958).

—'A Note on Melchizedek and Qumran', *IEJ* 15 (1965), pp. 152-54.

—*The Temple Scroll: The Hidden Law of the Dead Sea Sect* (London: Weidenfeld & Nicolson, 1985).

Yamauchi, E., *Pre-Christian Gnosticism* (London: Tyndale Press, 1973).

Young, N.H., 'τουτ' ἔστιν τῆς σαρκὸς αὐτοῦ (Heb. X.20): Apposition, Dependent or Explicative?', *NTS* 20 (1973), pp. 100-104.

INDEXES

INDEX OF REFERENCES

OLD TESTAMENT

APOCRYPHA

NEW TESTAMENT

INDEX OF MODERN AUTHORS

Murphy, F.J. 60
Murray, R. 24

Nairne, A. 15-17, 30, 47
Narborough, F.D.V. 26, 176, 214
Neusner, J. 45, 62-65
Nickelsburg, G.W.E. 157, 165
Nicholson, E.W. 117, 121, 157

Oepke, A. 23, 127

Pearson, B.A. 163
Peterson, D. 88, 101-103, 110, 210
Pierce, C.A. 98
Porter, J.R. 170

Rad, G. von 81, 84, 205
Richards, I.A. 224
Ringgren, H. 99
Rissi, M. 32
Robinson, J.A.T. 43, 47
Robinson, T.H. 51, 215
Rowland, C. 60
Ruether, R.R. 75
Russell, D.S. 132, 177

Sanders, E.P. 64, 65, 76, 184
Sanders, J.T. 189, 190
Schaeffer, J.R. 149
Schenke, H.-M. 61, 219
Schierse, F.-J. 23, 212, 213
Schmidt, K.L. 60
Schmidt, W.H. 60, 124
Schürer, E. 155, 159
Schweizer, E. 57
Scobie, C.H.H. 134
Scholem, G.G. 61
Scott, E.F. 23
Selwyn, E.G. 109
Sevenster, J.N. 47, 48
Skehan, P.W. 168
Smith, J.Z. 14
Sowers, S.G. 51
Spicq, C. 17-19, 31, 38, 39, 42, 45,

46, 49, 50, 51, 66, 81, 84, 90, 96,
134, 147, 148, 170, 176, 183, 203,
210, 212, 216
Starcky, J. 160
Stauffer, E. 189
Stewart, R.A. 111, 112
Stone, M.E. 112
Stowers, S. 187
Strack, H.L. 85, 125, 131, 150, 206
Swetnam, J. 18
Synge, F.C. 21, 22, 164

Taub, H. 205
Tcherikover, V. 100
Theissen, G. 35, 57, 212, 213, 215
Thiselton, A.C. 12, 218
Thompson, J.W. 47, 49-52, 55, 56,
59, 85, 213, 214
Thrall, M.E. 46
Thyen, H. 18, 19
Turner, N. 170

Van der Woude, A.S. 41, 161, 163,
164
Vanhoye, A. 17, 78, 213
Vaux, R. de 89, 99, 145
Vermes, G. 41, 99, 100, 121, 133,
158, 160-63, 166

Wacholder, B.Z. 40
Wendland, P. 46
Westcott, B.F. 170, 202, 203
Westermann, K. 106
Whybray, R.N. 191, 193, 194
Wilson, R.McL. 32, 72, 104, 120,
147, 149, 170, 175, 214
Williamson, R. 31, 49-52, 110, 123,
138, 195, 197-201, 213, 215, 216
Windisch, H. 23, 147, 203
Wolfson, H.A. 44, 131, 195

Yadin, Y. 38, 39, 40, 176
Yamauchi, E. 104
Young, N.H. 72